A River Called Titash

VOICES FROM ASIA

A River Called Titash

ADWAITA MALLABARMAN

Translated with an Introduction,
an Afterword, and Notes by

KALPANA BARDHAN

University of California Press
BERKELEY   LOS ANGELES   LONDON

The Bengali novel *Titash Ekti Nadir Naam* was first published in Calcutta in 1956. Sixth printing © 1986 Puthighar, Calcutta.

University of California Press
Berkeley and Los Angeles, California

University of California Press, Ltd.
London, England

© 1993 by
The Regents of the University of California

Library of Congress Cataloging-in-Publication Data

Mallabarmaṇa, Advaita, 1914–1951.
    [Titāsa ekaṭi nadīra nāma. English]
    A river called Titash : Adwaita Mallabarman ; translated with an introduction, an afterword, and notes by Kalpana Bardhan.
        p.   cm.
    ISBN 0-520-08049-1 (alk. paper).—ISBN 0-520-08050-5 (pbk.: alk. paper)
    PK1718.M2476513 1993
    891'.4437—dc20   92-46698
                                                                  CIP

Printed in the United States of America

The paper used in this publication meets the minimum requirements of American National Standard for Information Sciences—Permanence of Paper for Printed Library Materials, ANSI Z39.48-1984. ⊗

Contents

Translator's Preface

It was love for this novel that set me on and saw me through its translation. That, and also high regard for its unique place in the literature, and particular appreciation for a shared family heritage of riverine East Bengal. The desire to translate it took hold twenty-two years ago one summer when I read it over and over. In the last four years of working on the translation, I realized how apt is Boris Pasternak's remark that "the translation must be the work of an author who has felt the influence of the original long before he begins his work" (quoted in the foreword to *Selected Poems of Boris Pasternak*, 1983). I felt I was in the presence of a marvelously told tale of a people's capacity for joy and love, for music and poetry, that transcends their utter lack of material wealth and power; a tale of a community's vitality in ethics and aesthetics, and of being human and in harmony with nature. In the lives of the poor in Bengal, and in the literature relating to the lower depths and the middle classes, one sees the human spirit crushed and twisted; and, occasionally, one sees it survive and even triumph. But the life described here is suffused with a rare light as of the rainbow; a glow remains even as it goes out. The flowing narrative weaves scenes and viewpoints, events and reflection. And the friendship between Hindu fishermen and Muslim peasants affirms and honors Bengal's tradition of transreligious folk culture.

Beyond knowledge of the cultural icons and idioms, the text's evocative and affective meanings, the translator undoubtedly must have deep commitment to transmit both the knowledge and the personal affection for the work. If I have any measure of success in this, the credit goes also to the persons whose help I found invaluable.

In researching the author's life, the community, the time and location, and the songs, I received great help from Subodh Chaudhuri, one of the author's few surviving friends, who was closely involved in the novel's posthumous publication. He has been generous with his time—talking to me, reading an earlier draft of the translation, explaining some of the local terms and songs.

I learned much from a number of intellectuals, artists, and social workers in Brahmanbaria as well as from the Malo youths and elders of Gokanghat village, during my visit in 1990.

Puthighar, the novel's original publisher in Calcutta, by giving me the exclusive right of its English translation, propelled me to strive harder. I gratefully acknowledge Mr. Chaudhuri's mediation.

My husband, Pranab, gave unstintingly of his time and patience to read the entire manuscript and check with the original text, and to serve throughout as my trusty sounding board and most productive critic. My son, Titash, read parts of the manuscript and came up with fine suggestions for revision. My copy editor, Edith Gladstone, gave the manuscript the benefit of her skills and an uncommon combination of exactitude and sensitivity. The responsibility for any blemish that remains is mine alone.

Introduction

Titash Ekti Nadir Naam (A river called Titash), completed in 1950 shortly before the author succumbed to tuberculosis, and published in Calcutta in 1956 with the help of close friends, is considered one of the outstanding novels in Bengali literature. It made Adwaita Mallabarman (1914–1951) more a writers' writer in Bengal than a writer of mass popularity. A superb blend of ethnography and the poetry of folk expression, the novel takes up the lives of the Malo people at the turn of the century, communities of fisherfolk on the banks of the river Titash in Comilla in the northeast of what is now Bangladesh. The author grew up in one such community and became its first educated man and a writer; he lived in the village central to the novel until he was nineteen (see the brief discussion of his life in the appendix).

Mallabarman makes the Malos' rich oral culture, its ethics and aesthetics, the form and substance of this novel. He takes us into the community, the rhythm of Malos' speech and songs, the rituals of their daily and festive life, their light and dark sides. "Titash is just an ordinary river," he writes in the opening chapter. "But its banks are imprinted with stories . . . of genuine people of flesh and blood, accounts of their humanity and their inhumanity. . . . Although the truth of these stories is hidden, like most truth, it is as tangible as the feel of air." Autobiographic in a wider sense, *Titash* is a novel of self-understanding in relation to a community's sense of its own culture and view of the rest of society.

Himself a part of the community, its culture, and living environment, Mallabarman also journeyed out—through his education and occupation, his knowledge of contemporary and classical literature. He wrote this novel when the culture was embattled, the community dispersing. With an insider's insight he illuminates the soul of the community and its culture—

1

presumably for us, outsiders to the Malo fisherfolk. The community, its life, its characters are minutely specific in time, space, speech, moral codes, and symbolic world; yet their stories and feelings reach us unobstructed. What sustains wonder in lives that to others might seem deprived, closed, mundane? What sustains artistic sensitivity and joy of living in the face of material poverty? Where does the human spirit spring from? The key was in their culture, their cohesion, their love for one another and for the river. "Malos have a cultural life of their own. . . . People other than Malos themselves have no easy access to the heart of that culture to partake of its nectar." The narrative voice is imbued with that nectar.

The river's perennial fullness and modest supply of a variety of small fish were enough to give the Malos a steady livelihood, close community life, and time for singing, celebrating, storytelling, and reflecting. Along its meandering course the river sustained the cohesive richness of their cultural life. Wealthy fish merchants with large boats mostly stayed away on the big rivers. Labor-hirers and loansharks did not quite get a handle on these Malos because even in dry season the river spared them the desperation of other small fishing communities, living along summer-dried rivers or constantly having to migrate. Their settled life-style based on self-sufficient subsistence was destroyed when the siltbed formed. The river that had been the Malos' yearlong common resource became rich farmers' seasonal private property. As the community's cohesion began to falter, cultural and economic pressures broke up the Malo way of life.

The siltbeds have spread since the novel's time; for seven months of the year much of the river's course is used for wet-rice farming; but few of the Malos displaced from fishing have access to this new yield of the river. A few miles into the Titash basin, a huge modern complex taps a natural gas reserve; pipelines carry it to urban kitchens and to power plants that support industries and light nearby rural areas. The Malo communities that once lived alongside the river have dwindled. Many took to wage-labor, many went to West Bengal; of those who stayed on, the young have moved to other occupations. Gone is the unique vitality of their cultural life as described in the novel, though not entirely because of siltbed formation. The partition of Bengal in 1947 and communal riots contributed as well.

The Titash Malos owed their livelihood to a river dominated by no one, and counted this free access as a vital blessing. As yet independent of merchants and moneylenders, they filled their simple lives with graceful speech, songs, and depth of feeling. Perhaps the river's friendliness toward its gentle harvesters turned them inward, to cultivate familial and social relations and a satisfying cultural life of their own. In their singing and festivities, in their special ways of listening and dreaming, and in their keen awareness of life's cycle in relation to nature's, poverty and lack of power were no major impediment.

The Malo culture was a unique blend of Vaishnava *bhakti* (devotional sentiment) and Sufi spiritualism; as in the *baul* songs, it expressed the human being's unity with nature. Together with the river's gracious presence, it filled the Malos' life with riches of feeling and expression. The Titash Malos' relative freedom from excessive drudgery, though not poverty, nourished their culture. Their lives had the artistic integrity attainable in ordinary people's lives if they are not beaten down by weariness and oppression. The river's subsequent withdrawal exposed them to exploitation and despair; and social splintering brought alienation from their own culture. The author portrays his native community in the fullness of life and cultural spirit, ending with a glimpse of its disintegration.

A recurring note, relevant both to Bengal in the 1940s when the novel was written and to the subcontinent's current interreligious violence, is the harmony between low-caste Hindu Malos and Muslim peasants that prevailed in the area. Both knew the hardships and the joys of living with the river and had seasonal festivals attuned to life's cycle. This harmony thrived partly on the river's yield that spared the Malos from competition with the peasants, partly on their shared distrust of tricky exploiters and gentlemen oppressors. The Malos had simple nets and boats and used traditional knowhow to meet most of their needs from the familiar river. The peasants had small plots in the floodplain and lived by work and thrift. Neither knew affluence; both knew sympathy and friendship.

The narrative's lyric simplicity matches its harmony of structure and of dialogue. Scenes emerge and recede with seamless fluidity as nature's changes infuse the characters' lives and thoughts. Vivid water, sky, and landscapes of seasons and human rituals mingle and converse happily or sadly. Images change and moods shift, but so deftly blended with the face nature presents, with the intricacies of festivity or crisis, and with the nuances of antecedent events that even the mundane and the magical, the gruesome and the enchanting all become natural.

The novel's four parts, two chapters each, take us through large and small bends in the narrative flow. In them the narrative weaves together four interrelated journeys and quests. A young fisherman's first long journey becomes a catalyst for his social and sensual awakening, abruptly shattered. A young wife ventures out to find her lost mate and father of her child. An introspective boy sets out on his solitary quest for knowledge and education. A rebel woman struggles to keep her spirit and her sense of pride and purpose even in the wake of terrible misfortunes.

The novel moves along several interlinked levels. At one level, it relates the life and culture of a Malo community that lived beside the river Titash sixty to eighty years ago: a poignant account of the fullness of that culture and of its end through a tragic combination of natural and social adversities. At another level, it describes a boy within that community as he seeks an understanding of himself and of the wider world in the light of the Malo way of seeing, feeling, and expressing. At yet another, it tells of a young woman and a river. The river sustains the community's lifestyle and culture and then changes and destroys them; the woman fights violations of the Malo way of life. It also presents three women, each courageous in a different way. At still another level, the novel manifests a theme of friendship between Muslim peasants and low-caste Hindu Malos, in contrast with the contempt from upper castes and exploitation by traders and moneylenders that both groups encounter.

Within the narrative's riverlike flow, scenes change smoothly: one scene unfolds, then a tiny point in that scene—a phrase, a gesture, an image, a song, an aspect of the natural surroundings—makes a barely noticeable transition toward the unfolding of another scene. And this pattern recurs with a graceful, fluid ease throughout the novel.

The relationship between people, river, and seasons permeates events and images, metaphors and musings, songs and dialogues. This, as part of the life-style and the culture, also contributes to the narrative's flow. Daily life and festivals, events and reveries reflect the keenly perceived changes in nature. The river both evokes and affects lives and thoughts. This resonance has greatest dramatic clarity in the youth's journey up the Meghna and back. As nature's faces change through the novel from beatific to tumultuous to shockingly destructive, so do human expressions from sensitive and sympathetic to cruel to thoughtlessly violent. Indeed, Adwaita Mallabarman's *Titash* is unique in combining an unflinching portrayal of human complexities and contradictions with a loving description of a vibrantly beautiful culture.

Foreword by Friends of the Author (1956)

Today, on the occasion of the publication of this book, we remember with stricken hearts our dear friend Adwaita Mallabarman. He handed us the manuscript of this book on the eve of his admission to the Kanchrapara tuberculosis hospital. We could not have it published while the author was still alive—quite a few years have gone by even after his death. With financial help from *Ananda Bazar Patrika*, the newspaper he worked for, Adwaita was beginning to recover from his illness at the expected pace—but the history of the final circumstances of his death is different. We are unable to open here that sad chapter of the end of his life.

In the circle of journalists of Bengal, Adwaita had an established reputation—he started his career in journalism as a colleague of Premendra Mitra during the times of the weekly *Navashakti*. After that he worked for the daily *Azad*, the monthly *Mohammadi*, and the *Yugantar*; finally he was associated with the weekly magazine *Desh* and the publisher Visva-Bharati. When he started his journalism career as assistant editor of *Navashakti*, the salary of journalists in Bengal was not much. As a matter of fact, until he became associated with *Desh* and Visva-Bharati, he lived in acute financial hardship.

To worldly wise people, this financial hardship will no doubt seem to be largely a self-inflicted deprivation—because Adwaita had little in the way of conventional family responsibilities. He was not married; his parents died when he was still a child. But even his distant relatives and acquaintances did not fail to recognize in him a friend of small means but great generosity. We have always seen Adwaita sharing his fistful of rice with many.

Another cause of this financial hardship was perhaps Adwaita's love of books. All through his life, despite the extreme austerity of his living, he

5

collected books. After his death, his friends entrusted his substantial store of books to the Rammohan Library. Rarely does one come across such a thoughtfully selected and absorbing collection on literature, philosophy, and the fine arts. The authorities of the library preserve his collection of over a thousand volumes in a separate section.

This powerful thirst for knowledge was something that had been with Adwaita right from his childhood. He was born in a poor family in a Malo community, not very far from Brahmanbaria town [in Comilla]. The diligent boy passed each of the initial examination levels of his school life with a scholarship. As was true in the case of most other Malo boys, his parents could not provide him with any secure arrangement for food and care. Walking from the fisherfolk's neighborhood five miles away, when this boy came with dusty bare feet and took his assigned seat in the school classroom, at least some of the kind-hearted teachers, if not the boys who were his classmates, could easily read in this quiet pupil's wilted face the signs of an empty stomach.

Of the ascetic endeavor of mind and spirit to which this boy dedicated himself from childhood, we have no intimation of what he may or may not have accomplished. However, we do know that from his early years his literary achievements drew attention. He always read much beyond his years and published stories, essays, and poems in various magazines and newspapers—many of these even won prizes. After he finished his school education, his well-wishing friends and teachers pinned to his shirt the metal pieces he had won as prizes and sent him to Comilla for higher education.

Owing to various adversities, he could not carry on with his studies at Comilla College for very long. Then, around the time of launching of the newspaper *Navashakti*, it was probably "Captain" Narendra Datta who brought him to Calcutta. Adwaita's writings remain scattered in various magazines and newspapers. The issues of many of the magazines in which they came out may no longer be available—one or two complete novels appeared in special issues of magazines. However, *Titash Ekti Nadir Naam* is truly the crowning glory of all his literary achievements. *Titash* was first partially serialized in the monthly *Mohammadi*. As soon as the first few sections came out, it drew appreciative attention. Around that time the manuscript of the book was lost in the streets of Calcutta. Needless to say, this was the most heartrending event in Adwaita's life.

At the eager urging of his friends and readers, collecting his broken heart, the author sat down again to write the story of Titash. By then, although his family responsibilities had not increased, the number of his dependents had. Many of the Malo families, uprooted from their homes beside the river Titash, had come to West Bengal as refugees [following the 1947 partition of Bengal]. In gaps between his work, Adwaita would leave Calcutta to visit and look after them—and in order to help them even a little, he took up a second job with Visva-Bharati, alongside the one he held with *Desh*. Of his earnings from these two jobs, he kept barely enough for rice and vegetables for himself and gave the rest away to the Malo refugees. The two jobs and other freelance writing for supplementary income left him no spare time at all during the day. After working all day, he returned in the evening to his tiny rented place in Shashthitala on the eastern edge of the city. Most residents of that tenement building were railway workers and their families, the pigeonhole rooms and the corridors packed with their innumerable, spilling household units. But the climb through the dark untidy stairway took him to his fourth-floor room on the concrete roof, from where he could see the sky that is limitless—Adwaita dragged his tired body and sat down to write the story of Titash at night. Gradually, the soot of smoke would seem to fade from the city sky, which then would merge with the pastel skies that leaned over the bosom of the river Titash.

About this book we need not say much; it is best left to the judgment of its general readers. However, contemporary Bengali literature has very few depictions of life in terms as simple and natural as these. In many cases a lack of familiarity causes writers to adopt an unreal romantic perspective; in many others, a pretense of reality twists their artistic vision. Adwaita Mallabarman's writing is free of both this false romanticization and simulation of reality. In his works people, nature, joys, sorrows, all bear the stamp of a spontaneous relish for and deep understanding of life. Our friend Adwaita did not have a long life; perhaps his story of the river Titash will.

I

A River Called Titash

Titash is the name of a river. Its banks brim with water, its surface is alive with ripples, its heart exuberant.

It flows in the rhythm of a dream.

The dawn breeze dispels its lingering drowse; the sunlight warms its water by day; the moon and stars sit with it by night, trying to lull it to sleep, but they cannot.

The river Titash does not hold the awesome terror of the Padma and the Meghna. Nor the furtive beggarliness of the thin village stream that sneaks by the paddy storebin of Ramu Modal and the primary school of Jadu Pandit. It is a medium-size river. A daredevil village boy cannot swim across it, and a lone boatman never fears to cross it in a little boat with a young wife seated inside.

Titash flows in a regal mood. It is never crooked like a snake, never devious like a miser. The ebb tide with the waning moon draws away some of its water but does not reduce it to poverty. The high tide with the waxing moon swells its waters with restless energy but does not flood it.

On the banks of so many rivers once rose the ramparts of the indigo merchants' estates; their ruins still meet the searching eye. So many rivers saw the armies of the Pathans and the Mughals pitch tents on their banks; the thin swift cutters of the Arakanese Mahg pirates engaged in the fury of bloodspilling fights—so many battles raged along their banks. How the waters of those rivers ran red with the blood of people and of horses and elephants. Perhaps some of those rivers are dry today, but they have left their marks in the pages of scholarly books. Titash holds no such grand history in its bosom. It is simply a river.

No cities or large towns ever grew up on its banks. Merchant boats with giant sails do not travel its waters. Its name is not in the pages of geography books.

Never has it known the joy of descending the mountains, picking up water from springs along the way, touching the sprigs of hillside wild flowers, flowing over and around rocks. Nor will it ever know the ecstasy of losing itself in the gigantic kiss of the boundless ocean. Once upon a time the restless Meghna, dancing along her way, slipped in a careless moment—her left bank strained and broke. Her currents and waves flowed into that breach. The inflow there created its own course, finding and molding soft alluvium, cutting and twisting through hard ground. After making a broad sweep that held hundreds of villages along the two sides of its course and touched the edges of many forests and flatlands, this pride of the Meghna returned to the lap of the Meghna. This is its history. But is this something that happened in recent times? Nobody even thinks of its origin. All they know is that it is a river. A river that flows over a great distance between its two mouths joining with the Meghna. Like the little gap between the two ends of a metal bangle such as village women wear, a small gap separates the two ends of Titash, its deep arc in a similar circular shape.

There are many rivers that succumb to the profuse flooding of the rainy season. No sign is left of their banks' normal location, all distinctions disappear. Then no one can tell that a river had been there. In the dry season again, temporary bridges of two bamboo poles appear on those same rivers. Children and old men and women cross over them, holding on to one pole and stepping carefully along the other. Even women with babies in their arms can go across this way. Boats are immobilized, and boatmen tie ropes around their waists to pull them along. Crops are grown on siltbeds on both sides of the shrunken river. Peasants work there all day in the sun's heat. A peasant on this side asks another in similar toil on the other side how things are at home. The peasant on the other side wipes away his sweat and answers. Cows walk into the water to bathe, to have a good soak. But the shallow water does not cover their backs and they get only a crow's bath. Women, trying to immerse their bodies in the waist-deep water, squat and finish bathing by making waves with their hands and splashing water on their bent heads and shoulders. Since babies are in no danger of drowning at this time, the mothers do not worry even about allowing them in the water while they wash clothes and pots and scrub their feet with a paisa's worth of carbolic soap. Their homes are close by. They can hear if the men call; so they do these things without rushing.

But is there really no rush at all? There must be a rush in the mind of a wife who needs to give a meal to the man she knows is coming home, sweating hot from the morning's work in the field. Around noontime, the women do not stay long doing their chores by the water. But in early morning and late afternoon they linger. Their men do not ask them not to, as they know that no merchant boat plies that river.

In winter, bathing in such a river is too painful. You cannot get in and out fast enough. The water is so low that it does not come up even to the waist, let alone cover the entire body. There is no way to plunge into the chilled winter water for a quick full dip and come right out; the body gets wet bit by bit. It feels as if someone is slowly working a knife through your flesh. By the end of the month of Chaitra, parching dry heat reigns everywhere. Even the little water remaining in winter is blotted away drop by drop and is all gone one day. There is no way to wash the sweat off your body. The cattle make the mistake of coming to drink in the river and stand in confusion. In the middle of the month of Magh, the two sides of the riverbed were embroidered in mustard flowers and the verdure of peas and beans. And in the slight stream that still flowed there, fishermen pushing triangular scoopnets caught small batches of little fish like *chanda, punti, tengra*. But none of these survives the sharp heat of Chaitra. It now seems as if the month of Magh was a dream. Everything writhes in the relentless affliction of rough dry heat. Yet people do not become too upset. They know it is always so at this time of the year.

There is a river of such extremes thirteen miles away from Titash. It is called Bijoy. The fisherfolk on the banks of Titash have relatives in the neighborhoods next to Bijoy. The Titash folk sometimes go there to visit them and to look for prospective brides. They have seen in those villages how merciless a river can become in the parching heat of Chaitra. As the water drops to the bottom, the fish gasp for breath, thrusting their mouths out for air. The fisherfolk too, like the fish, are left gasping. A time comes when they despair at the sight of the shadow of *Mahakaal*, the god of time eternal, in the form of a dry skeleton. Those who went away in the wet season on fishing trips to the big river of Chandpur now leave their boats and nets in charge of the Muslim meat dealers and take the train back home. They are the only ones who do not have to worry; they cross over the hard time by spending the cash they have brought. But those who did not leave the attachments of home while the river held enough water suffer the most hardship. The river is now an empty vessel, and they cannot cast their nets. With a small triangular pushnet on one shoulder and a narrow-necked bamboo basket tied on the other, they roam the neighborhoods near and far, searching for some hyacinth-choked old pond or tank in the deserted estates of absent owners. They may find one covered on all sides in dense overgrowth and shrubbery. The fallen leaves have accumulated in layers, rotting, growing heavy, lying at the bottom. The small fish swim above the decomposing layers to take a gulp of air and let out a bubble. The neck-high water has dropped to waist-high, and to knee-high now. The fish are greatly troubled, but not for long. The thin elongated form of a Malo, his waistcloth tucked high, standing in the water with his scoopnet ready and watching with hawk eyes, snaps up the fish at some point. This ends the fish's trouble, but the fishermen's trouble seems without end; it stretches far, until the rainy season finally comes.

The rainy season is no longer very far away. Seeing the possibility of an end to the crisis, the Malos use their last bit of strength against a mountain of anxiety and hardship, catching small fish with pushnets in order to obtain half to three-quarters of a pound of rice. But for Gaurango Malo, to make it through another day seems impossible. The whole day he has worked in tanks and ditches, which yielded nothing but bubbles seething up from the decomposed leaves when he stepped in the stagnant water and a few frogs that leaped from the net this way and that every time he scooped up the muddy water.

A pomegranate tree stands in a corner of his yard, its leaves all withered. It was planted by his wife. She, too, withered away while still in her youth, cheeks hollowed out, chest narrowed into a rope, and breasts shrunk flat into her ribs. Then one day she died. By dying, she saved Gaurango; he doesn't think of her anymore. Today Gaurango remembers her as his eyes catch the pomegranate tree she once planted, now withered just like her. Oh, what a good thing she did by dying! Had she lived, his condition today would be exactly like his elder brother Nityananda's.

Nityananda lives in the hut on the north side of their yard. He has his wife, and he has a son and a daughter. Gaurango, worn out with worry and work for a single stomach, shudders even to look at Nityananda and his family. He does not understand how his brother, with the four empty stomachs on his mind, can sit by the door of his hut smoking a hookah, looking as if he has nothing to worry about.

Nityananda really does not worry anymore. He stopped after worrying all he could and seeing no end to it. His wife is dozing in a corner; the two children are lying down, their bodies limp but their eyes trustingly placed on the face of their helpless father. And Nityananda, seeing no way out, simply does his best to inhale tobacco.

Gaurango's hut is on the west side of the yard. He slips the net from his shoulder onto the ground by the pomegranate tree, and throws the basket to a corner of the porch. On the south and the east sides, where two other huts used to be, the mud bases stand empty. Their two uncles used to live there. One died, and his hut had to be sold to meet the cost of his funeral rites; the other dismantled his hut and, taking its movable parts, went away to live in another village.

Gaurango pointlessly snaps at his brother, "How's smoking going to fill the stomachs?"

"What else do I have?"

Not only his stomach but clearly his brain also has shrunk.

"Let's go and see Bodhai at his house."

Bodhai of Nayanpur village is more well-to-do than any other Malos there. His house has four or five rooms roofed with corrugated tin. He has two sons making money. He is big and dark like an elephant, and strong like one too. His fishing and dealing in fish is of a different kind. He leases large ponds and tanks and stocks them with fry. Later on, with the help of his two sons and some hired hands, he hauls up batches of the grown fish and supplies distant markets. Sometimes he hires many hands in this business. When the river dries and the Malos see nothing but darkness before their eyes, they go to Bodhai's house hoping to be hired.

But Titash is always so full of water! So full of currents! So many fishing boats ply it all through the year! In no way is it ungenerous.

And the Malos who have made their homes along the banks of Bijoy suffer so much. When the river dries, their boats not only become useless but crack under the wood-splitting sun.

Those of the Titash Malos who have gone there on visits have seen how merciless a river can become in the scorching month of Chaitra. Watching the hungry whirlwind over the empty fields as they went home again, they often wondered, what if their own river Titash someday became dry like that! Perhaps even before that their hearts and their lives would dry up and die. Thinking this terrible thought, they would remark with awkward abruptness to their companion, "The Bijna Malos are unlucky, brother, so very unlucky."

Those who have never seen the terrible state of the Bijoy river, those who have lived year after year only beside Titash, do not think this way. To them the idea of using the triangular scoopnet seems laughable: no more than three cubits long, such a net can be used only in knee-deep water to catch only tiny shrimps. They cannot believe that the water of Bijoy becomes too low to dip even this net. They lower a variety of large nets in Titash to catch many kinds of fish throughout the year. If the river Bijoy instead of Titash flowed here, their condition would be exactly the same as having the air they breathe removed from under their noses. They, too, would then find themselves like those others frantically roaming village after village with scoopnets on their shoulders, searching through clogged ponds for barely two-anna to ten-paisa's worth of little fish.

The wives, sisters, and daughters of the Malo fishermen of Titash think of a different kind of adversity—those who have heard about the big rivers, the terrible ones with the names Meghna and Padma. These rivers undermine their banks and make them cave in. Their terrible waves and frightening depths make boats capsize and sink. These rivers have so many crocodiles. Even without a glimpse of any such, hearts tremble. Catching fish is the life of Malo men. They are on the water so much of the time, late in the night and on nights of bad weather. How could they go out on those big rivers! And how could their wives and mothers bear to stay home, after they had gone on the river, waiting for their return! But Titash is so gentle. Even on nights of rain and wind, with their men out in Titash, the women do not really feel afraid. The wives can sleep, imagining their husbands nestled in their arms. The mothers can rest, imagining their sons in their boats on the gently rocking Titash, peacefully gathering up the nets filled with fish.

The bosom of Bengal is draped with rivers and their tributaries, twisted and intertwined like tangled locks, streaked with the white of foamy waves. This verdant land is like a maiden in the embrace of an ancient sage, held to his immense chest, locked in his wet kiss, his dense hair and beard tumbling in sinuous complexity over her youthful body and flowing on beyond. All these tangled wet gray locks are the rivers.

But all the rivers are not similar in appearance and essence. How they behave with people differs and how people behave with them differs too, the people who live beside them and the people who live away from them but use them. All the rivers meet a great many needs of people's daily lives; but each does so in distinctive ways. Merchant vessels with billowing sails visit the big ones. Fishermen's boats ply their huge expanses throughout the day and on for days at a time. The men cook, eat, and sleep in their boats and catch fish. Everything about those rivers reveals a harsh beauty. The bare banks of newly formed sandbars are lined with rows of coconut and betel palms. The sharp-edged currents undercut the lands along the banks. The hard-hitting waves make huge chunks of the banks collapse and fall in. People's homes, farmlands, granaries, and groves of coconut, palmyra, and betel palm all helplessly tip over, break up, and drown! Nothing is spared, nothing shown mercy. The river there is a frenzied sculptor at work, destroying and creating restlessly in crazed joy, riding the high-flying swing of fearsome energy—here is one kind of art.

There is another kind of art, with an exquisiteness made of serenity, poignancy, a soothing freshness, and the pleasure of finely turned moods and colors. The practitioner of this art cannot depict Mahakaal in his cosmic dance of creation and destruction—the awesome vision of tangled brown hair tumbling out of the coiled mass will not come from this artist's brush. The artist has come away from the rivers Padma, Meghna, and Dhaleswari to find a home beside Titash.

The pictures this artist draws please the heart. Little villages dot the edges of the water. Behind these villages are stretches of farmland. There in late autumn is the golden abundance of ripened paddy, and in the month of Magh the sparkling smiles of mustard in bloom. Beyond the farmlands, farther away from the river, are the larger villages. Here and there, all along the course of Titash, are the ghats that slope gently to the water.* The ghat slopes are alive with pictures of life through the day. Young mothers dip and lift their plump babies, dip and lift them again and again. Wives and daughters plunge into the water holding round earthen vessels in the curve of their waist and float up again a moment later. A little distance away from these, boats glide along their way, one after another. Some have a shed, an open-ended dome of bamboo panels; some don't. Sometimes a new bride sits inside the cover, being taken by her husband from her parents' home to his own—you can tell from the way some of her own saris are draped like curtains over the opening. When a young wife goes from her husband's place for a visit to her parents' place, then the ends of the dome are uncovered. So is her head as she sits near the opening and looks out at the ghats of passing villages. But not until the ghat of her husband's village has disappeared from view does she come out of the shed.

Women go back and forth on the river between husband's home and parents' home carrying within their breast so many different smiles and tears. The young wife going with her husband has the tears of parting in one eye and the dance of a butterfly in the other. The ones who travel sitting well inside the boat's cover belong to castes other than the fisher-

---

*Whereas the large public ghats on the banks of major rivers have a broad flight of steps to the water, the ghats of villages alongside small rivers such as this consist of a gentle slope entering the water and a common area for bathing, washing, filling pots, and tying boats.

men's—Brahmans, Kayasthas, all those upper castes. Fishermen's wives come and go in their fishing boats. They are not as delicately pretty; and they are not obliged to stay strictly under cover. The Malo youths blame the fate written on their foreheads—they will never get one of those fair beauties as wife. They do a good deal of watching, though. If they look long and hard, they will from time to time catch a moment's glimpse of a fair face and a pair of pretty eyes through a windblown fold of the sari draped over the open end of the shed. It prevents those outside from seeing her, but she can see all of them. With plenty of fish in the water of Titash, the Malo youths' spirits soar. Lowering their eyes to their nets, they send the passing beauty a song she will not fail to hear:

> A daughter I was of a Brahman,
> I worshiped Shiva for a husband.
> Then I fell in love with a fisherman.
> And now I spin flax thread for his net.
> Who'd have thought this was in my fate!

The boat moves down and slips into a channel beyond the village on the river. Like the sideways flick of a snake's tongue, the channel suddenly turns away around the village, far inland. Perhaps the boat will follow the channel past several more villages to take the young wife to the one where a home waits for her. Perhaps the home is beside the channel and small children are ready with a prank to startle her. Perhaps someone else also waits for her, with other plans. Perhaps the channel has grown too shallow beyond a point, and she has to get off the boat and walk some distance to reach the home. There, amid the design that the artist has laid out in the loveliest quiet shades of green in a mosaic of planted fields, she walks slowly along the narrow ridges between the patches of green. Perhaps then she thinks of the hardship of not living on the bank of Titash. For a young wife coming to a village right beside Titash, the boat pulls up by the ghat, busy with various activities, and she climbs out bathing in the empathic warmth of some ten pairs of female eyes. If it is her parental home, she runs up the slope and goes in to hug her little brothers and sisters. And if it is her marital home, she pulls down over her face the back part of her sari covering her head and slowly walks the path from the slope, taking restrained steps and staying between two to four women who lead and follow her.

In that manner, Jamila walks the path that leads from the ghat to the *maqtab*, the boys' primary school adjacent to the mosque of their neighborhood, and with one foot at the corner of the maqtab, she glances back at the riverside. Her husband is still haggling over the fare. Just a couple more annas and the boatman would go away happy. Old boatman, how hard he worked to bring them over! With her are only her two sisters-in-law, both even younger than she is. The evening is setting in, and the path is lined with overgrown grass. Doesn't the man understand that she is afraid, when after asking them to go on ahead, he himself is taking so long to come! What if a snake is out here and about to strike her big toe, taking it for a little frog!

Khamir Mian* is the accounting type; he never cheats anyone of a paisa and never gives anyone an extra paisa, carefully weighs everything he does. When the boatman gives up and turns glumly back to his boat, an unexpected daub of happiness dissolves its color through Khamir Mian's mind. The coming night is his night for what! On the eve of such a night, how can anyone ever make a boatman feel deprived! Let no one be deprived tonight!

From a moment's silence in defeat, the boatman gets four times what he could not get from ten minutes of arguing. He smiles at the four-anna bit on his palm shining in the fading light and heads midstream. When Khamir Mian comes near Jamila, she feels as if the snakes that have been wriggling around the big toe of her bare foot are suddenly all gone. How nice is this man of hers!

But today she has seen someone even nicer, by the ghat of a certain Malo neighborhood. She liked that person so very much; at the very first glimpse, she felt love for her. Did she too feel a similar love for Jamila? There was such fondness in the way she looked up at her. A wonderful person she must be, Jamila says to herself: Seeing her for the first time felt as if I'd seen her many times before! The afternoon was slipping away; a gentle breeze started blowing. And that breeze parted the curtain of sari before me; and in that very instant I saw her! If the breeze hadn't shifted the sari cover at that moment, I wouldn't have seen her. How many people do we thus miss seeing every day! Yet, if only we could see them, they might feel close to the heart in this very same way. Do we really see on our own, out of our will? The one who guides us shows us those we do see. How else could it be that the moment this person looked up, after waving clear the surface of the water and dipping her water pot, just then the breeze pulled off a bit of the sari tucked in before my face! It is to their village that my father goes in the rainy season with his

---

*Mian is a conventional title of courtesy, like Mr., for Muslim men; it applies to friends and relatives, as well as unrelated men.

boatload of soaked jute stems to have the hemp separated. Next time I go back, I'll describe to my father this young woman, who is about my age and like me, and ask him to locate her and say to her father: "My daughter wants to befriend your daughter. Do you give consent?"

As I was saying before Jamila came along: about the artist who cannot paint Mahakaal's *tandava* dance, the one whose brush will not capture the awesomeness of the tangled locks lashing out of their brown coil. This artist has left the sides of the Meghna, Padma, and Dhaleswari rivers and has settled on the banks of Titash to compose beautifully detailed pictures.

These pictures are very pleasant—little villages along the water's edge; behind those villages the farmlands, golden in late autumn and smiling with mustard bloom in late winter; beyond those fields, other villages shaded in trees and shrubs, leaves and vines; ghat after ghat with their lively scenes—mothers bathing plump babies, women taking dips with their vessels—and a little distance away boats gliding by, one after another . . .

Titash is a river's name. Those living beside the river hardly know the etymological source of its name. They never tried to find out, never felt any need to. There are rivers with significant names like Madhumati, Brahmaputra, Padma, Saraswati, Jamuna. And this one is called Titash! No one will find its meaning in the dictionary. But is there any proof that the river might have been dearer to its people if it had a more literate, meaningful name?

What after all makes a good name? It is only a phonetically pleasant collection of letters. If a girl named Kajal-lata is grandly renamed Baidurya-malini, her playmates will not be happy. To those who see this river every day, live by it, love it, to them, even if a royal decree comes and renames it Champakvati or Alakananda, they will go on calling it Titash in the informal conversations of their daily lives. To them it is a sweet name. They love it with their hearts, and that is why they string the name in their everyday speech and wear it like a garland around their necks.

They do not know who first used the name or even think in terms of anyone ever having named it. Nor do they want to. They cannot imagine that there could have been a time when the river was not known by this name, they cannot tell when in the distant past their ancestors came and first set up homes along its banks. To them, Titash has always been there, like an eternal truth, flowing on with its permanence in their lives, as their companion forever. They cannot do without it; their life would not be what it is. It is there overlooking every activity, its presence constantly mingling with their daily chores and concerns.

A river has its philosophic aspect, not only an artistic aspect. Like time, it flows on endlessly. Time in its ceaseless course is witness to events as they take place and subside, and to human demise. So many lives have ended in horrible deaths—from starvation, suicide, or another's evil deed. And then, again, so many lives are born through time, unmindful of the hundreds of deaths around. Titash, too, flowing along its course, has heard many cries of grief at the death of dear ones and has felt the tears of the grieving mingle with its waters. Then, too, perhaps its waters have cooled the smoldering cinders of grief in many, and perhaps its air has soothed the despair of the lonely and the bereaved. For ages Titash has quietly witnessed these and flowed on. It has also seen the birth of many new lives, the joyous celebrations for the newborn, and has contemplated the future sufferings awaiting the babies innocent of the shackles their lives are already bound in. What sorrow will come to them on the heels of joy, what pain in the wake of happiness, poison disguised as honey!

Who are the people who live beside Titash? They are Malo men and women. They are not those who live in brick houses with walls around, a pond in front, and a well on the side. They are not those with yards facing the roads that lead to the city and that cast out along the way branches reaching toward towns and large villages, roads that carry horse-drawn vehicles.

All the paths from the yards of Malo homes take them to the water of Titash. These are short paths. So short that a baby's cry at one end can be heard by its mother at the other end, the pitter-patter of adolescent girls' hearts can be heard by youths in their boats on the river. The only long road for them lies in the river's midstream and it carries only boats.

Titash is just an ordinary river. No one will find its name in history books, in any of the chronicles of national upheavals. Its waters were never tainted with the lifeblood of people from two groups locked in battle. But does that mean it is really without a history? True, its history lacks any grand element that could make you swell with pride as you read about it in books. But its banks are imprinted with stories of a mother's affection, a brother's love, the caring of a wife, a sister, and a daughter. That history perhaps some know, perhaps some don't. Still, that history is true and real. Along its banks appear so many vivid pictures of genuine people of flesh and blood, accounts of their humanity and their inhumanity. Perhaps some of those pictures have faded away. Perhaps Titash itself has wiped them away! But, having done so, it has kept them all hidden within its breast. Perhaps the river will never reveal them to anyone. Perhaps no one will need to know about them. Yet the stories are all there, deathless like the monkey king Angad. They are written in letters that children cannot practice on paper or on the banana leaves they use in village school. Although the truth of these stories is hidden, like most truth, it is as tangible as the feel of air. Who can say that the river Titash has no true history!

And true are the people who live along its banks. On winter nights, some of them sleep under their rag-stitched quilts, and some float on the water in their wooden boats. The young men under the quilts are awakened before dawn by their mothers or sisters or sisters-in-law, and they run straight to the side of the river. They see the sky growing light, although the sun is still some time away from rising. The water of the river is unruffled and transparent in the soft wind of the cold morning of Magh. Over the water hovers a layer of steam, like pale smoke. They dip their hands and feet in the water under that foglike steam to feel the slight warmth mysteriously stored there for them, so like the warmth of a mother's body as she sleeps next to her child under the rag quilt. How could they do without this bit of loving warmth!

In autumn, the fluffy white clouds float in the sky free of moisture; but the bosom of the river is still full. The low flatlands along its sides retain water deep enough to nourish the tall-growing wet rice, along with the vinelike grass and the submerged profusion of waterlily stems. The water lingers there for some more time, unmoving, containing the immersed mysteries of the silent growth of paddy and of the tangled stems underlying the flat expanse of lily pads. Then, toward the close of autumn, the overflow starts to disappear, sucked away as if by an enormous draft. Its excess water evaporated, Titash returns to its normal shape. The soaked flatlands dry and harden from butter-soft mud to clay. Comes the golden season, *hemanta*.

When hemanta begins to fade, the harvesting of rice has already started in the stretches of farmlands between the villages that dot the banks of Titash. After the harvesting on those fields, the peasants carry their loads of paddy back to their villages. They live in the villages away from the river, not right on its edge as the Malos do. From there, they come back soon after to plant mustard and eggplant in the fields close to the bank.

On the occasional sandbars along the river's edge, they plant sweet potatoes that grow plentifully in the sandy soil.

Jobed Ali's grown sons have been planting sweet potatoes all day on the land they own beside the river. With the daylight fading and the day's work done, they leave. Chanting "Ali Ali Ali" together, the three of them push their longish dinghy midstream and climb in. The two hired men, who work all year round at Jobed Ali's house and on his farm, will now have to prod and take across the river four pairs of bullocks and two pairs of oxen. The two men do whatever kind of work their employer wants done throughout the day and part of evening, have supper there, and go home only at night. Their near ones never see them awake. Sometimes their wives also work for a pittance in this home or that, husking paddy and rolling jute flax into bundles. They live from day to day like this. So, as the sons of Jobed Ali start off in their punt chanting "Ali Ali," the two hired men prod the reluctant cattle into the cold water of the river and, tying their towels around their heads like turbans and holding on to the animals' tails, they start to swim, chanting "Allah Allah Momin."

In the morning, when they came along the ridges between the mustard fields, the plows on their shoulders and leading the cattle, the fields all the way to the river's edge were smiling with the yellow brilliance of mustard flowers—a brightly embroidered wrap that had been festively draped over Titash's shoulder. So watchful they had to be then to keep the foolish animals from taking mouthfuls of the crops. Back across, wiping their wet bodies, they see darkness fall over the fields; now they needn't worry so much about the cattle feeding off the crops. The animals are worn out by the day's work. Also worn out are these two men. The whole day they have put demonic effort into their work at the field. Going home is the only thing on their minds now. But whose home! To their employer Jobed Ali's homestead, not to their own. Even birds go to their nests at this hour, but these men are going to their master's place. There they must first tie the animals in the shed, chop grass for them, and fill their feeding vats with bran, husk, and water drained from cooked rice. The chores in a landed farmer's homestead are endless. The big wide yard in the middle is enclosed by four large rooms on raised foundations. Adjacent to these, facing outward, are several more rooms and structures, including the cattle shed. In this immense homestead, countless chores await these two men's return from the field, all kinds of chores from mending the fence to twisting shafts of hemp into lengths of rope, chores they go on doing far into the night. At some point the call finally comes: "Ho, Karam Ali! Ho, Bande Ali! Come and eat."

After supper, they take the path home. Wiping his washed mouth and face with the towel from his shoulder, Bande Ali remarks, "Brother Karam Ali, I ate some rice and catfish curry. Don't know if my mate at home had a fistful of rice and some greens to eat the whole day."

"Brother Bande Ali, what you said is true. But our mates! You and I don't even have homes, let alone mates there. They kindly let us stay there at night—so we do. We get up before dawn and wake up only after we reach the employer's place. That's all the contact we have with home. Have I ever been able to take care of what she eats and what she wears? When I can't do even that, how can I think you and I have a home and a mate!"

Bande Ali thinks for a while and says, "I understand all that, brother Karam Ali. Still, when I'm eating rice and five things to go with it at the employer's place, I can't help thinking of her. And the food sticks in my throat—then it's hard for me to eat."

"Even that thought doesn't come to me anymore. It used to earlier, sometimes. Now I find it's better that the thought of her never occurs to me."

Bande Ali sighs and continues in his sad tone, "I go home all beaten by the day's work and find her lying on the torn mat. I slump down beside her. One night I woke up when her hand fell across my chest. I picked up her hand and couldn't recognize it, so hard and calloused it was from husking paddy day after day in other people's homes."

Karam Ali's wife doesn't husk paddy. She stitches cloth quilts in other people's homes. At this time of year, every family needs their old saris and dhotis stitched into quilts, and she works day and night, pushing and pulling the needle through layers of rag. Her fingers are scarred with a thousand holes and scratches from the needle. When he is finally home, she may still not be back from her work.

With a wan smile Karam Ali says, "At least you find her sleeping at home. I lie down on the tattered patch quilt waiting for her. She's sewing quilts in others' homes, and I feel that needle going through my heart. She comes home late in the night. One night of early darkness and late moonrise, I woke up and saw the moonlight shining in through gaps between the broken wall panels—as if someone were laughing at me."

Even when his words stop, the sad smile lingers on Karam Ali's lips. Somehow holding back the sigh that rises again from deep in his chest, Bande Ali says, "Karam Ali *bhai*, you're all right. You work, you eat, you don't think of her all day. You think of her only when you lie down. I have this trouble. No matter what I'm doing, I constantly think that I'm giving her nothing but misery. Not one bit of happiness and peace—we're such unfortunates, Karam Ali bhai!"

With almost a philosopher's detachment, Karam Ali says, "But I wouldn't sigh so easily! You and I work for a big employer, and we get good meals. Our wives work for little employers, and they get very little to eat. Because we have no land, no property, we spend our lives working on others' land. If we had land, our wives would work at home and they'd respect us."

Bande Ali's mind does not go along this path. It seems to him that Karam Ali's love lacks devotion. He is too cynical, always sounding as if love for a wife is of no value in life. Yes, of course, it is of no value! For landless peasants like them, love has no value. You value love when spring visits your life. Does spring ever come into their lives?

Spring does come. In spring, there is no color in the farmlands. But there are those whose homes edge the banks of Titash, whose boats are tethered by the ghat, and who live by selling and eating the fish they catch in this river. In their minds spring brings the excitement of color.

Spring is the season that seems to make everyone here a little tipsy with thoughts of love, with desire for color. The fisherfolk decorate themselves with daubs and smears of color. They also want to decorate the ones they are fond of. Even that is not enough. They want to be decorated just the same way by those they are fond of. Color spreads in the sky, in the flowers and the leaves, and in the minds of the people. They decorate even their boats. Young wives and daughters bearing small plates, each with a little mound of red powder and beside it the auspicious pinch of paddy seeds with sprigs of young grass, step into the water up to their ankles and hold out their plates to their men in the boats tied by the ghat. The men take from the offered plates some of the color and faithfully smear it on the bows and the sides of their boats, and they pick up with two fingers some of the paddy seeds and grass sprigs and respectfully touch those spots with it, while their wives perform the ritual ululation. As if tinged with their red *abir*, even the rippling bosom of Titash is imbued with warm color. This, however, is a reflection of the sky that the setting sun paints in shades of pink and red—the sky that looks at its own face in the clear mirror of Titash's water.

The end of Chaitra is signaled by gusts of the Baisakh wind, wandering like a *baul* singer; they herald the approach of the rains. Dark clouds rumble in the sky. The first showers wash the fields where plowing has just begun. The fields overflow and send streams mixed with their soil running into the river, turning its entire surface ocher brown in a day or two. The temporarily muddy, cooled water of Titash fills the Malos and their children with joy. The fish, unable to see then, easily swim into the nets of Malo men. Little boys, ignoring their anxious mothers' forbiddance, romp and splash in the muddy water, thoroughly enjoying this disobedient play in the coolness of the water at the end of a long hot summer.

The Journey Episode

The Malo neighborhoods are on the banks of the river Titash. Boats tied by the ghat, nets spread on the ground, in a corner of each yard a clay vat of *gaab* resin,* in every home a set of distaff, spindles, and reels to spin thread and weave nets—with all this the Malos live their daily life.

The village starts where the river takes a bend to become a deep arc. It is a large village, full of people and sounds, the day's noises not quite drowned even by the night's silence. The southernmost neighborhood of the village is that of the Malos.

On the last day of the month of Magh, this Malo neighborhood is astir with a celebration. It is only for unmarried young girls and marks the end of observance of a ritual called Maghmandal. Girls in this neighborhood never remain unmarried long after puberty. Before ripples appear on their chests, while their minds are still steeped in the colors of childhood play, their marriage takes place one day to the music of *shehnai* flute and drum. Yet it is for this marriage that they all observe the rites of Maghmandal.

On each morning of the thirty days of Magh, they bathed at the ghat of Titash and, back home at the porch step, worshiped the sun with water, wild flowers, and a tiny bouquet of tender blades of grass in their cupped hands, chanting:

> Please, Sun God, take this sacred water I offer
> Seven cupped handfuls I carefully measure.

Today is the last day of the observance.

About a cubit's length cut from a young banana plant, pierced with a few thin bamboo sticks, becomes the base for a float-home constructed

---

*The resin is extracted from the fruit of the *gaab* tree and used for toughening nets and coating the bottoms of boats.

with colored paper. At the end of today's ceremony each young worshiper will carry a float on her head and place it in Titash's water, accompanied by the playing of drum and brass plate and by women's singing.

On this day, Dinanath Malo's little daughter Basanti has a serious worry. For every other girl, either an elder brother or father is making a beautiful paper float—each one rich with flowery designs, swaying fringes, and flying banners. She has no brother to make this concluding ceremony of the ring of Magh a success for her by somehow putting together a float. She tried to ask her father, but he left grim-faced for his boat with his string-tied hookah set, bamboo tube of tobacco and charcoal, and clay bowl of embers, to spend the whole afternoon repairing his net. It caught in a stump last night and tore; he must have it ready before dark.

Basanti's heartbreak fills her mother with compassion. She thinks of Subal and Kishore. The two boys are inseparable and even at their young age are already known throughout the neighborhood for their daredevil activities. Basanti's mother rather likes these boys; they are not timid, and they fly in when someone asks for help, ignoring even their parents' forbidding. Kishore especially is a very nice boy, as fearless as he is considerate.

At the call of Basanti's mother, Subal and Kishore come promptly and sit down in her porch to make for Basanti such a beautiful float that all who see it pause to admire it and remark, "How Basanti's float glitters with beauty!" Proudly watching the decoration with ruffles and flags and flowers, Basanti finishes wiping the yard smooth with mud paste so her mother can draw a design with a solution of powdered rice. And then her mother says to the boys, "Now I'll paint an *alpana* design all over the yard. Come, my dear Kishore and Subal, draw an elephant and a horse and a few birds in it for me."

When the boys start to draw horses and elephants in the yard from pictures in the children's primer, Basanti's heart overflows with joy. No other girl in the entire Malo neighborhood has horses and elephants in her yard today; only her yard is going to have them. Watching with fascination the artists' unskilled hands at work, Basanti bursts into delighted laughter.

In the center of the alpana design Basanti sits on a low stool holding an umbrella over her head. She turns the umbrella slowly, and her mother pours puffed rice and sweet balls on the rotating umbrella, making a shower of treats around the girl. All the boys scramble and catch the sweet balls just as they catch those thrown at festivals in the name of Hari. Subal and Kishore catch the most.

By the side of the river, the women are singing.

> The bed of flowers, O my friend, waits there,
> My black moon Krishna has not come to share.

It is an old song. Seven years ago when Basanti came into her womb, the women sang this very song in celebration of this day. Today they sing it again; Dukhai the accompanist plays his drum, and his son plays the brass plate. Every year they play the drum and the brass plate with the same rhythm. Again today they perform it just the same way. All has remained the same; the only change is that Dukhai's drum looks even older and his son has grown up more.

Basanti's hair is groomed with oil, and she wears a thick new sari. She seems suddenly grown up a lot today, even compared to yesterday! She will go on growing like this, and so will Kishore, and Subal too. But Kishore is such a nice boy, and he'll look just right next to Basanti. Basanti's mother's thought is interrupted by the excited voice of her daughter. "Ma, oh Ma, look at what Subal-dada and Kishore-dada did! The moment I set my float on the water, both went for it. One said, 'I want it,' the other, 'I want it.' All the others were scared even to go near them. Oh, they really started to fight! Then I said, 'You both made it, you both keep it. Why fight?' When he heard that, Kishore-dada let go like a good boy. And, Ma, you know what Subal-dada did then—he grabbed it in both hands and ran off holding it on his head!"

Today the ghat slopes by the water near all the Malo neighborhoods display festive scenes like this. The drum and flute play, the women sing, and the water of Titash sparkles in the early afternoon sunlight. Unmarried Malo girls have come dressed in new saris holding up the colorfully decorated floats above their heads of well-oiled hair; they try to set the floats on the water. But the boys can't wait for them to finish doing it. The girls plead gently with them: "Don't catch it yet, let me set it afloat first, then you catch."

Nearly all the floats are launched. In high spirits the boys catch almost all of them, tear them as they scramble among themselves, and come home with the loot in various states of ruin. But a few floats, escaping their plunder, move out on the mild current and the gentle waves. Seen from the bank, floating in the distance, each one is like a peacock that has its feathers unfurled. But does the sight gladden the hearts of the girls they belong to? If the boys can't catch the girls' floats, then what's the point in setting them afloat?

Basanti feels awfully sad for Kishore. He didn't get her pretty float, Subal got it all for himself. But why did he let it go? He let go without a fight like a nice, well-mannered boy. But he must be hurt inside, no doubt about it. He's that kind of person! Others have friends too, but they don't do that! Maybe if their friends want something, then they don't clutch at it. But nobody just lets go of a treasure for the sake of a friend, not with eyes closed like that.

Subal's father, Gagan Malo, never owned a boat and net. All his life he hauled fish in others' boats with others' nets. When he was young, his wife often reproached him. "How long do you think you'll carry on with this sort of makeshift living! You were to get your own boat, your own net, and have a proper livelihood to support your family and household. You could marry me only after promising this to my father by swearing three times. Why won't you remember that?"

But it's useless to scold a man who simply lacks enterprise.

"You'll end up getting kicked by others in your old age!" she would say. "That'll serve a man like you right."

Gagan generally turned a deaf ear to these words.

When in fact old age came upon him, his wife asked him if he finally realized what she'd been saying all along. Gaganchandra then answered back: "I have my Subal. I couldn't get my own boat and net made, but my Subal will. Stop that buzzing."

Thus, Subal's father died without leaving his son a boat and net of his own. Now as Subal grows to a man's height, he joins Kishore in his boat and goes on casting nets with Kishore. Happy this way, he doesn't even think of having his own boat and net. Kishore is just three years older, they've been friends from their childhood, very close. In the wet season as kids they used to sit among the many snake-infested branching roots of the banyan tree, fishing with rods from inside their recesses. They made a net for trapping mud-loving fish, walked long distances in the darkness of night along the narrow ridges between jute fields flooded in chest-deep water to lay the net, and came back again before dawn to collect a netful of *koi* and *shing* trapped in it. Snakes often get caught in this kind of net laid in a flooded field. But such things never intimidate Malo boys. Not even when they know that many Malo boys died in this way, because they see that even so, many others are alive.

One day both fathers sent them to the village school. The first day they spent sitting quietly. But the next day, they fought with the boys from another neighborhood and got a beating from the teacher. The following day, the amount of beating they got after fighting with each other made them agree the punishment was more than they could take, and together they went out and never came back to the school. They took the beatings of their elders who wanted them to go back, and still they stayed away. Instead, that day Kishore made a pair of slippers out of two thick strips of banana trunk, put them on, and sternly told his companion Subal: "Hey, Subla. Look, I'm Baikantha Chakrapati. Pay me respect, touch my feet." Their teacher's uncle, Baikuntha Chakravarty, used to sit on his porch all day, wearing sandals, smoking a hookah, and receiving obeisance from the Pal moneylenders and traders who passed by. Kishore had watched him.

Then one day both of them were asked to take up the spinning of thread and the weaving of nets.

Along the wide bank of Titash in the dry season, they spread out the flax over a sweep one full sprint long before spinning. Inserting a stick in the wooden reel and saying "One, two, three," both boys gave the spindle such a mighty spin, trying to twist the strands that full distance, that often the stick broke and the reel tipped and fell. In the branch-dropped roots of the banyan tree where they fished in the rainy season they found also a perfect cool spot to spend hot summer afternoons. They took their nets and tools to sit there weaving. They devised a method of working together: they held the net with their big toes and moved their spindles in and out at the same speed. That made the weaving go very fast, even though many of the knots were not good.

Then came the time when the two boys, one shortly after the other, had their initiation with fishing boat and net. Soon the entire Malo neighborhood came to regard the youngsters as skilled fishermen.

The season of fishing slows near the end of winter. The Malos' endless daily demands tire Titash. But the two youths are tireless. After an entire morning of laying in and gathering up the net without getting a single fish, Kishore abruptly pulls in the net handle and says, "Subla, let's go to the lake of Jagatpur. Just can't get the net and the fish together here."

But even after roiling and churning the lake's bottomless waters with the poles of the net, they find no fish. Impatiently, Kishore moves his heel off the handle holding in place the net's enclosure and in one pull releases the net from its moorings. The lake's entire waveless surface shivers at the sudden impact. His eyes on that tremor, Kishore says, "Know how we can save ourselves, Subla? Let's head north."

One day in late winter, work begins on several boats that are to go on long fishing trips north. To go far from home. Kishore's boat is among these. The travelers replace the worn-out panels of each boat's domed cover with new ones. They pull the boat out of the water, turn it over in the sun, and coat the hull with gaab resin. They soak the nets in a strong solution of resin and set them out to dry for three days. They procure extra poles of bamboo and lengths of rope to go in the boat.

If Kishore's father goes along, there will be no one to take care of the daily needs at home. He must stay and do some fishing and buying and selling in the marketplace mornings and evenings meanwhile, to keep the household together. He has to find someone else to accompany them. He worries: they are both hardly older than boys, they've never gone away from their home region to follow the big river. They'll have to do all kinds of talking, they'll need wit and experience. If river bandits catch them and are about to snatch away the nets, they have to try to soften the bandits' minds, talk them out of taking nets away from somebody who's just a poor fisherman, not a fish merchant. They need an older man. They'll be out on unfamiliar waters for six months altogether. Tilakchand is an experienced fisherman. A bit too old, but that should be all right as the two young ones will be there.

His hands making little balls of tobacco dressed with treacle, Kishore's father instructs him. "Tilakchand has experience. Take him along. The name of the village you want to reach is Shukdebpur. The name of the fish-drying stretch is Ujaninagar *khala*. The chief's name is Banshiram Modal."

At dawn one day, the three get into their boat. Those who have come to the riverside to see them off are not many: only Kishore's middle-aged mother, Basanti's mother, and the unmarried Basanti—eleven years old.

The older woman asks the girl's mother to perform the auspicious ululation, as her own lips are not good at it. Basanti and her mother do so. The ululation of one and a half voices barely stirs the dawn air; it does not make a truly festive noise. Kishore's father has not come to the river. He sits at home anxiously puffing at the hookah. Back home from seeing her son off, the old woman breaks into tears.

Chanting the names of the five Pir Badars, patron saints of boatmen, Tilak pushes off with the pole. Subal takes the steering oar. At his strong pull, the boat hisses along like a water snake, cutting through the waves and making new waves in its wake. Tilak now goes to the stern and lowers the oars, but his old arms do not quite power them; they simply rise and fall. Kishore still stands quietly in the middle of the boat, one hand placed on the shed. He watches how first the homes and trees of their Malo neighborhood and then the boats docked by the slope disappear even in the transparent light past the dawn. Now the entire village goes, followed by the pasture grounds. Next to disappear are the open field of Kalisima and the twin banyan trees of Garibullah. He stands awhile feeling the sweet blend of warmth from the water and coolness from the morning air. Then he goes to the tapered end and asks Tilak to hand over the oars and rest inside with the hookah.

It is noon when they reach the point where Titash joins the Meghna. Lifting the oars out of the water, Kishore looks for some time at their surroundings, feels the immensity of the Meghna and the bottomless depths of her dark waters. At one time the hard bank on this side suffered much loss; it has stopped eroding now. But the sheer drop of its clifflike bank holds the triumpant river's banner of destruction. Small waves round out the huge chunks of felled land. On the other side, far away where the river is busy creating, he sees the wide silvery bed of white sand. Tree-shaded human settlements have been destroyed on this side, barren tree-less sandy expanses made on the other.

Asking Tilak to start the rice for the evening meal, Kishore scoops up some of the mighty river's water and pours it on the stern and touches his forehead to it. Then he lowers his oars and rows on.

When they reach the boat landing of Bhairab village, the sun is about to set. Some Malo families live here, as is clear from the tethered boats, the nets spread over bamboo stakes driven in the ground, and the tar-stained square pits here and there beside vats of gaab resin and cane baskets.

Though the sun has dropped behind the village, there is still enough light in the sky, and they can probably go past another bend. But as Tilak cannot remember a good place to spend the night within a short distance, Kishore says, "Let's sleep here tonight, Subla."

The huts can be seen from the boat landing. The village was once large but has shrunk since the railroads took away part of the Malo neighborhood. Mightier needs have pushed away the needs of small people. Still, the Malos of Bhairab are not poor. They catch fish in the big river, they live close to the railroad employees and supply fish to distant places by train. Their life here may not be at all bad.

"Do you know, Kishore-dada, what the Malos of Bhairab do?" Subal remarks, thinking of the same subject. "They put on rented shoes and shirts and walk near the houses of the rail company babus—and those rail babus too, they come to the Malo neighborhood to sit with them, smoke with them, and say to them, 'Send the children to school—get educated, get educated.' "

Tilak fumes. "Shut up! As if they'll marry their daughter into a Malo family even if it is educated! What would you know, Subla? Their mouths say sweet words, but their eyes are always on the Malo women."

Kishore smilingly intervenes and tries to soothe him. "No, Tilak-dada, you've got it wrong. Their eyes are always on the big fish. Otherwise, Nagarbasi of our own village would not knowingly have arranged a marriage in this village."

"Kishore-dada, let's go see the bride-to-be! Which house is it?"

"Can't tell which one. All I know is it's Dolgobinda's house!"

As the afternoon wanes, young women come to the ghat to fill their water pots for the night. Spotting a few unmarried girls in the group, Kishore teases Subal. "Why do you need to go into the village? Maybe you can spot one you like from here."

They sleep well in the boat all night and leave at the break of dawn.

Bhairab is a large port. Even a steamship anchors here once in a while. Numerous merchant boats have congregated, each full of people and activity. So many transactions going on in so many boats. Everyone is preoccupied with the business of making profit, everyone busy settling his own account down to the last pai-paisa. Those who have finished their business do not linger there. Those who finished late the day before and stayed the night leave with the light of dawn as Kishore does. Kishore and his companions are going beyond the port, while others are going in the direction they came from. The bustle of activity is only in the port area. As soon as they pass its boundary, the heartbeat of worldly life seems to stop.

All signs of the port gradually fade away. In front of them the vast river silently holds out her calm expanse. On the wintertime river the northern wind has fallen; the southern wind has not yet begun. There is no wave on the surface, no pull of current in the flow. All that the river has now is her boundless water, transparent, quiet, satisfied. Faintly disturbing this meditative tranquility of nature's fullness are only the two oars of Kishore's boat rising and falling.

They have been traveling close to that other bank so long this morning, the flat bank of barren sand with no village, no trees, no ghat sloping to the water, not a post anywhere to tie a boat, a bank of such ruthless desolation. The sun has meanwhile risen and warmed the air. The thought of the unknown they are now bound for stirs a wave of happiness in Kishore's mind even in the midst of this desolation. Looking at the vast expansive beauty of the river, tunes of many songs start up in his mind. He sees another boat coming and opens his throat to start singing.

> In those northern fields that my golden friend tills,
> the plowshare keeps striking pebbles.
> Alone in southerly Malay breeze, his moonlike face dims.
> Whom can I greet with leaf-nut betels?

As the other boat passes by, its occupants hear him singing this:

> Along the river's shores playing his flute he goes.
> Honey-sweet tastes the love of the stranger!
> In a bad moment I step out, at the ferry there's no boat.
> Rascal boatman's been devoured by a Lanka tiger!

One of the people in the passing boat remarks loudly, "Look at that! The old man rows, the young man lounges. Sings a juicy song too. 'Honey-sweet tastes the love of the stranger!' "

Hurt by the taunt, Kishore stops singing and takes the oars from Tilak, asking him to take a nap inside. Tilak promptly does as the young captain says.

Calmness surrounds him again—and the unbroken expanse of water. Pouring all the joy of his heart into pulling the oars, Kishore says, "Subla, steer midstream. I'm tired of watching the sandy bank. Move across diagonally. If you want to be close to a bank, then let's go near the other bank. Nothing on this side."

But they cannot make out the other side from where they are. Beckoned by the mystery of what is not visible, they move into danger perhaps. Kishore's heart flutters and he remembers the song,

> I beg at your feet, dear boatman,
> Cross only when you see the land.

But the last words of the song are beautiful.

> The boatman behind calls and says, tie the boat in love's land.
> Say Hari's name and untie it again, here's the tide you desired.

With this, Kishore consoles himself and, hearing the faltering rhythm of the scull, encourages Subal too: "Don't be afraid, Subla. Danger's always near the banks, nothing to fear in midstream. Mother Ganga reigns there and protects boatmen from harm."

Up from his nap, Tilak comes out of the boat's domed shed to look. The bank toward which the boat is moving seems uncertain. The bank from which it has moved now seems uncertain too.

Abruptly the winter afternoon ends. The light from the sky fades and then goes out. Losing both banks, they surrender to being lost not just in the vast Meghna, but also in the total darkness. Subal leaves the scull and goes inside the shed. Upset, he puts out the lantern Tilak lighted. Tilak goes on smoking silently. Only Kishore is not resigned. He takes the steering oar Subal left and gives it a few strong turns. Suddenly the boat goes aground and stops dead. Terrified, Tilak shouts, "All gone, Subla. The boat's on a pack of crocodiles' backs!"

"Crocodiles, my foot! The boat's struck a sandbar. Come out and check for yourself."

Tilak comes out and checks. "Tie it down here," he says.

When the night ends, they see the tiny ridge risen above the water level. It has been planted with all kinds of crops in little beds. The growing seedlings are beginning to flower; insects have made their homes in them; birds have found their way to them so early in the morning. It looks like a miniature fair in the middle of nowhere!

With sunrise, they untie the boat and move on closer to the eastern bank. They follow it until they reach what looks like a Malo neighborhood, with fishing boats tied near the ghat and nets drying on its slope.

"Do you know this village, Tilak?"

Tilak has no idea, but Kishore asks Subal to stop anyway to eat their midday meal. "As if they're waiting here to feed us," Subal grumbles. "We'll cook our own food. I'm not depending on strangers."

Subal pulls the boat in next to one of the boats in a row by the ghat. A man seated in that boat repairing a net looks out with interest at the strangers just arrived in another unmistakably Malo boat. He asks them which village they are from and where they are headed.

They learn from him that the village is called Nayakanda and has about forty Malo households. This is their new settlement. They used to live on the western bank of the river in a village that had educated gentlefolk. The big landlord there took away from the Malos the land near the water where they used to tie their boats and spread their nets, and he leased it to another community. That is why they left that place of injustice and set up their homes here. They live in peace here, under no landlord's rule. The markets are far off. But they have boats at their ghat and strength in their bodies. They can tackle distances easily.

Kishore listens in rapt attention and offers him the hookah he has just prepared.

"My hookah is coming too, but I'll smoke yours first."

Soon they notice a plump naked child coming toward the boat. She is bringing a hookah from home. As she walks swinging toward them, the hookah held in both her hands also sways back and forth. Down at the boat, she asks her father to pick her up. He does so, takes the hookah from her, and gives it to Kishore. "I've smoked your hookah—now you smoke my daughter's hookah."

Turning to his daughter, he says, "Ma, dear, what do you think of the groom? Shall I get you married?"

"Who's the groom?"

"This old man here."

"No, not the old man. Mother says my groom will look nice like Jamuna's groom."

"What about this groom?" The father points the spindle in his hand to Subal and says to him, "Have you brought your boat here to take the bride away?"

Subal plays along. "Yes. I'll take you far away. You'll never see anyone from here again."

Watching the worried face of his daughter, the father says, "No, no! I'll never let my mother be taken away. We'll have the groom stay here with us instead."

Before leaving his boat, the man tells Kishore, "Listen, Malo's son, your meal will cook in my home. My daughter invites you. What do you say?"

"You go home and eat. We'll cook ours here. Tell me, do you go out for the night net?"

"Here we don't need to go fishing at night. Casting the net a few times in the morning and in the afternoon gives us enough. No shortage of fish here. Catch as much as you wish."

The man bathes first his daughter, then himself. He puts the towel from his shoulder around his waist and his wrung-out sarong on his shoulder. Then he picks up the child and walks away toward the village. Watching him, Kishore fondly pictures a happy home tended by a woman with a dearly loved little daughter and a man who does not have to spend nights out on the water. A tune of detachment plays through his mind and he says in an indifferent voice, "Subla, do what you have to—I want to take off soon."

They do not have to do anything, for very soon they see a man coming toward them down the village path. His forehead bears a sandalwood paste mark and around his neck is a string of wooden beads. Face beaming with a broad smile, he addresses them without preliminaries. "Young Malo, I request you, and ask you also in the name of your father! Once you tie your boat at our ghat, you can't leave without having a meal with us." His words are so forceful yet pleasant, his tone so confident yet warm, that they sweep away Kishore's mild protestations like bits of straw.

When the men get together to eat the midday meal, the child's proud groom-searching father remarks, "Here! I knew it then. You could slip out of my invitation, but there'd be no escaping the sadhu's. So I didn't press you, I just came back and told the sadhu about you."

After the meal, the sadhu presents them with a further request: "Stay the night here. My heart longs to rejoice tonight!"

Tilak interjects, "But, Baba, we don't know how to sing."

"You don't sing! Where do you live?"

"Our village is called Gokanghat—,"

"I'm not talking about that. I mean does your spirit dwell in Brindaban or in Kailash—are you pledged to Krishna or to Shiva?"

Tilak has almost forgotten his religious initiation long ago when he was a young man. His guru did whisper into his ear one of Krishna's names. Though in all these years he has not been able to do anything beyond that pledge, he has not forgotten the three syllables of the main mantra. Without hesitation he answers the sadhu's question: "We are followers of Krishna mantra, Baba."

"Look at that—how the guru brings us together," the sadhu says with satisfaction. "Knowing how to sing is beside the point, son, when you sing to rejoice. All you have to do is let your ears take in the sweet beauty of the divine name. My dear lord is captivated by the harmony of the sixteen names in thirty-two syllables. The scripture says that Krishna, love incarnate, in a disembodied form, permeates everything in Brindaban. That is from the Bibarta-Bilas—talking about the eternal Brindaban.* But the lord appeared in the Brindaban that was his playground and engaged in light-hearted play with his cowherd friends such as Subal, and with Radha, the primary feminine power, accompanied by her friends such as Lalita. They are no longer visible in the Brindaban of their pleasure. But they are still at play in the eternal Brindaban within us. So you see—they are a graceful presence within this human body. Then think

*The Bibarta-Bilas is a body of philosophical enunciations concerning *maya* (illusion) that the sadhu refers to here: Brindaban is an actual place where Vishnu, incarnated as Krishna, played and grew up; it also stands for a universe permeated by the divine in all manifestations. The set of lyrics that follows comes from the collection of song-poems known as *Vaishnava Padavali*, created by a number of such *padakartas* (composers) during the sixteenth and seventeenth centuries. Baikuntha, in line three, is the celestial abode of Vishnu.

also of Lord Gaurango, Vishnu's avatar in the city of Nadia. As the *padakarta* has sung,

> There's one, my friend, and he's in Gaurchand's body-home,
> And, O my friend, he's in the mysterious heart of Brindaban.
> One form is in Baikuntha. Another is the beloved black moon.
> Another plays in this body, for pleasure and joy, O my friend.
> There's one, my friend, in the mysterious heart of Brindaban.

Perhaps Tilak follows some of the meanings of these words. Kishore and Subal, after listening to the speaker with a look of fascinated devotion in their eyes, say each to himself, The deep meaning of philosophy like this is not for everybody to grasp. Those who follow their meaning go to heaven. Little of it is for ignorant sinners like you and me to understand.

The evening's singing session takes them far into the night. The sadhu himself sings. A few others from the neighborhood who have gathered there also sing. Even Tilak sings one he knows well:

> The yard is dry and hard, the porch drifts in flooding.
> Ganga is dying of thirst, and of cold Brahma's dying. *

At the repeated request of the sadhu, Subal and Kishore too sing two or three songs they heard at the singing sessions of their own village sadhu and bring tears to this sadhu's eyes. The sadhu is touched by their singing, and even more by their guileless company. To himself he says, You're like the ever-young cowherd boys of Brindaban. May Krishna give you the joy of his heavenly abode. May the happiness you've given me make you happy likewise!

The next day they untie their boat and set off again on their journey. Powered by the two youths' pulling on the oars, the boat cuts the waves with a splashing sound. The sadhu stands by the ghat to watch them leave. The farther the boat goes, the more his eyes fill with tears. He has no family of his own. Though always with people, he is alone. Most people don't know how to rejoice and how to give joy. Those two youths, having given him so much joy, are going far away and leaving him with the monotony of daily life.

On the boundless waters of the Meghna, shining white in the morning sun, their boat shrinks into a little black mark; then it disappears. The

---

* Though the yard is dry, the raised porch is flooded; the river goddess may lack water, and the creator may fall ill—such paradoxes of life, and hence the foolishness of rigid notions, are a frequent theme of *baul* and other folk songs and proverbs in the Comilla region. This song (part of a longer song in chapter 7) belongs to a category of folk singing in East Bengal influenced by the mystic panreligious philosophy of Sufism and enriched by local folk idiom and imagery.

sadhu sighs. They've taken away even more than they've given, he now feels.

Here the riverbank has turned a convex arc. Around this curve the currents swirl with such ferocious energy that they saw through the hard ground, making immense chunks fall like severed palm trees. The bank, caught in this frightful grandeur of destruction, has grown steep like a hill, terrifying to look at. It is dangerous for a boat to go anywhere near that bank. Any moment a chunk of earth can fall on the boat! The current is so strong that progress against it is very difficult. Still, they must gain on it and move ahead.

Having rowed the whole morning nonstop, followed by the midday meal, Subal has fallen asleep. The body is so used to staying up all night on the water, and napping after the midday meal, that it demands its routine. The eyes are slow to close at night even when they are not checking the net, and they grow heavy with sleep once the midday meal hits the stomach. Tilak has just awakened from his nap. He was smoking and dozing, the hookah in his hands and his eyes half closed. Now he picks up the oars. Studying the water ahead, he says, "You're going to catch so many fish here, Kishore. Just one look at the water tells me this part of the river must be full of fish."

The immensity of the Meghna has diminished substantially. When they were downstream, the opposite bank looked like a faint dark line. As they move further upstream, they begin to make out even the straw-roofed huts of the villages on the other side. When Subal wakes up, he is so confused by the difference that he asks Tilak which river they are on.

"Same one we've been on all morning."

"The Meghna is so narrow here!"

"The farther upstream you go, the narrower she gets."

"How much more do we go upstream to tie the boat by the fish-drying khala of Ujaninagar? And how far is the home of Banshiram Modal in Shukdebpur?"

"Go back to sleep. I'll wake you when we've reached the ghat of his village and got the hookah ready for you!"

"Will you stop your teasing?"

They begin to see ahead of them a village shaded with the growth of green plants and trees. Up at the far end of the village, the river suddenly takes a bowlike turn and then, heading straight west, disappears from their sight. Just beyond the village the bank is a curved flat stretch, specks of sand glittering in the light of the setting sun. In total contrast with the village, the open stretch has few trees, little greenery, and a cluster of straw-topped structures, giving the illusion of a desert inn, except for the slithering python shape of the river that winds through the landscape.

When the village in the distance grows clearer, Tilak's old eyes soften and his voice trembles as he announces to the youths: "That is Shukdeb-pur village, and over there is the khala of Ujaninagar." Kishore says nothing. His eyes keep gazing farther ahead at the point where the river has turned and disappeared from his view.

By the time their boat arrives at the ghat of Banshiram Modal, evening has set in. The chief is a well-known and powerful man, controlling a five-mile stretch of the river near his village. Anyone wanting to fish here has to enter into a tenancy arrangement with him.

At daybreak they receive his invitation for the midday meal in his home. After bathing in the river the three of them go there. His house is large but in need of repair. It has four large straw-thatched rooms on raised foundations on four sides of the yard. In the porch facing one of the rooms, the chief sits with a cash box, counting silver coins. Admiring the rocklike solidity of his black body, strong as a demon, his heavy collarbones, and the skin and flesh that show no sagging even though he is over fifty, Kishore says to himself, Twenty-five men like you can easily match one hundred regular men. You deserve having people come to pay you respect.

The chief cordially receives the visiting fishermen and seats them.

"I now have your name, Kishore, but tell me your father's name."

"My father's name is Ramkeshab."

"Yes. I remember him. How many brothers are you?"

"I had a little brother. He died. I'm the only one now."

"Do you have a son?"

"I'm my son."

"I see! Which village have you married from?"

Kishore keeps silent. Subal speaks up. "He is to get married after returning home from this trip. It's fixed with a girl in our own village."

The dishes served at the midday meal are all of large fish. Kishore and the others in his village catch smaller fish. If a large fish ever strays into their nets, they sell it for cash to buy the rice they need for their regular meals.

The chief gives his undivided attention to a great quantity of food. He looks up just once from eating, remembering his guests, to say to them, "Fishermen brothers, you'll eat just with the help of your own hands, without entreaty from this side."

Kishore does not know what to say in response. Faced with the elaborate arrangement of food, he feels rather shy and tongue-tied. Chewing on the head of a carp, Tilak comments that there's no need for entreaty.

Kishore realizes that he too, the owner of the boat, ought to say something in appreciation. But he knows that he doesn't command the kind of clever language that an appropriate response calls for. He is a simple fellow, and his words come out painfully simple. "Where we live we don't get that many large fish. We hardly ever eat so much of it."

Hearing this, the chief's wife brings another large bowl of fish to him. And while Kishore is saying "No no, no no" as vehemently as he can, she cleverly touches the bowl audibly to his plate, so that now Kishore has to eat it, as it cannot be served to someone else and must otherwise go to waste.

She has served them with the sari covering her head pulled over her face. Kishore does not see her face until after the meal, when they are chatting on the porch and she brings the dressed betel. The chief, sitting straight on a plank seat, looks like a large-bodied mythical hero, like Bhima or Hanuman, right out of the stories heard in childhood. Kishore steals glances at him and marvels at the power the man holds without a trace of either conceit or temper. That powerful chest would give shelter even from a typhoon.

She comes out to hand her husband the hookah. She comes out again with a container full of dressed betel. When she puts it down in the center of the four of them, the covering over her face moves, and Kishore catches a moment's glimpse of a slim, dark young beauty. Kishore imagines her next to the chief, like the teenage Gouri beside the mature Shiva, somber and powerful. Seeing Kishore's thoughtful face, the chief asks if he is wondering about his wife. To Kishore's embarrassed objection he simply says, "But I've nothing more striking in my home. There used to be someone else, but she's dead. She'd have teased you and joked with you."

"Chief!"

"What is it, young fisherman?"

"You remind me of the Shiva on Kailash mountain. You're so powerful, yet your home is so simple, showing off nothing. You're amazing!"

The chief listens to him with approval, his gentle eyes intent on Kishore.

"The Shiva you remind me of is the old Shiva, the one everybody fears and respects, but who lives like a poor man!"

With obvious pleasure the chief says, "You call me the old Shiva, do you? Don't try to take my Gouri away from me, young fisherman. Besides, we're not in Shiva mantra; we're in Krishna mantra. Whose domain do you inhabit?"

Tilak's answer is prompt this time: "Brindaban."

"You're in Krishna mantra too! Krishna has brought us together. We'll have some singing tonight. Roll down now."

Encounter with the excellent feast has distended Tilak's stomach, which unabashedly declares its prominence. Becoming conscious of it, Tilak says, "You're right, chief. After the meal you fed us, we'll need to roll down to the boat; we can't count on being able to walk to it!"

The chief doesn't get the joke and tries to explain. "I didn't mean that, fisherman. I meant you could lie down on a mat here and rest before you go back to the boat. You'll be staying up late tonight for the singing."

"Oh yes, we can take a little roll if you have a smooth palmyra mat spread for us."

"You've got quite a way with words, old fisherman. I'm getting quite fond of you."

They do not return to their boat that afternoon. After a nap on the smooth cool mats, they go out for a walk through the neighborhood. Old Tilak doesn't bother to lower his dhoti below his knees. But Subal and Kishore arrange theirs to fall to their ankles, and with a towel over one bare shoulder they go out looking like images of the handsome young god Kartik.

Subal, with the obsession natural for his age, wants only to see which homes hold a girl ready for marriage. He selects each for himself, unable to leave out even one, and imagines with delight the silent plea that the parents of each one send through the air: "Come in, young man, and pick our daughter."

Kishore's thoughts are of a different kind. He marvels at the health of almost everyone in this village. Old or young, male or female, everybody here goes about on a flood tide of health. And everyone has very black skin. Not dull grayish black, but glistening deep black like smoothly carved figures of black stone. Most of the Malos in Kishore's village are very dark too, even the young women, but some are fair. Basanti's complexion rivals that of a Brahman pandit's daughter. Here the young women as well as the men are all black-skinned.

Another marvelous thing Kishore notices. The Malo homes in this village have not only nets but also plows, the tools for fishing on one side and the tools for tilling on the other! Almost every home has the vat of resin, the bundles of net, the fishing ropes and baskets as prominently visible as the plow and yoke, the weeder and ladder. Of the two less well kept rooms, one stores old nets from one or two generations, in bundles and piled up like old almanacs; the other is the cow shed dense with grass and dung and the foaming cud of cows and calves of various ages. The presiding deity of their life is like Adamsurat, the half-male, half-female

guardian of the sky, pointing two fingers in different directions, one to
the brimming river and the other to the smiling fields. If some invisible
demon one day unties the knots of their nets, loosens the nails that hold
their boats together, or drinks up the river's water in a giant draft, it will
not be able to destroy them, because they can survive on the harvest of
their land. Along with the work of raising crops in the fields, their hands
will be able to repair their nets and boats, return them to the way they
were before, and await the rains to replenish the river. These Malos will
never be ruined! And the Malos in Kishore's village? None of them have
any farmland. But they have the river Titash! Who could ever dry up
their Titash?

Tilak interrupts his thoughtful absorption. "Oh Kishore, where can we
get a smoke here?"

The singing session starts after the evening sets in. Tilak sings the first
song, supported by Subal playing the single-stringed little drum *gopijantra* and Kishore keeping the beat only by clapping and swaying his
head.

Gathered there are both Krishna followers and Shiva followers. After
the singing of the Vaishnava invocation that begins the session, attention
turns to one corner where batches of *ganja* are being prepared. Old Tilak
has smoked ganja only on rare occasions. Taking a puff with great gusto,
exhaling smoke through his nose, he turns his instantly bloodshot eyes
to Subal and asks him to play the accompaniment. Subal starts the beat
with the gopijantra pressed to his stomach. Stretching one hand toward
the chief seated in the middle of the gathering, Tilak sings a song about
the ascetic Shiva dancing with his horn and taboret in the cremation ground
in the company of spirits; this song does not quite appeal to the Krishna
devotees. One of them tells the chief that the singing is going off course,
that a different song would be better, like the one about walking the paths
of Braja all night with a three-wick lamp lighted with a paisa's worth of
oil. The chief is on the point of asking the critic not to show impoliteness
toward the visitor, when Tilak's brain gives in to the unaccustomed shot
of ganja and he passes out almost in the chief's lap. Subal and Kishore,
now feeling guideless, make no further attempt to sing and sit back to
enjoy the others' singing. After many kinds of song by the group of crit-
ics, the session ends with a song about the eternal union of Radha and
Krishna as one of the chief's men who is handing out raw sugar drops
from a pot in his arm reaches Kishore to offer him some. Awakened from
his dreamlike spell, Kishore accepts the sweet and calls Tilak up to return

to the boat. When Tilak opens his eyes, the gathering is already dispersing and people are going home.

Dawn comes on the river with the most exquisite beauty. The sun is not yet out and the transparent sky, taking on a hint of blue, spreads bluish creamy white light throughout. The sweet tones and soft serenity of this open expanse make all the pores of the heart sing with joy. The unobstructed gentle air rouses the delicate clapping of hundreds of millions of baby waves. The soft touch of that air fills even Tilak's old shrunken chest to its fullest.

To their east is the chief's neighborhood. To the north is the tree-covered bend on the left of which the river disappears. To the south the flow stretches straight as an arrow, with water as far as the eye can see. Defined only by the two banks, the flow appears unbounded in length. Tilak's gaze rests on the point where the expanse of water reaches the edge of the sky. The light breeze of this spring morning is blowing from somewhere even farther down south. Looking in that direction, Tilak fills his lungs with this immensely generous breeze.

A rope ties one end of the boat to a post and the wind pulls out the other. Standing in the middle of the boat, Tilak calls: "Kishore, time to cast the net."

Kishore has been coming out of sleep with the dawning of light and Tilak's voice severs the last link between sleep and wakefulness. Quickly he gets up, lights the hookah, and calls Subal, who is still in the stupor of sleep but wakes at the sound of the hookah.

They take the boat south of the neighborhood, alongside the gently sloping bank with its single footworn path of bare earth. The path follows the edge of an array of paddy fields dense with the young plants' light green tips waving in the morning breeze and rustling softly. In a delicate minor key, their sound plays a continuous counterpoint to the softly lighted sky, the ripples, the breeze, everything suffused with the morning's tenderness. Kishore's eyes fill with delight. People in the chief's village planted the paddy. They will harvest and store it, so that, unlike the Malos of Kishore's village, they will not have to fast on days of rain and storm when they cannot go out in the river. "Take care to work that pole gently, Tilak," he says, "so it doesn't hurt any of the rice plants. Don't know who this farm belongs to. That heart would suffer."

"Don't exaggerate," says Tilak. "So many cowherd boys hit them with their sticks as they go by, so many cattle sneak mouthfuls from the grain-forming tips. Who could tell we did it . . ."

Any other time, Tilak's lack of concern would annoy Kishore. But the balmy fresh morning and the sensitive artist inside Kishore's mind keep anger away from him. Already off the boat, walking alongside, he quickly catches the pole before it strikes the rice plants, deflecting and slowing it to save these speechless and helpless little things.

Pegging his net along the edges of those paddy fields, Kishore climbs back in the boat and puts his foot on the net's handle. Subal takes the steering oar and Tilak pushes the pole, floating the boat outward. When they are in midstream, Kishore lowers his net into the water. He takes a cupped palmful of river water in his mouth and spits it on his net in the ritual of starting. After waiting a little, he swings up his first catch of small slim silvery fish, replicating in his upheld net the lively ripples on the water. A turn of his wrists transfers the rippling silver from the net into the well of the boat, where the fish amazingly continue their lively dance. Kishore lowers the net and admires the beauty of his first catch, as fresh-looking as this dawn of early spring.

After a while the sun rises in a sudden leap and spreads golden light across the water. At the touch of the warm rays, all the fish dive to the deeper water. Now Kishore pulls up the net and throws it in a bundle inside the boat, indicating to his companions the end of fishing for the morning. Tilak comes forward to help him untie the ropes.

They return to the ghat of the Malo neighborhood and find the chief waiting for them. Happy to see their first morning's catch, he praises the young fisherman's skill and helps haul the fish to the raised drying area of the bank.

The spring breeze keeps blowing and stirring the transparent water into playful dancing waves. It stirs Kishore's heart, too, with ripples of joy in tune with those on the river. The sunlight grows with the morning, warming Subal's and Tilak's heads but showering Kishore's heart with golden light. He senses an invisible artist's brush painting the core of his mind, a brush dipped in the color of a still unseen source of happiness. Thoughts, some quite unfamiliar and unlikely, wander from time to time into his mind held in its spell. At one point, he goes with Subal for a walk through the neighborhood of Shukdebpur. He admires the leaves now emerging on the bare branches. Copper-colored leaves, soft and silky like the outer layer of Kishore's heart. One of the yards has a flower garden in a fenced area, beside the altar of sacred basil: a profusion of blooms, with beautifully colored designs on their petals. He stops before one flower that he has never seen before. Noting a young girl who passes with a skein of thread, he stops Subal. "Wait. Let me look at this flower. So colorful. But I don't recognize it. Ask the girl the flower's name."

Subal, neither a poet nor a companion sensitive to the moods that color Kishore's thoughts, says casually, "Ask her yourself if you're so interested."

"All right, I will."

Diffidently, like an accused before the judge, the muscular young man approaches the girl.

"I come from a different region, never saw this flower before. Would you tell me its name?"

Blushing, animated, she looks at Kishore and tells him the flower's name. But then she is unable to take her eyes away and stands before him like a small creature mesmerized by a snake, staring into his eyes and pulling the edge of her sari over her budding breasts. Then abruptly, like a frightened doe, she takes off and darts behind a hut.

Subal, sensing something, remarks, "Whatever you may think, I haven't seen even one girl in Shukdebpur as nice as your Basanti."

"My Basanti! Why do you say that, Subla?"

"She's going to be married to you when we get back with the money from the trip! Why shouldn't I say your Basanti? I can't say *my* Basanti!"

Kishore smiles. "No Subla, it's not a matter for teasing. I'll give my Basanti to you and see her go around the sacred fire seven times in step with you."

"Why do you try to confuse your own mind that way, Kishore-dada? Basanti cast her rice in your pot—you know that as well as I do."

"No, Subla. My mind seems to say, that's not right. How can I marry a girl I've seen from the time she was a naked baby, carried in my arms when she was a small child, amused and scolded and scared, and made the Maghmandal float for! I feel I can marry only someone I've never seen before Mukhachandi*—the moment when, hoisted on that wooden seat, she lifts her veil and opens her eyes fully to look, as the women sing and do the ululation. She alone can be my wife. All others are really sisters."

Subal is certain that Kishore is momentarily confused. But, if Basanti is really not going to be married to Kishore, then who'll be Basanti's husband? Subal starts wondering.

Kishore, aware of the sensation just touched off within his mind and feeling a bit awkward, suddenly loses interest in walking through the neighborhood and heads back to the boat with Subal behind him.

---

*Folk pronunciation of the Sanskrit *Mukhachandrika,* which refers to the bride and groom's ceremonial first viewing of each other's face.

The unfamiliar intensity does not stay with him very long. Otherwise Kishore would go out of his mind.

Another soothing bluish dawn of the month of Falgun arrives on the river. Kishore lays out his net and casts it into the depths of the lightly dancing river's bosom. He pulls it out and sees it filled with lively little silvery fish, all vividly alive. In the shallow water of the boat's hold, barely two minutes away from the end of their life, how they ignore death, to float and wriggle without a care! But watching them is so pleasant. Kishore loses himself in the swift rhythm of plunging and lifting the net. And all the restlessness that gripped his mind yesterday recedes.

Then it is the middle of Chaitra. Spring is at its peak. And it brings *Dolpurnima*, the full moon of the swing. Once upon a time somewhere two beings shared a swing; the swooping motion of their swinging lives on deep in people's memory, its waves restirred on this day every year. The deathless sensation infuses the air, the sky, the forests, and everyone's mind with the rhythm of swinging. People decorate themselves with color on this day and, still restless, smear their loved ones with color. Not yet content, they then smear all those around with color, ignoring who is related and who is not, wanting to make them all their own.

Such energy and abandon mark the festival of color in the congregation at the fish-drying stretch of Shukdebpur. Everyone will rejoice and celebrate Dol. The invitation includes all the villagers of Shukdebpur. As tenants of the part of the river in the chief's control, Kishore and his group are also invited to take part in the next day's celebration: singing, playing with color, and feasting, from morning till night.

Tilak informs his youthful charges: "Dolpurnima celebration in this khala is splendid. The way the women dance playing the cymbals! No mere dance—it's like a ballet of fairies. Bells around their ankles and cymbals in their hands. If you haven't seen this dance, you're still a baby in your mother's womb."

Subal is tempted by Tilak's description but feels unhappy that his dhoti and towel are both in need of cleaning. Kishore suggests the solution: buy some soap from the market across the river. But crossing the river for just a piece of soap seems too much effort.

At last the solution comes to them on its own.

A cluster of gypsy boats has anchored downstream. The gypsy women have come to do business by the ghat slope of Shukdebpur village, with their assorted wares of hand mirrors and combs, soap and hairpins, glass bangles and beads, even fishing hooks. They also have with them a basket or two of snakes.

Kishore and his companions are busy with the morning's fishing. The day is advancing and in a short while the fish will dive for the deep. He must sieve out as many as he can now, and he is getting a lot. At this point, the voice of a gypsy woman calls: "Ho brothers, got any fish?"

Knowing the trouble and distraction gypsies cause once let in, Tilak cannily says they have no fish.

But the gypsy woman does not believe him. Paddling her little boat that resembles a weaver bird's nest, she hitches alongside Kishore's boat. Holding on to her boat's rope, she leaps into Kishore's boat, looks in the hold and says: "So, fisherman, they said you have no fish. Give me four-paisa's worth of this fish."

The load in the net Kishore is trying to haul out is particularly heavy. Feet braced on the base of the bamboo stump at the boat's edge and hands pulling the net's handle, his torso straining backward as he pulls, his bare back touches the gypsy woman's breasts.

The gypsy woman is young, healthy; her breasts rise immodestly high. Their unexpected firm-soft touch sends an electric current through Kishore's body. He could have slipped off the bamboo stump, broken an arm or leg, and created quite an incident. The gypsy woman pulls him back with one hand around his chest and the other grasping his shoulder, holding him tightly to her. With this support, Kishore keeps from falling and steadies himself. But he loses his composure. The gypsy woman's breast feels cold like a snake. Slowly releasing her pressure, she teases him, "Would you rather trip over, brother? Can't you hold on to me?"

From the stern Tilak asks the gypsy woman to leave them alone and go back to her boat.

"You're an old man, what've I got to do with you? My business is with this one here." She puts her hand on Kishore's shoulder again and is about to brush her breasts against his back once more.

"In which birth was he related to you?"

"Keep quiet, lice-filled old vulture. How'd you know who he is to me?"

Kishore feels obliged to defend one of his own from her foul mouth. Caught in a dilemma, he finally says: "Ho gypsy woman, go back to your own boat now."

"I'll go as soon as you give me the fish. Think I came to live in your boat?"

"Here's your four paisa of fish. Now go."

"Got the fish now but not the man of my heart. You're the one!"

"Stop flirting. My Tilak here can get very angry."

"Don't care who gets angry. I just worry about leaving behind the man of my heart, and having to beat my chest later and cry. Can't carry such heavy losses in my business!"

Amused, Kishore says: "In one moment I turn into the man of your heart. Where's the earlier man of your heart?"

"Flew away—didn't tie him in time. Got to tie you in time."

"What've you got, gypsy woman, to tie me with?"

"Got snakes. Snakes in my basket."

She goes into her boat beside theirs, reaches into one of the baskets and with a snake in each hand thrusts them toward Kishore's neck. Startled, Kishore begs: "Please, gypsy woman, take your snakes away! They really scare me!"

"I will if you do what I want."

"Whatever, just say it."

"Give me two more fish as a bonus."

With a displeased face Kishore hands her some fish: "Here, take it and now go."

"I'm going. You're such a nice boy. You're my granddaughter's groom."

One nudge pushes Kishore out of Indra's court in heaven onto the bare ground on earth!

The gypsy woman is leaving victorious when Subal comes up and stops her. "Have you got soap with you, gypsy woman? Give me two paisa of soap before you leave."

Well before the singing is to start at the appointed place, the three of them arrive at the fish-drying stretch dressed and groomed. The two young men have arranged their dhotis, usually gathered up short and tight, to fall down to the ankles and have carefully draped the towel over one shoulder. In this clothing their bare muscular chests and arms look graceful. On arrival they are amazed by what they see.

The chief owns four large tanks. During the monsoon when the river overflows the banks, whole shoals of fish, some from far away, swim into the tanks and find shelter there. When the water starts to recede, the chief's men come and dam those tanks, locking the fish in—thousands of large fish such as *rui, katla, nandil, mrigel.* In the dry season of winter and spring, Malo boats from distant villages come here, each boat with four to five men and fifteen to twenty women. Malo men and women from many communities of many different villages come together in one spot in this way. Large sheds are raised to last for six months, each shed the length of a full sprint, in which they stay for the duration of the work.

Strangers gather here and become one huge family. They eat together, stay together, and work together. Heaps of rice and huge quantities of vegetables are cooked as at big festivities. People sit down in long rows to eat. After eating and washing their hands and mouths in the river, they return to work.

And what is the work they do all day? The women sit on the ground in long rows, each with the flat base of her fish cutter held down between her toes. One group of men brings basketfuls of freshly hauled fish and unloads them in piles before the women. The women's hands work with the smooth swiftness of machines. With three moves in the blink of an eye each woman guts and cleans a large fish, then precisely throws it over her shoulder onto other piles, where another group of men carries the fish in basketfuls to the raised ground prepared for drying. Day after day for three months this work goes on. When the dried fish is sold off to merchants, the fisherfolk prepare to end their six-month trip away from their home regions and head back. They call this trip "plying the fish-drying stretch."

A basketful of colored powder and a vatful of colored water have been set out. Between two lengths of bamboo stuck in the ground on two sides of a square set of four mud-plastered steps is hung a tiny swing made of a bit of red cloth. In it is placed an image of the crawling baby Krishna, an upturned hand held out for a sweet ball. With no Radha beside him, the baby god swings by himself, crawling and holding out his hand, hanging in the enclosure of red cloth. People come one after another to put a little colored powder on him and give the swing a gentle push. And thus he swings continuously.

The people here are ready, but the villagers from Shukdebpur have not yet come. One of the men receiving the guests ushers Kishore and his companions to the deity in the swing, gives them a little brass plate with a few handfuls of colored powder from the basket, and invites them to put some on the baby god's feet.

Can anyone tell where the god of love sets a trap and for whom, whose hearts are to be joined and where? Unseen, unknown to anyone, the knot is tied. And suddenly one day a person finds another never seen before but somehow known forever, from life to life. At the Dol festival in the fish-drying stretch of Ujaninagar, Kishore falls into just such a trap laid for him.

After the three of them touch the image of Bal-Gopal with color, several men come forward to smear them with colored powder, followed by a group of women. Three or four older women touch Kishore's forehead with color. Receiving it like mother's blessing, Kishore puts color on the feet of each of them, then makes the symbolic gesture of respect, touching the dust from their feet to his forehead. The younger married women, of an age that could make them his sisters and sisters-in-law, touch his cheeks and forehead with color. He accepts quietly with no gesture in return. Then he finds before him one who creates a problem for him.

She is an unmarried girl of about fifteen. Her body is blooming, but the flood of her beauty overwhelms every detail. Alive with the colors of this soaring spring morning, her body betrays the unfamiliar restlessness of her mind at this treacherous age. Such physical maturity rarely comes to Malo girls before marriage. Usually their bodies bloom like this two to three years after marriage. How could this breach of the rules arise, from where did it come to present itself before Kishore?

In touching his cheek with color, her hands tremble, her heart flutters. The soft touch of her tremulous hand opens up the petals, one after another, of a mysterious lotus bud hidden within Kishore's heart. Shivering with this sensation never felt before, he looks at her eyes. They have an eager entreaty and seem to tell Kishore, "Through many lives I arranged this plate of color. Only for you. Take it. Take me too with my color."

Her hand holding the plate of color shakes uncontrollably. Blushing red with shyness, she lowers her eyes but seems unable to walk away. She is saved by her mother, who quietly comes to put her arm around the girl and shelter her against her own body. Subal breaks Kishore's trance by tugging at his arm with a jerk and saying, "Ho *dada*, let's go to the place of singing."

Half the men of Shukdebpur village are out fishing at this time. The chief has gone to Basudebpur to settle an old dispute concerning an area of marshland. The women of Shukdebpur now join the women at the khala. The men too come soon after, closing the doors of their homes.

Tired after the exchange of color, the men all sit down on mats of woven leaves at one side of the gathering. On the other side, the women still greet one another and exchange color. The singing starts on the men's side. Dressed as the king of Holi foolery, one man wears a garland of a strip of banana trunk, a crown of banana leaves, a torn and worn-out waistcloth, and a torn vest. From time to time he springs up to dance, bending and twisting his hips, and then slouches back to rest. He is an old man.

Remembering and reexperiencing the abandon of festive joy, Tilak too wishes to play the king of Holi, like that man. Whispering his wish into Kishore's ears, he gets only discouragement: "We're strangers here. Better sit and behave. If you dance and do those things, they'll think we're crazy." But Tilak is not a man easily dissuaded. He waits for the right moment: when the singing picks up its tempo and the beat of *jhumur* dancing speeds up with it, then without looking at anyone he'll go to the middle of the stage and break into a dance. Somehow getting up there and making the first few rounds shatters all hesitation; there'll be no problem after that.

The male singers have divided into two groups, one Radha's and the other Krishna's, and exchange erotic songs in a rising crescendo. Radha's side starts with a song in chaste language.

> I beg you, O *koel*, to stop singing,
> though the springtime is so pleasing.
> The heart of this lonely woman
> burns without her beloved man.
> Burns harder with a dip in water.
> O, there's no cooling from this fire.
> The bee has forgotten the bud blooming.

Krishna's side answers vigorously with a louder song.

> The god of love, Madan, is here with spring—
> no more can I stay in alone, with my longing.
> Her husband gone far away,
> what's a woman to do, I say,
> how long her bosom to keep covering.

Radha's side still observes restraint and offers this song.

> The groves fill with flower,
> the bees drink their nectar.
> Sweet memories seize my heart,
> whom can I tell how they hurt!
> Merciless is the season of spring,
> with the branches all blooming.
> On an endless trip he stays away,
> the koel in the branch sings away,
> O my friend, O my friend, O . . .

Krishna's side now grows bold to the point of lewdness.

> Listen today, you Braja woman,
> O princess, 'tis your youth I come to summon.
> I'll take you by the hand—come, O playful one—
> On my open-lotus heart I'll seat you.
> I'll lift your sari to squirt red water, too.

Radha's side searches for an apt answer, when the demand comes from the women that the men now stop their singing and let them start, as the afternoon is getting on. Thrilled with the juicy turn, Tilak plans to get up to dance after the next teasing song from Radha's side, which would provoke Krishna's side to answer with a lustier song. His hope is dashed.

The women then take, the stage, visiting women mingling with village women to form the dancing circle of Dolmandal, their hands poised some to play finger cymbals, some to clap in rhythm. The cymbals strike out all at once, filling the air with the beat *jha-jha jham-jham* and the sound of innumerable bangled hands clapping. The women set their feet to dancing together. And many female voices joyously sing out together. Kishore's heart bathes in an unknown ocean of joy.

Suddenly his eyes spot the girl, next to her mother in the dancing circle, watching her mother's feet and moving in step. Then her eyes meet Kishore's and her steps falter. The mother, turning to the daughter with affection and noticing her unmoving feet in the circle and her face in a deepening blush, follows her eyes and turns to see the cause. Kishore stands nearby and gazes at her, devouring her with his eyes.

Seeing the rhythm of the circle of dancers impeded, the mother gently nudges the daughter out. Stranded outside the circle, the girl feels even more uneasy about what to do now, when a terrible clamor breaks out. A rush of angry noise blows in like a sudden wind, stops the feet, and snuffs out the singing voices of women. What seemed like a wave of noise then explodes into the fury of a storm. The Shukdebpur men present spring up, instantly gather their dhotis into tight shorts, bristling, ready to fight. Some run in a flash to the room that stores bamboo clubs and sticks and fetch several batches. The entire arena heaves in turmoil with hectic battle preparation.

By then the attackers from Basudebpur have entered the festive gathering. In frantic confusion the women mill around. Some of the attacking men have broken into the circle of dancers and jump about, brandishing bamboo clubs. One of them approaches the immobile girl. Bewildered, Kishore wakes up at this point. Throwing himself between the girl and the attacker, he deflects the club still in the air and now about to fall on his own head, when a Shukdebpur villager's club fells the attacker. Picking up the fallen attacker's club, Kishore is ready to jump into the fray when he feels a tug from behind and sees that the girl has caught hold of the end of his dhoti with both hands and is fainting.

The noise from hundreds of shouting voices contends with the sound of sticks hitting other sticks. Legs are broken, and arms, and even skulls. Many attackers are down on the ground bleeding. The rest back off to defend themselves with their bamboo poles thrust out in front of them until they reach the open fields, where they turn and run away.

Against this background Kishore holds the girl in his arms and shouts: "Where's this one's mother, where's her mother! She's fainted from fear. Bring water, bring a fan!"

The girl's long hair has come undone and her breasts are so close to Kishore's face that his breath seems to stir the cover of the sari. Amidst the melee her mother has been rooted to one spot, shaking fearfully. Hearing Kishore's call, she runs to the kitchen and brings water and oil and a palmyra fan. Kishore rubs some oil and water on the top of the girl's head until her eyes open.

Then he leaves, saying "Take care of your daughter now." His parting words resonate in the mother's ears, so like the words of a son-in-law.

That day, it turns out, has seen the start of open warfare. The Basudebpur men are numerous and skilled at attack. When in danger, the Shukdebpur Malos are eager to defend themselves and the visiting Malos as well, especially in circumstances like these when they know their chief is detained in their adversaries' village. The quarrel is an old one. In order to settle it without bloodshed their chief went to Basudebpur. He has not come back from there. How can the Shukdebpur Malos feel at rest? Hours pass in the uneasy sense of oncoming disaster. The air of Shukdebpur grows heavy with the men's grim preparations for fight and the women's sighs of apprehension. Assembling from each home whatever weapons it holds and readying the bunches of club sticks, sharpened bamboo poles, metal-tipped wooden spears, wooden bars, cutters and so on, the men tensely wait for a sign.

A somewhat abnormal hope has arisen in Kishore's mind—that he will be married to the girl. The hope is abnormal particularly because he is not going to tell anyone of his wish but hopes someone else will come to him asking him to marry her. He keeps imagining the possible ways in which it could materialize. Well, why can't it be that somebody from the girl's side comes to him and says: "Oh Kishore, we give you this daughter of ours. Take her along to your home and marry her."

For the afternoon fishing Kishore usually goes to a spot beyond the fish-drying stretch where there is a crosscurrent. On their way there this afternoon, he says to his companions, "Today I'll cast the net near the khala ghat." By the ghat slope of the fish-drying stretch, Kishore attaches the net to the end of the bamboo stump and keeps looking at the sheds with thirsty, eager eyes.

A young man of about his own age comes purposefully from the fish-drying area and approaches Kishore's boat. What could be the reason for his coming this way? Kishore is thrilled; he may be a brother of hers coming with the proposal. He grows quite convinced of it.

Indeed, the young man stops near Kishore and addresses him in a relation's tone. "I hear the area you're from is a very nice one. I wish I could go to visit your place. A good place it must be—with educated people, Kayasthas and Brahmans, living there."

No time for this. Kishore must cast the net. He has no time to explain in so many words how distressing it is to live in the same place with educated folk and how enjoyable it would be to live in a place like theirs. So he only listens, does not answer.

"I'd like to be related to you," the young man says.

All the veins and arteries in Kishore's body start throbbing in unison. Modestly he says, "We're poor. Are we suitable for a relationship with you?"

"We're poor too. Poor people are best related to other poor people. Don't you think?"

How would he convey to this inexperienced boy how eagerly he's waiting for such a relationship? Even if Kishore hesitates to express his wish in words, why can't the boy somehow sense it on his own? The sky of Kishore's mind glows with color. Prompted by sheer happiness, he asks, in spite of himself, "What kind of relationship do you want?"

"Friendship. I want friendship with you. I've traveled to so many places and seen so many people, but found no one I could love as a friend. Seeing you I feel I've finally found one."

"All right. I'm your friend now."

"Not just in words. I want us to become friends in a ceremony, with the playing of music and the exchange of clothes and towel . . ."

A ceremony with the playing of music seems appropriate for solemnizing the relationship only with that girl. For friendship, the exchange of words is enough. Falling from a heaven of happiness to a desert of sand, Kishore says, "Not with me. Have that friendship ceremony with Subla here."

Then one day the chief is seen returning to his village, walking in the midday sun beside one of his tanks. No one can quite look at his face; a mountainlike grimness has settled on its expression. No doubt something quite terrible is about to happen!

In the midst of these developments, Kishore is summoned to the chief's place. Preoccupied with his own different thoughts, Kishore has been wondering day and night what miraculous event could bring about his marriage with the girl. Life feels not worth living without that. Who will propose it to her parents on his behalf? Kishore might have opened up his mind to the chief, but he cannot approach him now, not in the present state of the chief's worries.

Almost fearfully Kishore answers the chief's summons. The chief has little time to talk and simply points indoors, saying, "My wife wants to see you."

The arrangement has gone so far at this end, yet Kishore was aware of nothing. When he enters the house and greets the chief's wife by touching her feet, she takes him into another room. In it is the girl, dressed in a new sari, her lips reddened with betel juice and cheeks rubbed with oil, and blushing over and over with shyness. The chief's wife holds two garlands. She hands one to Kishore, saying, "When you get back home, marry her with the proper customs. Exchange garlands for now." After they exchange the garlands, the chief's wife abruptly leaves the room, closing the door and latching it from outside.

The girl is afraid. Inside the darkened room each cannot see the other's face! At last Kishore puts her fear to rest.

Later the chief's wife unlatches the door to release the prisoners and, embracing the girl affectionately, leads her away like a sister, bathes her, and sits her down in the kitchen. To Kishore, now taking leave, she says, "Listen young fisherman, don't be restless and try to fly like a bird right away. Let gentleness and patience guide your coming in."

The girl's mother comes the next day and asks the chief's wife if the exchange of garlands went all right. When the chief's wife affirms it, the mother says: "Don't let them see each other anymore now. It's not auspicious until the wedding has been properly performed. Strange ways of fate, my dear! My daughter gets a husband and now must go away from me. I'm not unhappy about it, of course. I'm only worried about her father. No knowing what he'll do when he hears about this!"

When Subal heard about it from Kishore, he jumped for joy and then asked, "Now that you've found your own Basanti here, what're you going to do with Basanti back home?"

"I give her into your hands."

Now Subal's mind starts humming with the hint of a sweet hope.

The clouds of tension gathering over the village break loose like a summer storm. The chief, with no time at all to spare for talking, wastes no words telling the visitors in the fish-drying camp that they must break up and leave for home in a day or two. He hasn't forgotten Kishore and calls him up in the drying area before the girl's father to say solemnly to him: "You have your bride now. Take her to your village and marry her with religion as your witness. She's to be your lifelong companion, your partner in work and in virtue, your mate in this life and in the life after. Never neglect her in any way. And yes, one other matter: tomorrow your dried fish will all be sold and you can leave for home at the same time those in the drying camp leave. You won't see me again before you go."

With really no time to spare, the chief leaves Kishore facing the girl's father, who sits in silence, clearly not a man with a sweet temperament. Kishore stands before him feeling guilty. In a sternly formal tone the father asks: "What is your name?"

"Kishore-chand Mulyabrahman. Father's name Ramkeshab Mulyabrahman. Home in Gokanghat village, Tripura district."

The man writes this down on a slip of paper. Kishore bends forward to touch his feet and, straightening up, finds him already walking away in the direction of the camping sheds.

Near the ghat of the fish-drying camp of Shukdebpur all the boats are getting ready to leave. Already from this side of the river Kishore can see the Basudebpur men advancing, their dhotis worn like shorts and their hands carrying bamboo club sticks. Even from this distance their dark bodies and menacing approach remind him of a dark cloud that breaks away from the cloud mass in a far corner of the sky and comes rushing ahead of the storm. The thought of leaving the chief to his troubles saddens Kishore. He keeps thinking how helpless the man is even with all his money, his people, his business. And the chief's wife, she's even more helpless. But Kishore and his group must leave; the chief is unbending in his order—all his visiting tenants must leave before the trouble breaks out, he will not have outsiders caught up in it.

The trouble will most likely break out near the disputed tank on this side. The visitors quickly prepare to depart. Leavetaking in a boat is always deeply moving—this one in particular. Accompanying the new bride down to the boat is the chief's wife, who breaks into sobs. Seeing the tears in her eyes, Kishore's own tears well up inside and strain against his chest.

The bride first washes her feet in the river and then, after touching the feet of the elders, climbs into his boat. The two boats set off together, Kishore's and her parents'. For some distance they move out side by side. Then the parents' boat starts veering toward a branch off the western side of the main river. It moves away but is not too far off to hide the persons in it—a woman just past her youth, who has been sobbing hard holding a handful of her sari to her mouth to muffle the sound, now crying aloud, and even that hard-hearted man whose sternness finally dissolves as he removes his towel from his shoulder to cover his eyes.

They move farther away and become indistinct. Inside Kishore's boat, in the heart of a girl newly become a woman, all the dams now give way to an uncontrollable flood of tears.

After an afternoon of nonstop rowing, as evening approaches Tilak grows increasingly worried. He keeps the problem to himself until he thinks of a solution and then says to Kishore: "We're entering a part of the river where pirates rule, and we've got a young woman in the boat. I ask you, Kishore, to do this. Make a bed for her in the cell under the floorboards, so hidden that no one sees her and no one can tell she's here."

For his new wife's journey away from her home, Kishore makes a bed in the cell under the platform with patch quilts and a pillow. At nightfall they anchor the boat to cook and eat. The bride is let out, fed, and concealed again. Before going to sleep and watching Kishore's restlessness, Tilak sternly admonishes him: "Kishore, you must respect what this old man has to tell you. Don't even think of approaching the cell of the boat." Embarrassed, Kishore lies down next to Subal. Before daybreak they resume their journey.

Under Tilak's watchful eyes Kishore cannot even see her, let alone touch her. Subal has the task of feeding and taking care of her. Though the boat's master, he must in this matter obey Tilak.

Subal, working away at the boat's rudder at the back, says: "So, dada, you've finally found the wife of your heart?"

Smiling shyly, Kishore says, "How can I tell, brother? Haven't seen her well, haven't known her well. It's been so long since I saw her that I can't recall her face. May not even know if they put somebody else in her place!"

Although rainless Chaitra has passed and the summer is still in Baisakh, the water of Meghna river has already started to rise, sending upstream a strong opposite current. The swelling water has reached the narrow ridges of the paddy fields and jute fields on the bank. Picking up the handle of the towing rope, Kishore jumps down to the bank to pull the boat against the upstream current.

Kishore pulls with almost superhuman strength, making the boat swim like a water snake against the current. Using the full length of the towing rope, he pulls from quite some distance ahead of the boat. Subal, from his position at the scull, keeps his eyes on Kishore—he looks small against the backdrop of the river's expanse. Subal sees the bank slowly dipping

and the straining figure going down from ankle-depth to waist-depth. But
he has not quite realized what he sees. Kishore tows on unmindful of the
increasing depth and the wet cloth around his waist. Waking to the seriousness of what he sees, Subal shouts in alarm: "What're you doing,
Kishore-dada? Brake it, brake it. The jute fields are full of snakes. Slow
down and get back in the boat."

Kishore wakes up too and, slowing down, gets back in the boat. Subal
scolds him. "Kishore-dada, why do you sometimes act as if possessed by
evil spirits?"

Ignoring the question, Kishore asks: "How many more days are we
from home, bhai?"

Tilak answers. "The mouth of Aganagar is a day's journey from here.
From there if we can go one whole day nonstop, we'll reach Bhairab and
stop for the night in the inlet of Khalapura beyond Bhairab Bazar. From
there the mouth of our Titash is another half-day's journey."

They reach the mouth of Aganagar exactly as Tilak said they would.
They spend the night there and set off early. But then two entire days go
by with no sign at all of Bhairab Bazar.

Strong head winds start whipping up the waters ahead of them. The
boat barely moves forward one cubit before it loses another, even though
the two young men strain at the oars. Huge waves toss the boat high one
moment and fling it down the next. The two men at the oars sometimes
find the water above their waist, filling the boat in great splashes. Kishore
frantically bails out the water between strokes. Subal at the stern, in the
assault of wind and water, looks shrunken like a wet crow. From time to
time he still manages to throw all his strength against the steering oar.
The boat then goes forward a little, like a wind-up mechanism, only to be
pushed back like a broken-springed one by the current. Tilak has fallen
totally silent. In a frightened voice Kishore says: "Subal my brother,
we're not going to get back home." Pained by the despair in his voice,
Subal applies more pressure on the steering oar, taking it and himself
close to breaking point.

They have no time to cook and eat, no pause for a little rest, no break
to smoke the hookah even once. The look of the river on both sides makes
their hearts shudder. No shelter in sight anywhere, no banks, not even
the mouth of a canal or a branch river.

After three days of battling this relentless onslaught of vicious weather,
just as they are about to fall exhausted, the storm finally subsides. The
wind that blew and roared like a snoring giant now flutters like a butter-

fly's wings. The heaving waves fall asleep, the violently agitated waters of the Meghna grow absolutely calm.

They see the port of Bhairab in the distance and approach it feeling they are almost home. Riding a favorable current, their boat races on with hardly any effort, leaving the port and the nearby Malo neighborhood behind. They reach the mouth of Khalapura; they even see a good spot to anchor the boat. But with the exhilaration of the unimpeded speed, and seeing a bit of daylight still left in the sky, Kishore says, "Let the boat move on. We'll stop after we reach the inlet of the new tributary. Let's get on ahead all we can."

As the sun descends to the western horizon, the new tributary emerges into their view. Here they ponder the violent history of its recent formation, which Tilak now recounts.

The river once had just a little indentation on its western bank after miles of unbroken straight flow. Only the mouth of a canal in the west used to be there, filling with monsoon water and drying up by winter. In its shallow water boys from nearby Baikunthapur and Tatarkandi villages came to catch small fish with their thin towels. Then suddenly one day, the mouth of that same canal became the center of a grand transformation. A large eddy of strong current somehow formed in the Meghna right there and began an uncontrollable change in that mouth. Twisting and bending with furious energy, it broke up the ground and created a whirling wide mouth into which surged the boundless waters of the Meghna crashing on the two banks of the canal, and then started to breach those banks too. The water rushed on in whizzing currents, whirling at obstructions, hissing with violent energy. The swiftly demolished chunks of ground fell whooshing in one after another. Crossing vast areas of farmland and open fields, erasing villages small and large, tearing up the clusters of trees in its way, the surge of water kept up day after day. The speed of that motion was unstoppable, frenzied, deluging. Farmers, warned of the calamitous invasion, hurriedly cut their harvests and got out of the way of the blindly speeding water. Bewildered with terror, villagers left their homes, bundling their belongings and driving their cattle with them, and moved much farther west before pausing to set up shelter. In the course of time, many changes became permanent. What had once been only a canal became a body of water wider than the Meghna herself, full of even stronger currents and at least as terrifying.

Tilak's eyes shine with excitement as he tells the story of the new tributary. The story is not new to them; it is known to many of the Malos of their village who sometimes come here to fish. The fresh current brings plenty of fish into the new tributary. Kishore and Subal too have been here before, seen this horizon-spanning mouth of the young tributary, the site of the death god's awesome visit, and heard the story. Still, Tilak does not spare any emotion or detail in recounting it. For fishermen this is the very stuff of romance. They get enjoyment from hearing of the mystery and drama of rivers, as much as from detailing them. And if the listener has not heard the story before, and if moreover the listener is a new acquaintance of the teller, then the teller's inspiration knows no bounds. Tilak is keenly aware of the new person hidden under the boat's platform. She must be avidly listening to this mysterious story of the new tributary.

Tilak ends his account by saying, "After causing all these events, the new tributary in the end returned to the main body of the Meghna!"

The opening of the tributary is truly fearsome. From this side, the turbulence makes the location of the opposite bank hard to see. The on-rushing current keeps forming whirlpools, one after another, and opposite currents from the two sides at the mouth keep crashing headlong, sending the water up high in a fierce roar and shattering into gigantic sprays. A constant sound as of the whipping of stormy winds comes to the travelers' ears even when they are some distance away from it.

Next to this spectacle of ferocious clash the inlet is charmingly beautiful, a safe haven. A short length of the canal leads them into a wide lake. A placid body of water, not much ruffled even in strong winds.

Entering it, the three of them find a large congregation of boats. Most belong to traders of paddy or jackfruit or earthen pots. All are here for one night's shelter, all will leave at the break of dawn.

Their occupants are tired too, ready to lie down as soon as they finish cooking and eating. But these river roamers of eastern Bengal have treasures of their very own. They do not just lie down to sleep. They delight in those treasures before they nestle in the lap of sleep. Wonderful, different songs emerge from different boats. From one boat soars a Murshida *baul* song. *

> In life's immense waters at cosmic play is the pure.
> Rocks float away and rafts capsize on dry shore!
> Seeing rows of beings seated in water, clothed in water,
> Even the merchant flees, leaves his boat on a sandbar.

*Baul songs were traditionally composed by folk philosophers, both Hindu and Muslim. These composer-gurus gave rise to sects of wandering singers known as the Bauls. A Murshida baul song is composed by, or dedicated to, the Sufi guru Pir Murshid.

From another comes the *baromasi* singing of a heroine's lamentation month by month.

> Here is the month of Asarh, somber with clouds raining;
> On this night in Lila's abode there will be some stealing.

In one boat a man leans close to a dim kerosene lantern, melodiously reading out rhymed verses from an age-worn manuscript.

> Into the land of the foolish king . . .
> at long last they arrive sailing.

In some, episodic storytelling goes on, the talking interspersed with suitable snippets of song.

> All other nights on eastern or western sky the moon we see.
> Tonight on the paved steps to water the moon's come to be!

Kishore lies on his back listening and watching the bright moon climb up the transparent sky ahead of the detached tufts of white cloud that chase after it. Gradually sleep comes to the eyes of Kishore and his companions.

The muffled sounds of tiptoeing and whispering first catch Tilak's drowsy attention. He thinks it must be the shameless impatient Kishore and, feeling annoyed, turns on his side to go back to sleep. Then, feeling something pull his foot, he emerges from sleep. Fully awake, he finds that all three of them are lying outside the covered section of the boat where they went to sleep; their ankles are tied with ropes to one end of the boat. And the boat is no longer inside the inlet. It is speeding toward the dangerous mouth of the new tributary. He screams in terror. "Kishore! How long can you sleep? Open your eyes, a terrible thing has happened!"

In one jerk Kishore frees his leg, snapping the rope. In the same breath he reaches the floorboard over the cell inside the boat's shed and opens it. She is not there.

"Oh Tilak! This one of mine is gone! Stolen on the lake by pirates."

Tilak looks for the hand box with the two hundred rupees from their business on the trip. The money and the box are gone.

Kishore lets out a throat-shattering insane scream: "Oh! What's happened!" The sound of that cry fades and drowns in the exuberant waters all around. Not even a faint echo comes back. The noise of effusive turbulence at the mouth of the tributary grows increasingly louder. Like a pin to a magnet the boat is being drawn toward that mouth. And the sky pours forth an abundance of moonlight.

Coming to his senses, Tilak orders: "Subal, go to the back and take the handle of the scull."

Violently objecting, Kishore says, "No, no, Tilak! Don't hold back the boat anymore. Let it go where it's aiming."

Subal's and Tilak's life-or-death struggles at the oars through the night somehow save the boat from imminent destruction. In the perplexity of night, they cannot make out any direction, any bank. After some time they get back their sense of direction too. The night seems dreadfully, abnormally long. Even this night ends at last and morning comes. But the bird's wing broken in the night's storm does not mend ever again.

Kishore sits at the oars, but they keep slipping out of his hands. Moved, Tilak takes the oars from him and sends him into the covered part. Kishore goes in and sits by the board under which she was but is no more. Where is she now?

Subal's grip on the steering oar weakens too. And only the feeble effort of Tilak's old arms moves the boat slowly on.

Here is the mouth of Titash. They must enter it now, ending their relationship with the Meghna. With the recent rains, the mouth is much wider now than when they emerged from it. After the boat has gone some way into Titash, Subal says "Enough!" and abandons the scull. He picks up the pole, lowers it to the riverbed, and pushes it in with a few turns. Then tying the boat to it, he goes to the covered area and lies down. The afternoon still is not spent; they could have gone somewhat farther before sunset. But Tilak does not find the courage to mention it.

Evening comes again. Night deepens. And at some point it ends.

The eastern sky is beginning to lighten. Prompted by some thought, Kishore gets up. He stands in the middle of the boat watching that sky for a while. Then he goes to the stern end and touches the water with his hand.

His hand meets not water but something else. Something very soft and terribly cold. He bends over and looks, and he sees very clearly. After seeing, Kishore gives a loud scream.

A female body is floating there, almost vertically under the water from her waist down, horizontally from waist to neck. Her chest is above the water, her throat stretched out, her head dropped back in the water. And the gentle current of Titash pulls her long tresses this way and that.

"Oh Tilak, come here and look!"

Tilak rubs his eyes and asks: "What is it, Kishore?"

"There she is."

Tilak comes up and, seeing the dead body, goes back muttering Rama-Rama against evil spirits and wakes up Subal. Then without lingering for another moment, he unties the boat.

Kishore has been sitting quietly for some time inside the shed.

Tilak, exhausted from rowing, comes in to sit down. At first he notices nothing. When, putting a few pieces of pressed coal in the ember bowl, he asks Kishore if he has seen the bamboo tube of tobacco and gets no response, he looks up and notices. Kishore's eyes have become abnormally dilated and hibiscus-red. His face has taken on a terrible demonic expression. From time to time his eyeballs wildly roll up and down, side to side.

Terrified, Tilak screams, "Oh Subla, come here and look! Kishore's gone mad."

II

New Home

Four years have passed.

In a silted-up river on a winter dawn, the water level is dropping. Water brought in by the night's tide is drawn away by the morning's ebb, in a current moving like a hunter's arrow. In a short while all of it will be gone. Two old men struggle hard to get their boat started before the creek shrinks to a trickle. One of them, fitting the rowboat with a panel of woven bamboo, calls the other in a harried, gruff tone: "Oh Gaura!"

The gnarled fingers of Gaura's hands are too stiff to untangle the pile of rope he has been struggling with for some time. He becomes angry as over and over his fingers try and fail to unravel the knots—this he simply must do. The sun is still some time from rising; he needs a bowl of embers to warm his fingers so he can move them faster. But they don't have the bowl of embers here.

"Gaura, go up to the *barun* tree and call them."

Unless they start off while the downstream current is still alive, they'll be stranded, and then they'll have to wade the muddy creek bed, one pulling the boat tied to his waist with rope, the other pushing it with his shoulder.

From another rowboat leaving across the creek, a man calls to them: "Oh Nityananda-dada, oh Gaurango-dada!"

The two old men cannot hear him as their heads and ears are wrapped in rags against the chill. The man brings his boat closer to catch their attention. Gaurango looks up hoping for an ember bowl in that boat but, finding that it has none, returns unhappily to the untying of knots. What he unravels gets tangled up again. Nityananda, having fitted the platform and now setting up the oars, asks the man if he is going to market.

The man says, "Yes, dada. Fish in plenty have come into the river. How can I miss a day now? Aren't you coming too?"

"Tomorrow, not today. Today we've got to take the princess to Gokanghat."

Finished straightening the rope and tying the steering oar in place, and shivering from cold, Gaurango starts for their hut. Angry and annoyed, he is out of words, muttering only "Princess, princess." When he sets foot in the yard, all his irritation and anger melt away at the sight. Despondently, her legs stretched out before her, the princess sits crying for the home she is leaving.

Tears come to the old man's eyes. Both brothers are really full of affection for the unfortunate girl. But they also know that the fatherly love in their old hearts won't calm the unfathomable sorrow that sways her heart. The boy is busy in a corner of the hut arranging in a paper box his fantasy treasures: fragments of a few pictures, empty matchboxes, pieces of weaving equipment, some thread, a disintegrating copy of *The Essence of Devotion*, and a small length of pencil. When he finishes his careful packing, he comes and takes his mother's hand. The young mother wipes away her tears as she gets up, as if answering the unspoken wish of the thin little boy. The time has come for them to leave.

In a tearful voice, Gaurango asks if there's anything else to do before leaving. Yes, there is one thing. They go to the altar of sacred basil in the yard and touch their foreheads to it.

Pulled by the ebb tide, the boat moves on nicely down the creek. A shallow country river it is, almost a canal, and lining both sides are picturelike arrangements of villages, then farmlands, then still other villages. The sun has risen, and all this is bathed in soft sunlight. The boat moves on, leaving the villages behind one after another.

Ananta sits close to his mother's lap. This is his first trip in a boat. His happiness today is boundless. In his eyes is the wonder of seeing a whole new world. The two banks are so close that, as the boat passes the villages facing each other, he can see inside the homes on both sides. When a village ends and farmland begins, he can see the farmer smoking a hookah as he squats on the ridge between fields, and the two yoked bullocks nearby look back at him.

After some time, the boat gets stuck. The last pull of the current slackens and, having drained the canal's water, the current expires. The current in their pathetic canal began to die quite a while ago, quite a way back; its expiration, like death that travels from the lower parts of a person's body up to the head, is now complete. The boats are stalled wherever they happen to be.

In disappointment Gaurango unties the steering oar and pulls it in. What they have to do now is a most unpleasant task on a cold morning.

Ananta's mother, having already lighted the tobacco for them, hands the hookah to Gaurango. As he sits holding the hookah, he looks ahead of him and sees that the river Titash is only a little farther away—not a great distance to pull. Turning his gaze to Ananta, not much longer to be with them, he feels a rush of affection. The boy was so eager to see the river. How his eyes light up as he listens to their stories about the big river, about laying nets there, and floating all night on its water! This boy is bound to grow up to be a big fisherman one day. Not like Gaurango and Nityananda, who wade through the knee-level muddy waters of this dead river catching little fish in scoopnets. He'll go out on the deep waters of Titash and lower all kinds of large nets: the floating net, the great Bhairab net, the trapping net, the sieve net. Perhaps he'll journey out onto the vast Meghna and even cast the "roundup" net. Will he then remember these two old men? His mother, whom they found and sheltered like their own daughter, will become the mother of a big-river fisherman. Will she remember to tell him about how once on a terrible night, when he was in her womb, she escaped from the bandits' boat by diving into the water, how swimming for life or death with the last bit of strength in her body she barely reached a sandbar, beyond which she has no memory of what happened! Then these two old men, these two grandfathers of his, brought her to their own home from the strange place where she lay unconscious, from nowhere to a village called Bhabanipur. "See Ananta, how strangers turn into the closest of relatives! How a path appears in pathless wilderness, how a slope to the water forms where there was none! These two old men aren't related to us, but they're all we have, they're my father and my uncle. Never ever forget these two people, Ananta!"

Feeling the blood circulate through his cold limbs, Nityananda smiles at the boy and says to him: "Look Ananta, my little one, over there is the big river you're so crazy about." Ananta is too short to see ahead far enough. The old man's upper body is wrapped in layers of old cloth. He lifts the boy across his swaddled chest to his shoulder to show him the river ahead of them.

The oars are useless between here and there. Gaurango ties the boat's rope around his waist and proceeds to pull it. Nityananda goes to the back of the boat and puts his shoulder to it. To lighten the boat, Ananta's mother also gets off, with the boy in her arms, and walks down the bank toward where the creek takes a bend and joins the river Titash.

Here finally is the big river.

Ananta gets down from his mother's arms and stands on the ground, his eyes on the river. A little field mouse has come out of the maze of paddy fields to find itself suddenly beside the fairy-tale river brimming with liquid silver. Not a mere river—it is a thousand years of untold stories flowing on between the bounds of two banks.

Ananta is speechless. Silently he does as his mother does: he touches a cupped palmful of the river's water to his forehead before washing his face and his feet and climbing back in the boat at the mouth of the creek.

His mother lights the hookah and holds it out to old Nityananda. She cannot bear to look at the sad-faced, exhausted man without crying. Two helpless old men, their wives dead long ago when they were still young, now seeing off the only family they've known in a long time.

Ananta bends over the boat's edge to look into the crystal water. First he sees the reflection of his own small face. As he keeps gazing into the transparent water he sees the sandy bed, shallow near the bank. He sees the silver tracks left by a snail or two that moved along the sand, and a group of small *bele* fish resting still on the sand, so still that he imagines he can pick up a few by dipping a hand in and leave the others unmoved. The sandy bottom gradually dips away from the shore. The snail tracks go on toward deeper water until they are not visible anymore. He'll never find out about the mysteries that live in the depth where the snails went and their tracks disappeared, where your feet can't touch the ground. And farther in where even the rowing oars can't reach. Even greater mysteries may be there. No matter how hard Ananta tried, he'd never find out about everything there. Moving his gaze back to the surface, he reaches out and stirs the water, and the little fish skitter along the bottom and retreat to deep water rather than float up. Ananta could spend a long time gazing under the water where the snail tracks go out of sight. His mother pulls him back near her and runs her fingers through his hair.

Watching the mother and son with affection, Nityananda worries how they are going to live through the summer. He says, "Titash's water is so clear now! More fish get caught when the water grows muddier. I keep thinking what you'll live on meanwhile in the hard months, daughter!"

She has thought about it. For the coming fishing season, fishermen are already busy making strong nets. For that they want plenty of flax thread. If she can settle down in that village, she will be able to make thread, both thin and thick kinds, and sell it to feed herself and her son.

"My days and nights will pass somehow, with belly full or half full. But how shall I bear never being able to see you again!"

If only they too could come and live with her in that village. But she knows when people are old, it is hard for them to leave their old home; they grow so attached to their birthplace that they cannot let go of it even if they have to let go of all else. Ananta's mother's eyes blur with the flow of tears clear as the water of Titash.

The two old men are now warmed by the sun, their exertion, and the tobacco. Securing the scull in its rope knot, Nityananda gives it two or three vigorous turns and asks his younger brother: "Gaurango-sundar, take this wrap off me. The cold has fled." Gaurango has been washing the stern area; he comes up and, untying the knot in the back, frees Nityananda from the snug layers of old cloth that make their winter wear. Then Gaurango, silently invoking Mother Ganga, pushes off with the pole into the river.

Ananta's mother holds him close to her. Although he sits quietly in her arms, his mind is far away from his mother and his two grandfathers. He forgets even that he is sitting in a boat. All his sensations are absorbed in the river that flows around him. Ceaselessly and as lightly as gossamer, the river draws out all his feelings, all that is the essence of his existence. Forgetting both past and future, he floats in the continuous flow of this freshly awakened, eloquent present. It is as if the real journey of his life starts here.

The sun has crossed midsky. The afternoon is on its way. Ananta's mother tries to imagine the village where she is going, the village she has never seen. All she knows is it is by the river Titash, near where after following a long northward course it takes a westward turn. The shadow of every village the boat comes to startles her and she looks out, overwhelmed with anticipation and agitation. Is this the village? The village has drawn her mind not just today but from the time Ananta was in her womb. Through the storm of dangers that night, and forgetting so many other things, she remembers the name of the village. The village from where he took the trip. She can't recall his name or even recollect his face very clearly. After all she hadn't seen him that many times.

That first seeing! All my heart wanted him in a way it never wanted anyone else, but I couldn't look at him very well. Before all those people at the festival, the music, the noise, and the melee of the sudden attack— didn't all that make me feel faint? He saved me from falling and being trampled by the rioters, perhaps to death. I remember the second time, the day I really got him to myself. I felt a kind of fear in the dark inside that room. I was waiting for him with my wildly beating heart. He came and he took me in his arms and calmed all my fears. That happened as if in make-believe, like playing with dolls. After that, I saw him once or twice; but with others around, I felt too shy to look at him. And so—not even getting a clear, full look at him—how would I be able to remember his appearance! I remember when I stayed like a prisoner in the cell under the boat's platform, his friend came and fed me, but he himself kept away. Once I heard him tell his friend he barely remembered my face. Why didn't he take a good look at me? I couldn't, not with all those confusions, but he could have; he had no such problems. Will a man who forgets so easily still recognize me now when he sees me? Whether he does or doesn't, I'll have trouble. If he recognizes me, he may refuse to acknowledge his relationship with a woman who's been touched by bandits. If he doesn't, he'll think that a poor widow is just trying to get shelter by faking the relationship. I don't wear the colored and bordered sari, the ornaments, and the vermilion of a married woman, because they look odd when I have no husband with me, and they stir up curiosity. I always tell people that my father forced me to dress like a widow; he overruled my objections, arguing that either my husband was killed by the bandits—who'd have killed me too if I hadn't jumped into the river—or he drowned and his boat sank at the mouth of the new tributary. I tell them the old man wanted to keep me always with him as a daughter, with no marital home to go to, and so he told people my husband had been killed. Since then I've worn widows' garb. To others it seems plausible, but I know it's only a story. In my heart I know he's alive and back in his own village. But I don't know his name. I don't even know his friend's name.

The sun has grown strong; it has heated up the boat and the leathery skin of the two old men with the oars. Watching them strain so, her affection wells up and makes her long again and again to sit near them and make a soothing shade for them with a part of her sari. But she can't do that, embarrass the grown men with the shade of a young woman's sari. She shades Ananta instead, and lying in the soft sweet shadow of her sari gently takes the boy off to sleep. Thus he misses many more sights on the trip. Perhaps he sees all those things in his dreams.

With a thud the moving boat lands at the slope. Although Gaurango used all his strength to brake the boat as it veered in, he didn't quite succeed, and the remaining energy of its motion causes a shudder as the bottom strikes ground. The bump stirs Ananta's mother out of her reverie, and she starts to arrange her clothes and wake Ananta up. Rubbing the sleep from his eyes, Ananta looks out at the ghat slope nearby, at the people on the ghat doing various things, and at the tree-shaded village not far from there. As far as he can see are fishing boats, one after another, tethered in a long row to bamboo stumps along the water's edge. The boats are of similar size and shape, each with a domed shed near the back, and both ends of the dome open.

It is early afternoon. The women by the ghat, the late bathers, look up at the unfamiliar boat just arrived, and they watch with friendly curiosity the new people getting off. Ananta's mother looks at the faces of the women she has never seen before, knowing they are going to be her neighbors; her own hut will be among their homes. With them from now on she will spend her good times and her bad times. With them she will merge in a woman's routine of daily work and concerns. Looking at their faces fills her with happiness, with the comfort of coming home—as if they all were her relatives. The little waves of Titash rush in like children to rest their heads in the lap of the gently sloping bank. The waves held back inside her heart grow restless for shelter in the arms of these women on the slope.

An old man and an old woman come out of the nearby neighborhood, dragging a reluctant madman toward the ghat. The lunatic is a young man—perhaps handsome once, but now in a terrible condition and ugly. His bones stick out, his skin is dry, flaky. He mutters frantically, incomprehensibly, and lurches from time to time to escape the old couple's grasp. The old man raises his bony hand and strikes him with all his strength as he tries to control him. The lunatic moans in pain but refuses to go into the water and keeps trying to get away from the old couple, who seem equally determined to take him into the water and give him a bath. Suddenly the madman, as if possessed of an elephant's strength, jerks out of the old man's grip and starts running away from the water. Picking up a length of split bamboo that lies within her reach, the old woman lashes the madman. He cries and howls in pain at the top of his lungs. Tears fill the old man's eyes too. Sighing a long-held sigh, he laments: "Oh God, oh ruler above, what have you done! For what sin have you given me this punishment? Such hopes I had for my old age! How I hoped to live on the earnings of my strong young son, have him bring home my daughter-in-law, hold a grandson in my lap. My wretched fate . . ."

The old man's lament trails into uncontrollable sobbing as he cradles the head of his son. The son, too, crying in pain and lamenting incoherently, hugs the father and goes with him down the ghat slope into the water. The only one without tears is the old woman. Perhaps she is his mother, but how hardhearted she seems! Perhaps all her tears have dried up and condensed inside her chest. She simply lifts water in her cupped hands to wet the madman's body and scrubs him with a length of loosely woven towel. The women on the slope watch them in somber silence. From their eyes flows sympathy. And in some eyes tears also well up. Ananta's mother feels very close to all of these women. Feeling her head almost resting on the bosom of these women, she too looks at the madman with silent sympathy. She too lingers with tears filling her eyes, forgetting to move on, go home. How she wishes she could put her arms around the lunatic's neck and cry aloud with him for a while!

Instead she holds Ananta tightly to her.

Their village is going to have a new resident and a new home—everyone who comes to know of this feels happy. The matriarch of the richest family in this Malo neighborhood, a woman known to all as Kalo's Ma, persuades her sons to sell an unused part of their homestead to the newcomer at a reasonable price. Boys and girls come in a noisy bunch and clear its weeds. Several men in the neighborhood lend their hands to raise a little hut for them to live in.

After settling Ananta and his mother in their new home, the two old men take their leave one day. Seeing them off at the ghat, Ananta's mother holds back her tears for a long time. The women on the slope watch this leavetaking, absently stopping whatever they have been doing.

The little rowboat with the two old men leaves the landing, enters the midstream, and slowly moves away. It may be their age that tires them to row only so far; it may be only their sweat that they wipe from their brows onto their wrists in between pulls on the oars. But Ananta's mother knows that the gesture of wiping away sweat hides the wiping of tears. The boat is moving farther and farther away. It looks very small now. And the two men in the boat also look very, very small. Like children, like two children from the land of the moon they float away, dressed in old men's costume from a *jatra* show.* They are not of this world. They came for some reason—but will stay no more; gradually they grow smaller and rise upward. Any moment now they will disappear completely.

Ananta's mother now breaks down. Sobbing uncontrollably, she is on the point of slumping to the ground when someone steps forward and puts her arms around her. Through the blur of tears, Ananta's mother

---

*Jatra is an open-air melodramatic play describing the heroism of mythological or historical figures and featuring elaborate costumes, makeup, and songs by a chorus and other characters. The performance is staged either by a traveling jatra group, for money, or by a village's own group.

sees that the woman is about her own age and wears, as she does, a widow's plain white sari.

The more curious women in the neighborhood exchange whatever they know or guess of the newcomer: who she is, where she was married, whether the boy's father died when the boy was still in his mother's womb or when he was an infant or had perhaps just started to walk.

Kalo's Ma is an imperious woman, with no time for gossip. Her husband left a lot of money at his death. Her sons too make money. The people in the neighborhood defer to her. In a year, four to six hundred pounds of thread are spun in her home. Great big nets are woven with that thread, and a great deal of fish is caught with those nets, bringing a lot of money to her home. Even this woman, Kalo's Ma, is curious about the young widow. She has been to the newcomer's hut in the morning but comes again in the afternoon to investigate. Not sure how to ask her directly, she begins: "Tell me, daughter, is your poor mother a bit like me?"

"Yes, mother, she's just like you."

"Where is she? Is she alive?"

"I don't really know."

"What a fate!"

After Kalo's Ma leaves, she sits worrying about what they will live on, having spent almost all her money on buying the land and raising the hut. How will she get through the coming days?

But she cannot sit and think of it for long, for soon a group of older women come to visit her. To offer them something to sit on, she considers the white sari she washed and set out to dry on the bamboo fence that separates her hut from Kalo's Ma's house—the big house, as they call it. But the women promptly seat themselves on the floor of her hut. One of them asks her if she has any betel leaf at home. Another asks if she has a hookah and tobacco for them. Ananta's mother has none of these in her home, and she feels like shrinking into the ground with embarrassment. One of them takes out a small, nicely embroidered, colorful bag from her waist and from it hands out rolls of dressed betel to the others. She gives one to Ananta's mother, too. That woman's teeth are stained black from chewing betel. She puts two or three rolls of betel in her mouth and a daub of lime on her fingertip, adding a bit of it from time to time to the contents of her mouth. Ananta's mother is amazed at the way her mouth fills with crimson juice from the mix of lime and catechu in the betel. Noticing her fascination, the woman says: "You look surprised, my daughter, at the amount of banyan leaves I chew. You should have seen the amount my mother-in-law chewed in her own time!"

"Banyan leaves?" Ananta's mother asks, even more surprised.

The woman signs to her companion, who explains: "Her father-in-law's name was Pandava. She can't utter *paan*, which sounds like part of his name. So she calls paan banyan leaves."

"And the amount of tobacco my father-in-law smoked," adds the betel enthusiast. "He had a full head of shoulder-length shaggy hair and big angry eyes like a messenger of the god of death. We all feared him. He was always playing the drum and smoking."

"Do you know what the mother-in-law of my sister-in-law used to do?" pitches in another. "Whenever one of her sons-in-law came on a visit, she would tease and shame him in front of all who watched. She would offer him a dressed roll of betel, singing,

> Witty son-in-law, have a paan
> and answer this riddle in a pun.
> With which avatar did the betel come?
> If you can't tell us of the betel's origin,
> Be a goat, chew leaves from the tree ghosts live in.

You suppose any of her sons-in-law dared chew a roll of betel in front of her?"

The jokes and lively banter do not quite engage the mind of Ananta's mother. These older merrymakers do not capture her heart. They conclude that this woman is distant; they feel a bit offended that they cannot win her over, this mere fist-size girl. So haughty underneath the appearance of simplicity!

But Ananta gazes at their faces with intense curiosity and listens avidly. To him they seem like visitors from the land of fairy tales, their minds so well stocked with tales that, no matter how many they tell, they will never run out.

Another woman opens her story chest: "The stories about my father-in-law are like legends. He was a master in casting Tumri spells. Two masters would stand at opposite ends of the yard fighting each other's spells. One would send a snake by the power of his chant and the other would send a peacock with his chant to kill the snake before it could reach him. Not knowing the counterspell would've meant certain death. The first one would then reply by sending fire, and the second one would put it out by bringing clouds with his Barun chant. * Once a gypsy woman, a spell master from the far-off Kamrup-Kamakhya, came to challenge my father-in-law in Tumri. Her first round was with another master from the village. The gypsy woman put her chant into a mustard seed and sent

*Barun is the god of the oceans.

it to grab his life, and then she tightened the knot of her spell around his life inside her mustard seed. The more she pressed the seed, the more that man bled from his nose. He didn't know the counterspell. Luckily, my father-in-law was nearby. Quickly he pushed the gypsy woman down, breaking the spell in her mustard seed, and saved that village master's life. Furious, the gypsy woman challenged him, 'If you're your father's son, then save yourself from my wasp chant.' My father-in-law cast his spell for a shower of dust to blind the wasps and promptly followed it with another spell that pulled the gypsy woman's sari up and up again. Frantically she tried with both her hands to keep her sari down. But each time she pulled it down, up it went—*fraat!* Finally she ran to her boat and stayed in there to save her modesty . . .''

The rest of the story remains untold because of the appearance of Kalo's Ma. Just as sunrise dispels the dream-filled night, so the coming of Kalo's Ma disperses the gathering of these storymongers. They leave, making brief excuses about the day running out.

To Kalo's Ma too, the day seems too short for the work in her charge. Last night, her three daughters-in-law went to bed late, after hours of spinning. Before they could sleep even a little, they had to get up: it was time for Kalobaran and his brothers to go to the river with their nets, which they do before dawn. The poor wives can do little about that. Soon after the husbands leave their side of the bed for the river, taking with them the containers of tobacco and charcoal, the ember bowl, the bundled nets and fish baskets, the eastern sky starts to lighten and the first chirping of birds begins. As long as Kalo's Ma lives, the wives must get up at this time. Her daughters-in-law must finish bathing at the ghat before the wives from other households. Then, as the sun comes out and reddens the eastern sky, they must set out the previous day's partly dry catch under the tent of fishnets covering three or four unused foundations in the homestead. Meanwhile, Kalo's Ma walks to the side of the river, taking in the young sunshine, and waits at the ghat. She stands facing the boat landing of the marketplace, now crowded with the night fishermen's boats loaded with fish. Traders go up and down its slope in hundreds. There is no end to the din at this time. One of the men in the crowd draws Kalobaran's attention to his mother waiting at the village ghat. Her manner of standing is quite regal, it catches attention. Kalobaran's brother runs along the bank to hand her a basketful of fish. She brings it home and sets off a rush of scaling and cleaning the fish. After a quantity is put aside for the day's cooking of two meals, the fresh fish is placed under the net to dry. All the village crows come to the Malo neighborhood now, and they are up to their worst tricks here. By sheer persistence they may slip past the watchful eyes and drag a fish from under the net. But Kalo's Ma keeps a good watch. She sits on a squat stool holding a length of split bamboo with several crow feathers tied to its tip. Crows don't come near those waving feathers; they just caw and fly around. She has several grandchildren who gather about her at this time with little baskets filled with puffed rice for breakfast. Holding the smallest child in her lap, the one who can stand but not walk yet, the old woman waves the length of split bamboo and chants rhymes that please her grandchildren:

> The crows' grandma died,
> With a winnowing fan hide.
> Go away crows, now go away.

For Kalo's Ma, so busy as she is regulating her household, time has value. To her Ananta's mother is a beginner, a mere milk-fed infant. When those women who came to spend time away from work have gone, she asks Ananta's mother if she has no work to do. The only work Ananta's mother can think of is to fill the water pot at the river and bring it home. Though at a loss now about what else she can do, she knows she must do a lot of work to make a living. But who will lead her by the hand and show her where to find the work and how to do it? Kalo's Ma knows only how to prod others to work, not how to show them the way to do it.

The one who comes to show her the way to work is Subla's wife. A young widow, she is the one who held her close when she was crying at the ghat. Ananta's mother still feels that breath of sympathy on her face, eyes, and breast. The past few days Subla's wife has glanced in on and off. When alone, the young woman's face is grimly sad; there's no point trying to make friendly overtures to a grim face. When she's with people, most often it is Kalo's Ma; and Subla's wife cannot stand this Kalo's Ma character.

Ananta's mother senses the yet unseen presence of Subla's wife in her life the way a doe senses the source of musk about her. Subla's wife has noticed the disorder of her household. A fisherwoman's home must have some spun thread and unspun flax, a net or two in the making, and the tools for spinning thread and weaving net. Without these, how is it different from a Kayastha woman's home? Even the unscrubbed pots and pans do not escape Subla's wife, and she tells herself that this lethargy must be broken in a couple of days. She has also been admiring the bounty of her hair, rare even for goddesses, and longing to undo the careless bun, to comb and groom the hair with her own hands. The face is untended, but still beautiful. How nice it would be to hold the chin, and give the face a shake. Those downcast lovely eyes were once opened fully to look at someone at the auspicious joining of eyes at the wedding. What kind of man was he? But he is no more, and she too is a widow like me.

"When did the boy's father leave for heaven, sister?"

"I don't know, sister."

"But he's dead, isn't he?"

"I'm not really sure, sister."

"Which village were you married into?"

"I don't know."

"I'm asking: you did have a marriage, didn't you?"

"I don't know!"

Subla's wife grows annoyed. "Bad luck! Tell me, is the boy born of marriage, or what?"

"I really don't know, sister."

" 'Don't know, don't know, don't know.' Is that all you can say? You really don't know? 'I slap my forehead and bite my tongue, Whence did Lord Jagannath come!' Did the boy just drop from the sky into your lap?"

Silently Ananta's mother takes the remark, dying of shame, and Subla's wife fumes on. "This place looks like a Shudra wife's home. * Not a bundle of thread, no spindle. Even so, she herself looks like a dainty Brahman wife . . ."

"I'll get some flax fiber this afternoon, from the lady of the big house."

"Oh, from Kalo's Ma? At what price?"

"Don't know. She'll give it on credit."

Subla's wife falls silent, worried. Here a large trapping net has been spread out and the big *boal* fish swims happily into it.

"You've fallen into quite some clutches, sister!"

"How can you say that, sister? She's a woman of gold—cares so much for me and Ananta."

Subla's wife smiles bitterly to herself.

"Why are you suspicious of her?"

"Why am I suspicious of her? Because she's caused a terrible burning in my heart. A burning I have no way to talk about, no means to show anyone."

---

*Shudra is the generic term for the lowest castes in the four-order ranking of the Hindu *varna* system—Brahman, Kshatriya, Vaisha, and Shudra. Since Malo fisherfolk are themselves Shudras, Basanti might be referring to Namoshudras, a subgroup of Shudras.

"I see."

She never spun thread at her parents' place nor had opportunity to learn. With twenty pounds of flax to spin, she finds herself in deep water. In the afternoon Subla's wife comes back with several spinning tools. She lays them out on the floor and explains. "Here's your large spindle to make thick thread. Here's the small spindle to make fine thread. And here's the wooden platform you'll take to the river to thrash the wetted hemp on—that's the first thing. Then you'll set the fiber out to dry in the sun. I'll come back in the evening to show you exactly how to do it."

The result of her first attempt at spinning gives Subla's wife a laughing fit. She says, "My sister is such a spinner that a strand of her thread can trap an elephant."

The result of the second day's work makes Subla's wife happy. "Now pick up the small spindle and try to spin finer thread."

In seven days she produces fourteen skeins of thread, seven of the thick kind and seven fine. A trader from the Kaibarta neighborhood comes by one day and buys all her thread, thick ones at one rupee a skein and thin ones at two.

After she has sold her thread, Kalo's Ma drops by and asks her: "These blasted eyes are giving me such trouble. Who's the person who comes out of your place and goes off like the demon-fighter goddess Chandi? Who's that woman, my dear?"

"Don't know her name, mother. Know her only by face. She helped me with the thread."

"Ah, Subla's wife. Subla is no more, but his wife is. Before, they called her Basanti. I used to call her Ramdas's niece. Once there was a proposal for her marriage with my youngest son, but then she was married to Gagan's son, Subla. Subla died. The girl remains like a big drum that beats out his name. Now everyone here, young and old, refer to her as Subla's wife."

"There was a proposal for her marriage to your youngest son?"

"Yes, dear. Long before that, her marriage was fixed with Ramkeshab's son, Kishore. That Kishore who lost his head and now roves the strange forests of his mind."

At noontime one day Mangala's wife walks by the porch of Ananta's mother instead of taking her usual route to the river to wash utensils; she glances inside her hut. On her way back, again walking this way and glancing into the hut, she is greeted by the sharp voice of Subla's wife: "What is it, Mohan's mother? The moon seems to have risen in the wrong place today!"

Mangala's wife is annoyed by the way Subla's wife guards this woman day and night, leaving no scope for others to see her alone for a minute. And annoyance often makes a person cruel. Mangala's wife steps forward to stand under the eaves of the thatch, but without coming in she leans forward, one foot on the porch and one below, and striking a pose of seriousness with her palm on her cheek, says: "Oh, Subla's wife, have you heard the sort of things that are going around today all over the village and the marketplace?"

"What sort of things?"

"They say that in the meeting of the ten notables, her case will be mentioned."

"Whose case, Mohan's mother, whose!"

With sarcasm in her voice, Mangala's wife says, "The boy's mother's case."

Subla's wife cuts short the exchange with a scolding. "Have you asked yourself why she might be mentioned in the meeting of the ten notables? Has she fed anyone's father's wealth to snakes, or has she taken in a stranger from the streets, that the ten notables will need to judge her! I don't go about saying things in the offhand way you people do, Mohan's mother, without listening carefully first."

Indeed, Subla's wife does not let her off simply with this correction. She takes the opportunity to explain all about the evening's meeting of the notables. "The leaders haven't been home at the same time for a while. Some went north on business; some went to buy paddy from upstream areas; one was down with fever. Now they're all home, and the one who was unwell is feeling better. Now the village is brimming over with all its people. This is the time for a meeting to talk over community matters. So many matters have collected over the months. Complaints against some to be acted upon, matters of conduct to be settled. There are things to decide about the coming Kali puja, about the poll tax for fishing in the river. After all those topics, someone may also ask about what group Ananta's mother will be part of on social occasions—whether she'll go with you, with me, or with Kalo's Ma."

The blast of words from Subla's wife sweeps off Mangala's wife. But Ananta's mother feels afraid. Her heart pounds at the thought of being mentioned in a community meeting of the notables. Coming to live in a village as an unrelated newcomer is such a problem.

Shortly before that evening, two boys go door to door with invitations to the meeting. Starting from one end of the Malo neighborhood, the two stop at each home, saying: "Honorable ones, if you are at home, we have a message. The notables are going to meet in Bharat's yard this evening.

You are invited. You'll have betel and tobacco, and you'll listen to the things people have to say." Standard words of invitation, for Ananta's mother as well. The announcers are instructed to make especially sure they invite those whose concerns may be raised at the meeting.

Ananta's mother would definitely not have gone to the meeting by herself. Subla's wife drags her out and takes her along.

When they arrive at Bharat's yard, the gathering is humming and full. Bharat's yard is uncommonly spacious. Surrounded by four large rooms on four sides, the yard is somewhat raised, like a courtyard. Some time ago, this yard did not look so expansive. Bharat does business in dried fish. Nine months ago, he had dried fish stored in clay containers in a large hole dug in the yard, covered and mud-plastered like a dome. At this season's high price for dried fish, he sold all his stock at wholesale rate. After dismantling the storage, he leveled the yard. But even after the hole was filled, the excess earth smoothed over it made the center of the yard swell up like the chest of a proud beauty.

The part of the yard where the women of the household cook food and parboil paddy, oil one another's hair and pick off lice, is enclosed with a fence. From inside it they can see all those in the yard outside, but from outside it no one can see them. All the women gathered sit there.

Over the whole yard a canopy of sails has been put up. At the center, on a spread of fine bedding, sit the most respected of the Malo community. All of them are high up in one way or another—some in money, some in physical prowess, some in powerful brothers, others in intelligence. However, those with good judgment or presence of mind or talent for cleverly twisting words to confound simpler persons have preeminence in all these meetings. If such a man happens to be strong also in money and in brothers, then few can muster the courage to rebut his words in public. Such an eminent person sits in the middle of the row of notables, one whose expression and manner of sitting catch the eyes of Ananta's mother at once.

Subla's wife explains, "That's the one known as the big leader," and whispers in her ear, "The name is Ramprasad."

"Calm, meditative eyes like Shiva's, and a beard like a great ancient sage's! This man reminds me, sister, of my father's elder brother. Where in the neighborhood does he live?"

"He doesn't live in this village. Ten years ago, after a dispute with Kalo's father, he moved with his family and hut belongings to Jatrabari. It's across from the Kurulia canal, just beyond the monastery at the bend of Titash—the one you can see from the ghat of our neighborhood. That village has no other Malo family, only Kaibartas."

The man who next draws her attention among the notables has a severe expression, eyes and face angry red like the sage Durvasa, and back as straight as a young man's although he is advanced in age. Subla's wife explains: "After the big leader this one has the most respect. At jatra performances in the Kayastha neighborhood he plays the sage's role. When he enters the stage in his loincloth, wooden thongs, and *namavali*,* the audience falls fearfully silent. When, holding his sacred thread, he leans forward and roars his curse at the king, even the king with his shining sword and glittering clothes bows trembling at his feet, not to mention all the poor folk sitting on four sides of the stage. Such is the power of this one's personality! The name is Dayalchand."

There are some others in the group at the center worth knowing about. With little time left before the meeting is to start, Subla's wife describes two or three others in a few words. "That one's name is Nitaikishore. Bloated with bribes, but his worn thatch doesn't get a fistful of straw. And this blind man here, his name's Krishnachandra, his judgment puts, as they say, 'a daughter-in-law in her father-in-law's bed and a son-in-law in his mother-in-law's bed.' For this perversion of justice he lost his precious eyesight."

And all those people, gods in human forms, sitting around the notables, they are there to listen and to smoke the tobacco their host will offer. Already several boys are busily working with dozens of hookahs, clay tops, bowls of live charcoal, and containers of tobacco. Their hands swiftly prepare batches of *chillum* and pass them on. No sooner is a fresh batch finished than an exhausted batch comes for refill.

On a large brass plate, cleaned to a brilliant shine, are neatly arranged wads of washed and wiped betel leaves, finely shredded betel nuts, and several scrubbed clean bowls of lime and spices to dress the betel leaves with. The brass plate in his hands, Bharat approaches the center of the gathering. He bows and says: "Honorable notables, I am ready if you think it is time I offer you paan."

The elders look at him in consent. Following Ramprasad's assenting eyes, Bharat himself offers the betel to each of the notables at the center. Then he hands the plate to a neighborhood boy in attendance. The boy swiftly goes through the forest of people, distributing the betel. Before that operation is quite over, the meeting opens its proceedings.

Dayalchand surveys the gathering with his Durvasa-like sternness. Then he places his eyes on Ramprasad inquiringly. Ramprasad is advanced in

---

Namavali is a saffron-colored cotton sheet draped on the upper body and hand-printed with some of the names of Krishna, commonly worn by ascetics, Vaishnava devotees and singers, and by priests.

age. His complexion is a shade of lustrous copper, in his youth it was golden. The big bones now prominent beneath the skin are reminders of the demonic physical strength this man must have had in his youth. But his eyes have the serene expression of a god's eyes. Yet they also reveal the power of a warrior's courage underneath and hint at great creative talent that still seeks expression. Filled with endless unanswered questions, these immense eyes gaze off into the distance, in search of an essential truth.

Responding to the silent question in Dayal's eyes, he first turns those thoughtful eyes of his to Krishnachandra, saying, "Come, Nagar's father. Bring up your question."

For the blind, to look up or not in conversation is the same. Krishnachandra keeps his eyes steadily downcast and after some rapid blinking inquires in a polite voice, "Where're you, Bharat?"

"Here. I'm here, uncle."

"Is your being here enough? Tell us the reason you've brought all these people together at your place."

What he has to tell the meeting is more or less known to all. A hut's owner is its inhabitant, but the land it stands on some landlord owns. The owner of the land has no connection at all with the hut. He lives his sumptuous palace life. He hires a *tehsildar,* who collects the rents, lodges complaints about defaulters, evicts them with the landlord's signature, and puts other tenants in their place. The landlord himself never comes there to set up home and live. If he did, then there'd have to be many, many landlords. In fact, then everybody would be a landlord. The landlords are so few because their existence is not genuine—it's only a contrivance. They are the exception among mankind. The real people are the tenants and therefore, at the end of the twists and turns of history, they are recognized as the real owners of the land—not holders of paper claims, but owners of the right to live on it. Similarly, the true owners of the river are the fishermen. The king of Agartala owns the papers. But the Malos own the right to fish in the waters of Titash.

The rule set long ago was that the Malos were to deliver ten head-loads of fish once a year. On the designated day, ten selected men heaved onto their shoulders ten huge clay containers filled with fish and ran all the way there, making waves in the air with the energy of their exertions. But the river's yield of fish cannot be taken for granted. On the specified date, the catch may not be enough to fill the ten containers. In Krishnachandra's youth, he was the one who went on behalf of the community to see the king's ministers, taking care to pick a time when they were in a good mood, and begged at their feet for an alternative arrangement. The

Malos' plea was granted: they no longer had to deliver the fish, but instead once a year they were to deliver to the king's treasury a poll tax that they themselves would collect. Krishnachandra was also the one put in charge of collecting and delivering the tax. In the last three years, all the Malo families duly handed him the tax. But some months ago the king's collector informed them that the taxes due for three years hadn't been delivered, and that the Malos of this village must immediately produce before the king's administration the entire unpaid amount.

Although in today's meeting the chief topic of discussion is going to be this threat issued by the king's messenger, other social questions and some personal ones also wait to be raised. Fearing that the subject of his default would come up before anything else, Krishnachandra smiles a forced smile and, without raising his head or his blind eyes, says: "Bharat hesitates! It's to find a groom for his daughter that he called the meeting. The palate can be seen when the mouth is opened."

Bharat, having just shifted from his lap the naked little daughter of two and a half who was crying and clinging to him, promptly answers this joke at his expense: "Why should I worry about my daughter's marriage when our leader uncle is here. If the uncle agrees, I can hold the seven sacred circlings with the groom right in this meeting."

This kind of joke usually brings out warm laughter. Krishnachandra has a broad smile on his downcast face; a few have a faint smile; but most have no smile at all. Soon, when Bharat raises the main topic of discussion, those who have not smiled produce a hum of discontent that rises over the gathering and hovers for a while before subsiding. The common people seated in rows around the notables restlessly occupy themselves with taking puffs at the hookahs and coughing. Perhaps these people do have the words to express their discontent. But the insecurity of their lives has made them naturally bereft of courage and kept them subdued time after time. Hence they cannot promptly come forward to express their minds' unrest in forceful words. Although they have lost the voice to protest injustice, they never swallow that injustice. Hence, time after time, place after place, the multitude of the speechless, even if they cannot storm to the forefront of protest, unfailingly express their objection, however indirectly. Sometimes they express it by laughing, sometimes by crying, sometimes by whistling. And elsewhere, inside their homes, the speechless protest by smashing utensils, by banging their heads against walls, or by setting a lighted match to a kerosene-soaked end of their own clothing. This evening, the ordinary Malo folk of Gokanghat village protest the wrongdoing of one of their leaders by producing a chorus of coughing on the pretext of having inhaled a bit too hard at the hookah.

In a perfectly audible low voice Dayalchand censures Krishnachandra. "In your place, I would have saved my honor by drowning in the waters of Titash."

"Please, Dayal merchant, don't start the episode of Rama's Forsaking of Lakshmana at the community meeting. No good can come of turning a friendly gathering like Brajalila* into a battle on the scale of Kurukshetra."

"Take advantage now of having done something for us in some Treta Yug† long gone!"

The leaders, sensing the impropriety of extending such angry exchanges among themselves, keep quiet. Only Ramprasad chastises in his dignified way, "Krishnachandra, are you not willing to preserve the prestige and responsibility of the position of a notable of the community!"

Krishnachandra, feeling embarrassed, says apologetically, "Grant me a few more days to mend the matter."

"Honorable leaders, I've something to tell you all."

Ramprasad turns to look at the speaker, in the row behind him, a man wearing a silk wrap. "Go on, say what you want to say."

The Malos who do a small trade in fish—buying it here and taking it to town to sell—face a new problem. The speaker is one who will be affected by it. With the chief's permission, he tells the gathering that the landlord's men are demanding a tax from fish sellers in Ananda Bazar. Unless they pay two annas for each container of fish they bring, the Malos will not be allowed to sell there.

Ramprasad's calm eyes and expression harden a shade, as instantly the events that started off Ananda Bazar flit across his mind like shadows on a screen. At one time Ananda-babu and Jagat-babu, two prominent landowners living in the town, each started a marketplace bearing his name and each wanted his own to thrive and the other's to fail. Both sent campaigners to the Malos. The Malos listened to their appeals, were not sure what to do. Knowing that Ramprasad was pivotal to the community, Jagat-babu's men came to Ramprasad in the morning, and Ananda-babu's in the afternoon. Those who saw him in the morning secretly offered him

---

*Braja, which includes Brindaban, is the place where Krishna grew up; *lila* means divine play. Brajalila refers to the happy gatherings and amorous play of young cowherds and milkmaids in which Krishna took part as a child and adolescent.
†Treta Yug is the second of the four long eras into which Hindu philosophy and mythology divide the history of the world—Satya, Treta, Dwapar, and Koli, the last being the recent centuries of the modern age. In each age Vishnu appears in a different form as a savior-avatar.

three hundred rupees if he would give his word. He did not. Those who saw him in the afternoon offered for each Malo fisherman twenty-five rupees and a dhoti. He served them paan and tobacco.

The next morning, the Malos of the village took their containers of fresh fish to Ananda Bazar. Not only all the trading Malos, but also those who normally sold very little stopped by and, tying their boats near the ghat, sat in the market each with a container of fish. The marketplace looked spectacular that day, and Ananda-babu's grin was wider than his mouth could hold. From that day on Jagat-babu's market was a sorry sight. Ananda-babu is no more. But his men now want to impose a tax on the Malos of Gokanghat for selling fish.

"Listen, trader, tell the babus straight: the Malos never paid a tax in order to sell their fish and never will, no matter whether they're allowed to sell there or not. Tell them the Malos know how to start a market as well as they know how to end one. Where they go a path appears in wilderness, and a market appears where none was before."

Perhaps the only person there who listens to none of these exchanges is Tamasi's father, preoccupied with his own anxiety. He knows he will be censured in this meeting. He has been judging himself in his own mind, and finds himself guilty. A Malo's first duty, he knows, is to maintain unity in the community, to care for the feelings and interests of other Malos in the neighborhood, because they have only one another. Those other communities, who are they to me? They don't let any Malo in their homes. They consider anything touched by a Malo to be polluted. At their festivals and worship, even the Malos who are invited must themselves get rid of the banana leaves they eat from, because the high-caste status of those others will be polluted if they touch such things. They hold Malos in contempt: Malos don't know how to read and write as they do, nor how to walk as they do dressed in dhoti and wrap and shoes. But is that supposed to make them unworthy of even being touched? Are Malos not human beings just because they're Malos?

At this point he hears his name called by Dayalchand: "Do you hear me, Tamasi's father?"

"Yes, uncle, I hear you. Say what's on your mind."

Dayalchand goes on, setting out everything. "Your hut is near the marketplace. We hear the Kayasthas come to your home to practice tabla-playing and to eye your daughters. Think of this—your mixing with the Kayasthas will not confer on you the rank of a Kayastha. You will always be just a Malo. Even if you seat them on thrones when they visit you, they'll give you a broken old plank to sit on when you visit them. Even if you serve them tobacco in a silver hookah, they'll hand you only a detached clay top, not a hookah they themselves use. No, what you're doing is not right."

Repentant, Tamasi's father manages to say only this: "Please, honorables, I've already been crying. Don't make me cry even more."

At the very end comes the question of Ananta's mother. Her heart starts pounding. This matter too Bharat has to set before the meeting. "You've all heard of the new person who's come to live here. Tell us, how should we relate to her in social matters—which group of families will you put her in? Uncle Krishna's group, or uncle Dayal's, or that of Basanta's father and uncles . . .'"

Krishnachandra says, "First find out her kinship group, the places where she has relatives."

According to the instruction, Subla's wife asks her those questions.

With tears in her eyes, Ananta's mother addresses the women in the gathering. "Dear sisters, I know nothing about my kinship, my relatives, and where they may be now."

After hearing that, all seem discouraged and none come forward eager to take her into their own subgroup in the neighborhood.

Krishnachandra says, "My social group has twenty households. Don't want to add any more."

Dayalchand's has ten households, each one rather large, and there's really no more room. Mangala is sitting in the very last row. He gets up at this point, nudges his way forward, and says, "My group has only three households."

Ramprasad asks, "Who are the others in your group?"

"Subla's father-in-law and Kishore's father."

"With the new family now you're a group of four households."

"Yes, Uncle."

Later on that evening, perhaps the tenth or eleventh of the fortnight of new moon, Ramprasad wanders alone through the village in ink-deep darkness. Age has put its mark on his body as if by force; only lately has some slackening come over the large joints of his limbs. The vision of his dreamy eyes has been robbed of very little strength. Yet something curious happens to him this evening. He loses his way.

For one who walks purposefully, aware of his destination, there is only one path, the right one; and for one who walks absently, absorbed in thought, there are hundreds of paths to wander. As Ramprasad steps onto another path just beyond the one that goes toward the gardener home, a wave of memories suddenly breaks into the quietude of his reflection, memories of the flower woman who once lived there. Sometimes it so happens that a thought enters one's mind all of a sudden, possesses and engulfs it without giving the slightest notice. How the thought comes, unconnected to the stream of subconscious thought, how it appears as if by tearing open a hole in the sky—that is a puzzle for psychologists to solve. But if we go back a little, we can see that the thought so sudden in its appearance is really complementary to the preceding thoughts, pulled in by them. Thus, though to Ramprasad the flower woman's appearance seems quite sudden, she traveled in an indistinct, barely visible boat into the surging tide of his thought. Perhaps in the darkness the cluster of nets hanging in Ramgati's yard gave him the illusion of the bamboo clump in the flower woman's yard. Perhaps walking past that path also reminded him that a little to the right of it is a place known as the gardener home. The home is deserted now and nobody at night walks the path that goes by it. The spirit of the flower woman, who died helpless and alone, appears there in ghoulish forms to make faces at the stray traveler. And snakes of all kinds move along that path catching frogs.

But that home was not as it is now. Small clusters of trees and shrubs made a beautiful screen around it. Inside, there was a flower garden on one side, a patch of eggplant on the other, a neat clump of bamboo and a mango tree on the third side, and a little pond at the eastern end. Bees hummed among the flowers; the springtime thrush sang among blossoms in the mango tree; the bamboo clump was alive day and night with all kinds of birds. Even when the flower woman was a little girl close to adolescence, she used to walk down that path every day to go to the village school, carrying a roll of banana leaf to write on. Ramprasad saw her also in the full bloom of youth. He still remembers her sitting in the porch together with the gardener, weaving flat baskets. Then one day the gardener died. Still brimming with youth and guarding undiminished her irresistible beauty, the flower woman lived there alone a long time. The home was still surrounded by the screen of boughs and shrubs. As the fence around her mind grew slacker, she drew tighter the knots in the fence around her garden. No one was ever able to go in there to touch the flowers. Even with honeyed love words in their mouths, the enamored hovered near the threshold of her yard but stopped short as they felt their hearts shrink with apprehension. And now with poison in their mouths, the deadliest of cobras hunt there without hesitation.

Why did it end like this? Why were there no children in the flower woman's youth, no grandchildren in her old age to fill the yard of her home with their play? Today, why are there not ten more strong men and women descended from her, their sweaty bodies busy tending branches heavy with flowers and fruits? Multiplying, and finding the home too small, why aren't they here to clear the weeds behind the hut, fill the ditch with earth to extend the house, and thus form a few more gardener homes around it? What kept these possibilities from being born? And left the great potential of these simple ways to wither in a crevice of the flower woman's heart? Why did her home become so totally empty! How do people make their homes and live their lives, and then disappear leaving no mark, nobody to take their place! So many times, the flower woman trained pumpkin and white gourd vines to climb bamboo props and produce bounteous crops. Why couldn't she find a strong support for herself to become fruitful in its shelter? Her home would have stayed fresh and attractive, not ended in this way. New people with the promise of new life and a new era would have played about in its yard. New artisans would perhaps have filled new needs now or inspired other ones and developed skills to meet those needs. Cobras would have come nowhere near that home.

Returning home at this late hour of the dark night are the two brothers Baharullah and Shariatullah. They went to town that afternoon. After walking the paths together, they part near their homes, which stand next to each other with a fence in between. Baharullah waits till his younger brother is inside his hut. Then turning and taking the few steps to enter his own property, he is startled. In a corner of his yard, near the four-mouth hearth for parboiling paddy, a shadowy figure bends forward and gropes about. Sliding the large fish off the stick on his shoulder, he grasps the stick and confronts the figure. Then he recognizes him. "You, leader! Here so late in the night?"

"Brother Baharullah, I've lost my way. Came for the evening's community meeting. This forgetfulness I've never known before!"

Baharullah takes his hand and helps him up to the dark porch. His wife is asleep inside, but as soon as he calls, she lights the lantern and opens the door. He goes in, puts down on the floor the bundle tied in his thin towel, and, asking her to prepare the hookah, steps out with a squat stool to seat his guest.

Baharullah's wife is not young, she is the mistress of a large household. Her three sons with their wives have gone to sleep in the three rooms. Quickly preparing the hookah, and leaving it propped against the wall for him to pick up, she goes to the kitchen to put together the food waiting for him. Inside the middle room is the wide bed in which she had been sleeping. With the door partly open, it is visible from the porch. There she had lain asleep, her many sleeping grandchildren nestled against her, some at her chest and some at her back. Ramprasad smokes and glances there once and then back at Baharullah. Baharullah is about his own age. His family is full. All of the land he tills he owns. With three sons, he plows his fields using four pairs of bullocks. The paddy they harvest and bring home his wife stores in large containers with the help of her three daughters-in-law. From the abundant crop this year, he brought home a lot of paddy; a lot more is still to be cut. At the crack of dawn, his wife will wake up her sons and see them off to the field and then wake up her daughters-in-law to help with the daylong work of parboiling and drying the paddy in batches. They cook meals in the two-mouth hearth, but at this time of year they light the four-mouth or the six-mouth hearth to parboil paddy. Before cockcrow they start four to six large pots, and by the time the sun rises they are ready to spread out the parboiled paddy in the cleaned yard to dry through the day.

The smooth, whitish mud-plastered floor of the yard shines in the faint yellow light of the lantern. Handing the hookah back to Baharullah, Ramprasad says, "I hear the crop is good this year."

"Yes, chief. Quite good."

"Are you arranging for *jari* singing after the harvest?" *

"No. I had to let it go this year. The way the paddy are rushing on to ripen all at once, where's the time for me to go around looking for a jari *ustad?*"

Blowing smoke from his mouth, Ramprasad glances at the clear wide yard, where jari singing has been held so many times. The best master in the whole area was brought in. For a whole month the jari master stayed in the village and trained the young boys. Once they were ready, another troupe would be invited to compete with them. Groups of boys and young men did the heroes' dance in step, holding waists and shoulders in formation, sending tremors through the whole yard. The music was so absorbing that people forgot all else.

"Baharullah bhai, how lovely those songs were! The tunes of two songs are stuck deep in my heart—'How I long to fly like a bird to the tract of Karbala' and the other one, 'At Jainal's crying, how can the heart be held, when even the trees their leaves they shed.' " †

---

* Sessions of *jari* singing are held in rural East Bengal on the occasion of Muharrem. The songs commemorate the martyrs of the siege of Karbala (A.D. 680). Although Muharrem is in August, the jari singing sessions in villages are held in late November or early December after the harvesting of the main crop, autumn paddy.

† Jainal (Hinduized pronunciation of Arabic *Zainul*), the son of Imam Husayn and Safina. Tormented by the crying of a thirsty baby, Husayn braved the siege to open an access to the Al Furat river (the Euphrates) and became a martyr.

"You're right, leader! Those songs were so absorbing. Do you also remember this one—'Don't go to the battle, my lad, with the Kafirs' lands all around, where jewels may be but no water is found!' It's been a few years since we heard these songs. In this yard of mine there was jari singing so many times."

The Malo fishermen were also invited to come and listen to the jari singing. Ramprasad has listened to those songs many times, sitting in this very yard. Filled with the moods of heroism and tragedy, those songs held the audience in rapture, riveted to their seats. For several years in a row the crop has been poor, and the farmers have got deep in debt. Those who borrowed from the loan company and failed to repay on time because of recurrent bad harvests must take heaps of rebuke and threat when each installment falls due. How can they find the joy in their hearts to sing jari songs? This year the harvest is plentiful, but they are working day and night reaping and carrying the paddy. They do not have time to organize their jari singing.

"The time for the Malos' Kali puja isn't far off, is it, leader?"

"Not very far. On the fourteenth night of the coming new moon."

"They've arranged singing for the occasion this year?"

"Yes, eight sessions. Four of jatra and four of singing poets' duel."

"Eight sessions! With all that money they could have started a school in the Malo neighborhood."

"You're talking about a school! The Malos are thrilled the way they are; what do they care for a school of their own!"

"You know, leader, I myself never learned even the first letters of the alphabet. Now I understand a little how valuable is the stuff in those black letters. Every morning when I go past the school I persuaded Ezmaili to hold in the corner of the mosque, I stand there and listen. The boys recite the alphabets aloud and it sounds so sweet in my ears."

"Baharullah bhai, Malos can't stand criticism even when there's a reason for it; they want to hit back with sticks. It's because of this frustration that I left my native village and went to live away from it."

Baharullah takes a long puff at the hookah, puts it down, and says in reply: "The Malos have an easier life. We farmers take the grind. We may have rice at home to eat, but can we buy even a thin towel to wear around our waist? After selling the jute, we see a little money, but most of it goes into paying taxes and loans. Then so many farmers are forced to sell their land. With your prayer and theirs, my land has so far escaped the pressure to sell. But who can say what'll happen later on."

"Never do such a thing, Baharullah bhai. Never let go of your land as long as you've got life in your body. It's different in the case of the Malos.

They live in perches set up on water! The water rises when the tide comes in and falls when the tide goes out. Can water ever be trusted, can it ever be depended on? Without the relation to land, man's life has no security, Baharullah bhai."

"Come, leader, let me walk with you part of your way."

From under the thatched eaves over the porch Ramprasad steps into the smooth open yard and sees the moon rising. A powerful, splendid orb—riding forward as if in a mightily driven chariot.

"The moon is up, Baharullah bhai. Stay home and eat your meal. Now I can find my way alone."

The new moon that crawled out of the horizon like an infant a little earlier climbs steadily up toward the center of the sky. The sky—transparent, bluish, starless—seems to have dropped from the faraway unseen world down very near, to hold a canopy of moonlight over the sleeping Malo neighborhood. The rows of huts, close together and of similar height, with their sloping roofs of straw, stand tall and bathe in the stream of clear moonlight. Into corners here and there fall little pieces of shadow. Ramprasad walks on, stepping into them and watching this bounty of moonlight in the Malo neighborhood; its full smile spreads a shimmering wealth of dreamlike beauty over the homes that stretch up to receive the passionate embrace of the transparent sky. No one else in the sleeping neighborhood sees this scene except Ramprasad.

Another person does see it; but his seeing is meaningless, feelingless. Stepping into Ramkeshab's yard, Ramprasad sees him flitting across the yard from one side to the other. The moonlight is a bit less bright here. Fishnet spread all over the yard on bamboo poles casts its shadow on the ground. Fish cannot get their heads through those net holes, but moonbeams can; through each hole moonlight falls on the yard's bare ground. It is as if a marvelously clever Malo girl with unearthly ability has woven a net of moonlight and spread it over the ground of Ramkeshab's yard.

To the north of the yard is Ramkeshab's hut, a two-roof hut with a length of porch facing it. The low foundation is broken in places along the corners and the edges. The eastern room was built as the inner quarter and once had a protective fence with a one-way view. It came apart long ago. Attempts were made earlier to cover the gaps with fishnet; there is no such attempt anymore. It is obvious that in this home the need to protect privacy is over.

On the porch, some tangled ropes, carelessly stored in the rafters of the roof, hang clumsily along one side. Next to this, old nets in need of repair are thrown on the floor in a big pile, one over another. Perhaps the man lay in that pile, in the twisted posture of a sleeping dog. Suddenly he springs from the porch into the yard and darts across its entire length in three strides with the speed of an apparition. Except for a towel around his waist he has nothing on his body. His head supports a wild growth of uncombed hair, his face an untidy beard. During his swift passage through the light and shade woven in the yard by the hung-out net, his dust-covered dark body glimmers, a somewhat abnormally swollen body.

In that glimpse Ramprasad recognizes him. Rapidly moving his hanging arms and thrusting his head out, the man comes forward as if to attack. Bringing his distorted face close to Ramprasad's, he smiles faintly and addresses him in the quiet tone of a wise man: "Oh, it's the leader, after such a long time. Now come onto the porch and look at the terrible thing that's happened."

"What happened? Why don't you say, brother-in-law, what happened."

"Go and take a look yourself."

He takes Ramprasad's hand to help him onto the porch and shows him. In the mud-plastered floor of the porch, he has cut three or four long trenches with a fish cutter. Pointing his finger there, he says with extreme agitation in his voice, "Look at what's going on. A girl is being stolen! This is the Meghna river, and the inlet's in there. The boat was well inside the inlet. How did it get into the big river? I wake up to find the girl's being stolen. The outside bright with moonlight and the inside dark and a young woman being abducted. What do you say to that, leader?"

Ramprasad says nothing. He sighs a great big sigh, the way porpoises swim up from deep in the water of Titash when they sense the evening's shade, and release long-held breath. Sitting down in the pile of nets, Ramprasad lets out such a deep long-held sigh.

Inside the hut, Ramkeshab is fast asleep without a care; his snoring can be heard outside. He'll have to go out before dawn to cast the net. It would be cruel to wake him up now. A prematurely awakened man cannot keep his head steady to work with the net. It would ruin his day's income. The last hour of the night can't be very far anyway. Ramprasad is unable to think much further. The slight warmth in the pile of nets pulls at his mind abstracted in thought and his body numbed by exhaustion, and sleep overcomes him.

His sleep lightens once before the night is over and he vaguely sees that the madman sits close by. The cutter he uses to dig the mud floor rests next to him. It would not be unnatural for him to do something terrible with it. With this unease Ramprasad comes out of his sleep. He opens his eyes when he also feels the presence of someone sitting so close to him that the person's face almost touches his own. Before fear grips him, he rubs his eyes and looks again. The man is Ramkeshab, sitting close in a posture of guarding him, his beard and his chest almost touching Ramprasad's. Ramprasad even feels the warmth of his broad hairy chest.

Ramkeshab is older and his body, though it shows a strong structure like Ramprasad's, has broken down much more. But the hair on Ramkeshab's head, beard, eyebrows, and ears is only partly gray. In the light slanting into the porch from the new moon on its sideways course along the sky's path, he seems almost boyish next to Ramprasad, with his flaxen white hair and beard. They look like two ancient infants in an unearthly association, its history unknown except to the still night. And the only human being who sees them can no longer think or feel.

Drawing together, the two old men talk in soft, fond voices. "My dear leader, you didn't call me. I didn't even know when you came. You suffered the cold of the night out here."

"No, my dear Malo, I didn't suffer much in the cold. Once asleep, one doesn't feel cold. I thought that when you went out to the river at dawn, I'd go in your boat and get off at Jatrabari."

"I came out once in the whole night and saw a strange man out here. I came close and saw it was you. Didn't want to wake you up. With the lunatic here, I stayed on, sitting near your head. It's no longer possible for me to go out on the river before the end of night. The cold wind chews on my ears and my forehead, cuts into my chest as if with a blunt knife. At my age, my dear, the time for catching fish is over. The time has come to spend my remaining days sitting inside my hole and smoking tobacco. But fate made him a lunatic. Other lunatics get well; my lunatic gets no better. Come, sit inside. I'll light the tobacco."

Inside, the open-wick kerosene lamp in a clay container holds a little blinking flame. Ramkeshab must have lighted it when he got up to go out. Its sooty dim light accentuates the dismal gloom of the interior. The bed is made of dirty, torn rag quilts spread on a disintegrating mat. One of the two pillows spills its cotton filling at the broken seam. Ramkeshab has been sleeping on it, as is evident from the bits of cotton in his hair and beard. The person whose head is on the other pillow sleeps covered from head to toe with a heavy rag quilt furred with disintegrating fiber. She is Ramkeshab's wife.

"Ho old woman, get up and see who's here!"

The bundle of quilt stirs. From behind the drab quilt emerges an even more drab face to ask: "What kind of relative visits in the middle of the night?"

"Shut up, lowborn crone. The son-in-law's here."

Son-in-law! She struggles again and again to link the torn threads of her worn memory, but she cannot figure out who with the status of their son-in-law could come to her home visiting. The mucus-filled eyes dulled with sleep; the blotchy, flaky skin smeared with the grease of lethargy; the gaping mouth with missing teeth—all this makes the old woman's confused gaze seem so ugly to Ramkeshab that he cannot bear it anymore. With a jerk, he pulls her up by the hand to a sitting position. Struggling now to fix her loose clothes over her chest and around her waist, she asks: "How can I know if you don't tell me, from where the son-in-law comes?"

"The son-in-law from Jatrabari. Basanta's father."

Husband of a niece—now she knows. Respected everywhere, he is not an obscure man. But since the niece died, he rarely visits their home. As the old woman's head clears a little, she remembers the custom and reaches for the end of her sari to cover her head.

Through the stillness of the receding night comes the sound of a rooster crowing far in the distance. Those who live by the labor of their bodies regard this as the most sacred moment. At this time, a farmer's wife lights the hearth to prepare for the morning's work of parboiling paddy. And a Malo woman washes her face and sits down to the morning's spinning of flax thread. Men who have not been to the river earlier in the night now set off with nets on their shoulders.

Stepping out of the porch with the net on his shoulder and the hookah in his hand, Ramkeshab says, "Leader dear, don't leave today."

The morning's golden sunlight falls in the yard of each home. In no home is there a wife or a daughter not busy with some work. In no home are there children still in bed. They are all out in the yards, their upper bodies protected from the lingering chill of the morning by their mothers' saris folded and lovingly draped around their necks. Warmed by the sun, they now take off those wraps, and in bare bodies they are absorbed in play. Beautiful children, fair and dark and in between, all glowing with health and nurturance.

Ramprasad walks toward the river, eagerly watching the children playing in the yards of Malo homes. In his eyes, the golden light of this magical morning has turned everything golden. Today they are all golden children. Play-cooking in their golden little pots and pans the rice of silver sand, they have sent their invitation to those in the land of the sun and the moon. The invitation, though, is only for the mundane reason of eating a meal.

Ananta, too, plays in his yard, his mother's folded white sari still tied around his neck. Ramprasad stands nearby watching him. The child looks up at the white-haired, white-bearded man. Suddenly struck by a thought, he runs up the porch and calls his mother. Stepping out into the porch, she is so astonished to see this distinguished man standing in her yard with such an expression of deep emotion that she is unable either to go back inside or veil her head with her sari.

Ramprasad comes closer and, taking Ananta's hand in his, says with a smile, "Are you afraid to see me? But I've come to your place not to do any judging. I've come only to see you. I live in another village. In my home there is no mother like yours. No little grandchild like you plays in my yard. If your mother came to live in my village instead of this village, then there'd be two Malo homes, not just the one which is my own."

Birth, Death, Marriage

On each of these three occasions—birth, death, marriage—Malos spend their money. And the entire neighborhood gets involved in celebrating or solemnizing the occasion.

Certainly not all can spend money. Not those who have no money. Still, into each home come birth, death, and marriage. We live with these three and with them nature maintains the equilibrium of life's flow. After birth and a long interval comes marriage, and after another long interval comes death—this is nature's rule. But in some homes death comes soon after birth; these are unfortunate homes. Because, although Malos spend their money on each of these three occasions, a wedding, with its unfailing promise of youth's fruitfulness, is what gives their spending its greatest joy and meaning. The path into the realm that fulfills this promise is as short as its two sides are enchanting, with flowering groves, butterflies, and rainbows. Its first steps are covered with a fresh green scarf of spring leaves. The path goes on through a glorious profusion of blossoming trees and ends where all the green trees show the tiny beginnings of fruit where blossoms were a short while ago.

But the fruit, grown and ripe, cannot stay to dry on the tree. The ripe fruit must come off; there is no other way. In time even the tree becomes barren, loses the clusters of green leaves and the flow of sap. Then, as the weakening roots loosen their hold in the ground, the tree must fall, uprooted. For fruit that is too ripe to stay on the branches, people do not grieve. For an old tree that falls in a storm, they do not shed bitter tears.

Because birth, marriage, and death—these three make up the stuff of life in all homes. Although these events occur in a natural cycle in almost every family, occasionally we come across a home that in the past perhaps knew the cycle but, in the present and as far into the future as we can see and anticipate, has no chance to resume the natural succession of these events. The past we can smile about, cry over, arrange our dreams around, but never get back. The present we want to hold in our hands. The future makes us string up our hearts with hope. What is there to gain by dwelling on what happened in some long departed past!

Those who are born must die some day. So each household is bound to be visited by death. Yet the certainty of death's appearance in a home does not necessarily bring a birth and a marriage. Such a home is a rarity, that's all. In this Malo neighborhood, the sole site of this misfortune is Ramkeshab's home. The old man and wife have reached their time to drop off. Even a lunatic hesitates to hope this dried old tree will bear fruit. And marriage? For the young man who went mad before marriage, even the remotest possibility of it he himself would hesitate to consider.

Never will this home ring with the ululation at a birth or fill with the singing at the turmeric bath the day before a wedding. Sooner or later, one sound alone will echo through this home. That sound can only make the heart tremble; there will be no drop of consolation, no flutter of joy.

But Ramkeshab's household is an exception in the Malo neighborhood. Kalobaran's household is also here; it, too, is an exception in the opposite way. It has received three red-veiled brides one after another at short intervals. All three young wives are like fruitful vines; all three are now in a race to bear children. The birth of each baby and the ceremony for its first rice-eating are celebrated extravagantly in this family, the only rich Malo family here.

The middle wife became pregnant some time ago. After the midday meal, when she comes near the refuse dump in the yard to clean her husband's plate of fish bones and food scraps she didn't want to finish, she has a full view of Ananta's mother's hut. At that hour Ananta is usually inside the hut, absorbed with a few pieces of cane and bamboo, a small cleaver, and other insignificant playthings, dedicated to the task of giving these paltry objects a degree of appreciation far beyond their dreams. The middle wife's tired face and abnormally swollen belly puzzle him; he can make no sense of her transformation.

One day Kalo's Ma is seen in a great flurry of rushing about. She rushes into their yard too, yelling, "Ananta's mother, come for the ululation," and rushes back home.

Ananta's mother goes. Other women from other homes have collected there and stand in a knot outside the threshold of a little dark room, silently waiting with anxious faces. Ananta's mother joins them. Ananta stands close to his mother, unaware and uninformed about what is happening. One of the waiting women says to the others in reminder, "Five rounds if it's a boy, three rounds if it's a girl." To Ananta this too is meaningless. Kalo's Ma, who seems to be frantically busy inside the little dark room, sticks her neck out of the doorway and says, "The danger is over, my dear women. Do the ululation happily." The women's energetic rounds of ululation burst into the air over that yard.

After welcoming the newborn with this auspicious rite, the women try to get a look inside the room. Ananta, too, looks in with curiosity. The middle wife's swollen belly is gone. Looking abnormally thin, she slumps on the floor face down, with her long hair loose and tangled. Some of the hair that immediately before the climactic moment had stuffed her mouth still remains in her mouth; she lies clumsy and unconscious. And amid the blood all over is a tiny blood-smeared human being, soft as butter, helpless as a doll. How could such a weak little person tear through the swollen belly of the middle wife!

Kalo's Ma picks the baby up in a rag and brings it near the door to show to the gathered women, who all bend forward for a look. Ananta takes one look and backs away.

On the sixth day after the birth, a pot of ink and a pen are carefully placed in the birth room. On that night Chitragupta* will come unseen to all, to write the baby's destiny on his forehead with the pen after dipping it in the pot of ink. On the eighth day comes the eight-peas celebration, for all the little children in the neighborhood. Ananta, too, is called to the home of the newborn and gets popped rice, different kinds of roasted peas, and brown sugar drops that fill the fold of his clothing he holds out for them.

Thirteen days after the birth, mother and baby come out of confinement. On that day, after everything in the household is washed, the barber comes and shaves the scraggly thirteen-day beards of Kalobaran and his brothers. The priest comes in and chants the mantras, then goes out. Next a new palm-leaf mat is spread on the porch and some unhusked paddy set out on it. The middle wife comes out, wearing a new sari and holding the baby wrapped in a colorful new handkerchief. As she steps on the new mat and spreads the paddy over it with her foot, the women gathered on one side join their voices to sing:

> Look at the queen, the lucky queen,
> with the kind lord in her lap bouncing.
> Eat cheese, my little Gopal, and dance with joy,
> dance and we'll give you the stick of a cowherd boy.

*The record keeper of Yama, the god of death.

Dance once, dance twice, three times for us dance,
we'll make for your hands the flute that enchants.

While seeing the priest off with his fee, Kalobaran asks: "Will you check, master, if there's a good date for putting sacred rice in a baby's mouth? We'd like to get both ceremonies over at the same time. What do you say?" The priest checks the almanac and says an auspicious date for the first rice-eating ceremony will come after one more day. The youngest wife's baby now sits and holds his head steady and, more and more greedy, puts anything he can grab in his mouth. Kalo's Ma says it's time to have the baby started in on rice.

Thus, only two days later, there is another celebration in the house of Kalobaran. Ananta's mother is again invited along with several other women to sing. First the bathing ceremony. Surrounded by singing women, the youngest wife walks with the baby in her arms to the ghat slope at the river. There, she touches her joined palms to her forehead in respectful *pranam* to the river, three times for herself and three times for the baby; then lifting a bit of river water in her cupped palm, she washes the baby's head and wipes it with her sari; she ends with another series of pranams to the river. Then she walks back as she came. After a little rest, the group sets out again, singing and bearing a large platter of rice pudding, to the temple of Radha-Krishna. The food is offered first to the divine couple, then after a bit of it is put in the baby's mouth by his mother, it is all distributed among the children present there.

The occasion that thrills the Malos the most is a wedding. Marrying is a happy thing to do, an enjoyable thing to watch. The one getting married is, of course, boundlessly happy. Even all the neighborhood folk feel that the celebration makes the day an excellent one. Seeing their dearest and closest ones get married and make merry with the new bride is most pleasing to Malos. Only a man who never married spends this night in his boat. Gurudayal is such a man; he is over forty.

One day he got into a quarrel with Kalobaran's youngest brother, when both men were out in their boats by the ghat at the marketplace. Gurudayal insisted that the trader Shyamsundar, being a father of three sons from three marriages, was as likely to marry again as the moon of the eastern sky was to rise in the west. Kalo's brother objected: "Nonsense. For what do you think the trader saved so much money from his lumber business? Without a wife next to him in bed, will he spend the nights in the last part of his life hugging a cotton pillow? Once he mentioned his wish: he'd somehow marry again, not let it pass."

"Yes. You've got a point there. Without a wife nearby, who's going to put a little water in his mouth the moment before he dies? A son's no better than dog piss."

Kalo's brother had recently become the proud father of a baby son. Outraged at this general disparagement of sons, he replied: "What you said can come only from such a king of the childless as you."

King of the childless! The reference to his childlessness felt so intolerable that Gurudayal could not stop himself from uttering a curse: "From now on may God make you, too, childless!"

"Go away, crow of the ghost-infested tree! Now we see why your hair's graying, your beard's graying, yet the sola cap of wedding has never come to your head."

"Listen to the words of Naida's son! Has my never having the sola crown on my head caused you a loss of face at a meeting of the ten notables? Did I ever go around in the night breaking the fence of your home because I'm not married? Can you say that?"

"Stop there, you son of a bitch Gurudayal! Now I'll show you your father's marriage and your mother's remarriage!"

From his boat Kalo's brother swung his pole at Gurudayal's head, and from his own boat Gurudayal raised an oar to hit him. The others in these two boats and in other boats nearby now became concerned and intervened. Some said, "Listen Ramnath, let it go"; others said, "Ease off, Gurudayal, young Ramnath may lack sense, but you don't."

Eventually, Kalo's brother's prediction proves right. Trader Shyamsundar gets his lumber supply from the north for his business here. From that distant land, a man one day brings, by train, a girl who is to be married to him. Shyamsundar didn't have to go himself; it was all arranged by letter. On the day of the wedding a group of older women, visiting on the porch of Ananta's mother in the course of their afternoon round to neighborhood homes, start right away on the topic of the night's wedding.

One remarks, "Nanda's mother was the trader's first wife. Her parents' place was in the same area as mine. She and I were born in the same year and were married off in the same village too, she in a rich family, I in a poor one. The golden stick came into her hand, the cooking stick into mine. But I'm not talking about that. What I'm saying, my dear, is that the girl he's marrying tonight could be Nanda's mother's granddaughter. What'll the old man do with her? When her buds come out, the old man'll be ready to drop off."

A second woman tries to draw Ananta's mother's absent attention by saying to another, "A red-gold mango in a crow's beak, my dear."

A third one seems tinged with the color of youth. Although she's past middle age, erotic thoughts absorb her mind. Perhaps the music of others' weddings brings back the night of her own wedding. Unable to keep the pleasure within her mind, she turns to Ananta, teasing him: "Well, my little slave, you want to get married?"

Ananta has been hearing so much talk about the wedding for the last three or four days that, even without quite grasping what it really is, he senses that getting married must be something nice. With absolute ease he answers yes.

The woman goes on, "Can you tell me what a man does after marrying?"

Ananta finds this question a bit difficult, but after some thinking, he answers easily, "Makes her cook the rice."

"Hee-hee-hee. You're wrong, my slave, you're wrong. After marrying, men take their wives' legs on their shoulders. Hee-hee-hee."

Ananta does not like the answer at all. He feels quite sure it can't be true but worries about what it could mean if it is true.

"Want to marry me?" the woman then asks him.

Glancing fearfully at her thick legs, Ananta says no.

Shortly after evening sets in, when Ananta accompanies his mother to the wedding, amazement overwhelms him. What he sees is not a wedding ceremony but sheer magic, the stunning performance of a marvelous story. Only the storyteller is unseen and his words are unheard, but the wondrous story he tells plays itself out right before Ananta's eyes.

The man sitting quietly with a wedding crown on his head is a huge giant. His men have abducted the little girl and kept her imprisoned in his cave. The girl, now brought out here, looks around and, seeing the giant's men everywhere watching her, realizes it'll be useless to try to escape. For now, she decides, it's better to do this: she walks round and round the giant and tries to keep him pleased by putting flowers on his head. As soon as his men relax their watch, she'll run away from here. But where can she go? How nice if she comes to Ananta's home. His mother will hide her for some time. The giant will search for her throughout the neighborhood and, failing to find her, will be so disappointed that finally one day he'll drown himself in the water of Titash.

Ananta is awakened from his musing when a man stands by him and, holding out a handful of raw sugar drops from a large clay pot in his arm, says gruffly, "Here, take the sweets. Which way are you looking!"

Absently Ananta holds out a cupped hand and takes the sweets. The wedding is over by then, and the barber is reciting an appropriate verse as the honey-sweet ending of the solemnization.

> All you gathered here, listen with your hearts
> About Shiva's wedding in this wonderful verse.
> On Mount Kailash was Shiva in deep meditation,
> Narad brought about with Uma the lord's union.
> On seeing Shiva laments young Uma's mother:
> To such an old man will I give my Uma never . . .
> Uma is filled with joy, having Shiva as her husband.
> Shiva's wedding is over; utter the Hari-Hari chant.

The middle of the passage recited seems to give Shyamsundar a start. Has the passage been selected with his age in mind, are the words addressed to him? Be that as it may, the end of it is encouraging. No matter what Uma's mother thinks, Uma herself is happy with her aged husband.

Before the wedding compound starts to empty, Ananta's mother takes the path home, holding Ananta's hand. As he walks back, he grows aware that the sweets still in his other hand hold less value as treats than they had up until now. What he took in this one evening makes him feel much more grown up. Closed windows that hid certain mysteries seem slowly to open up before him.

Shyamsundar spent a lot of money on his wedding and gave a good feast for all the Malos in the village.

But for Malos the grandest of festivities comes with the annual Kali puja. Image makers come from another area. The making of the image starts a month ahead. Even the huge bamboo framework they construct for the image brings wonder to Ananta's eyes. They need five days to set it up. When a boatload of straw comes, they make padded constructs of torsos and limbs of the central figure and other smaller figures by spirally winding jute string around measured bunches of straw. Next they put the headless figures in human shape onto bamboo sticks and attach the backs to the upright framework.

One day a boatload of clay lands at their ghat beside Titash. Unloaded and mixed with finely chopped jute fiber and water, the whole pile of clods becomes the responsibility of the Malo boys to work on. Stomping and treading on it, dancing and walking in it, they soften the clods of earth to pliable clay. It will now go to form the sky-high image. The boys feel very proud of this role of theirs in preparing the clay.

The craftsmen then spend days applying the smooth clay layer upon layer to construct the body. The day they complete the neck of the image and set the head on top, the immense figure seems to want to talk. Then when a coating of chalk solution goes on, and the entire surface area of the image is polished and smooth, Ananta thinks the work is over and the image ready for worship. He asks one of the craftsmen, "Now the image is made, when is the worship?"

"No, stupid!" the image maker explains. "We still have many more days of work left. Now we'll apply colors on the whitewash. Then one day we work on the eyes and end by giving them life—then our work will be complete. The worship will take place on that night."

Treasuring the assurance of this knowledgeable new friend, Ananta goes home and returns to the scene next morning. But he is disappointed to find that the arena of the image has been closed off by a curtain of sails in front, with a small opening in one corner to let only the craftsmen in and out. Fixing his eyes to a tiny gap in the closed flap, he sees an array of countless small bowls of dissolved colors. The craftsmen dip their brushes in those and work swiftly, deftly, and the image changes in appearance from one moment to the next before his mesmerized eyes.

Kalo's Ma designates the three women who are going to observe ritual abstinence for doing the next day's work of Kali puja: Kalo's Ma herself, Ananta's mother, and Brinda's mother. The abstainers are to eat only vegetarian food the day before and start the day of the worship with a predawn bath in the river. They are to fetch the water for use in the worship, pick through and arrange the flowers, prepare the offerings of food, and place them before the image. They are to do everything that needs to be done near the image and fetch various items at the instruction of the priest, who simply sits before the image wearing his garland and his namavali wrap. Not a matter of small pride! They are the priest's helpers. Half the worship is really their work. The priest is important only for chanting the mantras. Ananta's mother feels proud of the role she is given, but sad for Subla's wife. She is so skilled in this kind of work, yet Kalo's Ma hasn't asked her at all.

The craftsmen do their finishing work, taking not even a drop of water that whole day. When they complete the last strokes with their fine brushes and remove the curtain around the image, the light from the sky is going out and gas lanterns are being readied under the canopy of sails.

Ananta's mother told him to look first at the feet of the image, because of the immense size, and then slowly raise his eyes to the crowned head—if he looked all at once at the face, he'd feel scared. Ananta forgets all about that and looks straight up at the face of the just unveiled image. But he does not feel afraid at all.

Soon afterward he sees his mother enter the arena of the goddess bearing the offerings, dressed in the pure, quiet, graceful white of a worshiper. She is wearing a new sari. Where did she get it! But how beautiful she looks in it! The arena of worship, separated by a horizontally fixed bamboo pole, is out of bounds for all the people gathered there under the canopy. Anyone trying to cross that boundary is stopped and turned away with a scolding. He himself had the same experience. But his mother is in there, bearing so many ingredients for the worship and standing so close to the image! The few who have been able to go so near the goddess must be above ordinary people. Certainly not insignificant like Ananta, they must also be capable of having a conversation with the deity. He feels an inexpressible reverence for his mother. Yet she is his mother— she has fed him, dressed him, and held him in her lap. Eagerly he longs for one glance from her, for the grace of her look into his eyes and on his face. But no, he must be one of the unfortunates, because not once does she look in his direction. She leaves after finishing her work there. She doesn't see her own son waiting like a forlorn destitute apart from her. Yet pride fills Ananta on account of his mother.

For a long time after that, he does not see her reappear. Perhaps she has gone home. Coming out of the brightly lighted world within the canopy of sails and enclosure of burlap into this night of new moon, Ananta at once falls into an ocean of darkness. Somehow groping his way back, he reaches home but finds the door locked from outside. His mother is not back. So late in the night, in such deep dark, where can he go now for shelter? Even the thought of walking alone all the way back again is forbidding. Yet he has to do it. From this moment he has to embark on his journey of fearless conquest. Steeling himself with dauntless courage, he walks the dark deserted paths without looking in any direction. He cannot help worrying about chancing on those beings he heard about in stories. No, he encounters none of them. Maybe they don't know Ananta is going alone in the dark on this path; they'd come if they knew. Their business of scaring people keeps them occupied. It's possible they just overlooked a little person like Ananta. That hurts his self-esteem. He knows so much about them, yet they know nothing about him.

In the house adjacent to the lighted yard are stored all the ingredients and offerings of food for the worship. Perhaps his mother is in one of the rooms somewhere here, sitting alone by an oil lamp with the ingredients before her, like an image of a goddess. Will she ask him to leave if he goes near her? The clothes he is wearing are ones she washed just for this occasion, but they're not as immaculate as the clothes he has seen her in this evening. And he'll never look as beautiful. In that case maybe it's not right for him to approach her now as her son. But, if only his mother knew about his daring trip home and back, she'd certainly call him to her side, if not exactly to her lap, and ask him never to walk the paths alone like that in the darkness of night. He'd tell her it was quite all right, assure her he wasn't that afraid. She'd say she feels afraid even if he doesn't, because if he gets lost in the dark she'd never find another Ananta just like him. And she'd be telling the truth: where can she find another one just like me? I don't see any such person. With this thought he decides he must find her and tell her what he has just done.

He approaches a room with its door partly open and a lighted oil lamp inside. In its light he can just see the yard facing the room. As he hovers there in that light, someone nearby suspects he may be trying to steal some item of worship. The man shouts at him, roughly, scolding. Ananta gets no chance to say he's only looking for his mother. When the man comes toward him and points outside with his finger, Ananta silently goes to the lighted pavilion.

Seeing him standing alone and at a loss, someone there is moved to pity and asks, "Whose home are you from?"

Ananta does not answer, because he does not understand what the question means.

"Ho boy, who's your father?" the man asks again.

Ananta has some vague idea what the word father means. Most boys his age in the neighborhood have a man they call father, who buys them roasted peas and beans, biscuits, and oranges from the marketplace. In the morning when those fathers come back home from a night of fishing, they lift some boys into their laps, kiss others, and for no reason at all tease still others to tears. At noontime fathers rub oil onto their bodies and onto their little boys' and take the boys along to bathe in the river. A father feeds a boy from his plate, takes the roe from the fish he is eating and puts it into the boy's mouth. These things Ananta has seen many days and many times. He has thought a lot about what he has seen and reached the conclusion that only fathers do these things. He has also found out that the nice colorful garments he has seen other Malo boys wearing in winter are bought by their fathers. Boys having fathers do not suffer the winter cold. Ananta suffers the cold, because he has no father, for such is not quite the work of a mother. But whether he too might have a father or if he ever had one—the question has never occurred to him. Nor has his mother ever told him anything about this, even though she has told him about so many other things. A strange question it is; nobody asked him this question before. He finds no answer at all.

"With whom did you come here?" the man tries again.

This is an easy question, he thinks, for someone who just conquered the fear of walking alone in the dark. He says he came alone.

The man, exasperated, asks a man next to him: "Which home is this stupid calf from, Bipin?"

The young man called Bipin puts an end to his curiosity with a rebuke: "You talk as if the village you live in were other people's. Can't you keep track of who comes to live in your own village and who goes away? His mother is a widow, new here. Set up home near the house of Kalobaran merchant. In the morning, go take a look at the little hut in which she lives and eats." Bipin finishes wrapping a thin rag quilt around his upper body while he talks and brings his lips near the man's ears to say: "'In a little hutment lives a woman of great talent!' Tee-hee-hee."

Assailed by some thought, Ananta frantically objects: "No, no."

But seeing him shiver in the cold as he stands apart from them all, a man sitting in another knot motions with his hand, beckoning Ananta to him.

A large area facing the arena of worship has been roofed with tin sheets atop bamboo poles and, with the front left open, three sides have been covered with burlap; the bare ground inside is covered with more burlap. The worship will take place later in the night. Men, young and old, and children, wrapped in rag quilts they brought from home, already sit or lie on the broad expanse of burlap spread there. At the center of the space separating the people's pavilion from the arena of the goddess, a fire has been lighted with thick logs of mango trunk to burn through the night. About ten or twelve men sit huddled near the fire. Tobacco and charcoal are on hand in clay pots and five or six hookahs glow on and off; the men are being warmed simultaneously by the heat of the fire and the charge of the inhaled tobacco.

These men all appear old, heads and ears swathed in rags, bodies covered by cotton blankets or rag quilts, and faces partly hidden behind bushy beards and mustaches. If the glaring bright light of the pavilion makes them seem unearthly to Ananta, that is not the fault of his eyes. At the beckoning of one of the men, Ananta slowly walks over and hesitantly stands near him.

"Are you cold?" the man who called him asks.

Ananta tilts his head to one side, indicating yes.

"You don't have a shirt?"

Ananta shakes his head, indicating no.

"Come, sit here. Move a little, Uncle Sarat, give him room to sit. He's shivering."

Ananta sits among them just like one of them. Just like them, he holds his palms out at the fire and rubs the warmth he snatches over his face and cheeks.

Subla's wife comes out to look at the arrangement of offerings before the image. She turns and goes to the porch of the storeroom, calling his mother: "Oh sister, come here for a minute. Oh Ananta's mother, come and see what your son is up to. He's become an old man sitting among old men."

Ananta's mother, having finished preparing the food offerings, has been thinking of her son, of using the break in her work to look for him, when she hears Subla's wife. She too is amused by the sight but is also filled with compassion for the boy. Only half of his bare back is visible, the rest of him lost in the confusion of rag-muffled old figures, the way a beaming moon is covered by seven layers of scraggly clouds. She lingers, regarding him in this condition. At one point, as the two old men flanking him try to move closer to the fire to escape a cold draft, she sees his small hands try to push away the rags and wraps smothering him from both sides. For a moment his face appears clearly before it is lost again. The moon emerges from the clouds for a moment, for an eagerly waiting mother to catch a glimpse. Presently it disappears, and the mother leaves to return to work, remarking that he is in good company.

Ananta misses the worship. At some point when he felt sleepy, he joined those sleeping inside the shed, snuggling close to them. Some time after that the worship took place with the ringing of bells and gongs. All the other children were awakened. They saw the worship, bowed to the goddess, received the distributed offering, and went home with the fathers or uncles they came with. Ananta came with no one; no one woke him up either.

When he wakes up, it is late in the morning and no one is asleep in there. The people from other neighborhoods and other villages, on their way to or from the morning's marketing, now stand in a little crowd before the image of the goddess.

Ananta recalls the room inside that house where his mother was last night. Maybe he can find her there now. Rubbing the sleep from his eyes, he heads in that direction.

His mother is there, in that very room. And gathered near her, watching her work, is a large bunch of children about his age. In a huge copper bowl she mixes together some of the food offered at the worship—bananas, golden-yellow raw sugar drops, sugar, sweets made of thickened milk, soaked fragrant rice, and many other delicious ingredients. She blends them with utmost care, and the children quietly watch as the food is prepared for distribution, looking at her attentive face and her hands preparing the treat.

It does not seem right to him to go straight up to his mother. Instead, Ananta joins the band of children and, when she is ready to distribute the food, extends his palm to her like the others. Like the others, he too receives from her a large soft ball of the sweet fragrant blend.

As he receives it, Ananta clearly sees her look at him and smile a little. She smiles only a little—the pale, transparent, tenderly affectionate smile of the departing moon at the end of her nightlong vigil.

The four days starting from that day are sheer marvel. Eight sessions, one after another, of jatra opera and songsters' competition grip the neighborhood. For those four days Malos do nothing but watch jatra acting during the day and listen to poets' dueling at night. Boats remain tethered for the four days by the ghat landing and nets, after a soaking in gaab resin, dry in the sun. For those four days everyone forgets about eating and sleeping.

After the four days of nonstop excitement, the Malo neighborhood slumps back in exhaustion. With the low that inevitably follows a period of extreme enjoyment, the big and small homes in the neighborhood stay similarly, drowsily inactive.

The only exception is Ramkeshab's home. The home that knows only sadness every single day does not share the dark wave of sadness that comes at the end of joyous celebration or experience the cloud of exhaustion that follows hectic excitement.

Aware of Ramkeshab's poverty, the leaders had asked him for the Kali puja subscription only for himself, waiving it for his lunatic son. They were sitting in his porch by the lantern they had brought. He couldn't bring himself to say no. Offering them a hookah to smoke and leaving them seated there, Ramkeshab got up, brought out his only good net, and called to his next-door neighbor:

"Mangala, didn't you want to buy a net? If you've got the money with you, bring it now."

With a sense of the stormy waves crashing in Ramkeshab's heart as he came out with the net, the leader who held the subscription slip said to him, "Don't sell the net for this, Kishore's father. The puja and all the celebration will take place without your subscription, but if you sell the net, you will lack one for a long time. I'll explain it to the leaders."

For this reason Ramkeshab felt hesitant; with his subscription waived, he was reluctant to go to the worship, partake in the food offerings, and attend the drama and singing sessions financed from others' subscriptions. How could he sit with them and listen without paying for the cost? What would they think when they saw him?

The night of the worship and the four days and nights of the singing he kept the lunatic locked in and stayed away from the festivities himself. The four nights he spent working hard near the mouth of the canal, laying his net there alone for long stretches of time. He caught a lot of fish and sold it at a good price in the market, coming home with some money. But when money comes into a poor man's hand, it is always restless to fly away. He tells his wife that for the well-being of the lunatic he will invite some people and feed them on the day of the harvest festival.

"On that day," she points out, "every home makes plenty of good things to eat. Who's going to jump in to eat at your home?"

"You're right about that."

What Malos spend on the occasion of the Kali puja goes mostly for the performance of music and plays. But they spend on food for the celebration of the winter solstice on the last day of the month of Paush. For five or six days ahead, women in every home are busy grinding rice from the new harvest, drying the ground rice in the sun and in hot clay pans, making popped rice, and grinding it—ingredients for the sweets and pudding on the day of celebration. Women stay up throughout the preceding night to prepare those treats for the morning's feast. Every man, woman, and child rises with the break of dawn and goes to the river for a dip. Even those who go out on the river to fish take a quick bath like everyone else, getting into the boat draped in a thin towel and changing into dry clothes before they set off. But then out on the river they shiver from the cold dip; and as shivering hands do not do well in fishing, they give up. After throwing the net a couple of times, they gather it back in and tell themselves they can give fishing a rest for the day of festival. The women in their homes and their children out on the ghat by the river know this and keep an eager lookout for the fishing boats. While waiting for their own to come back, they watch whose boat returns before the others'. Getting home earlier means having the treats the women prepared at night sooner. And finishing the feast sooner means getting to start their singing procession ahead of the others. The singing procession through the entire village starts out from the Malo neighborhood before any other. After their group has been out for a while, singing groups from the neighborhoods of the Saha traders and the Jugi basket weavers start out. But the Malos' *kirtan* singing tour is far livelier than any others'. The others' singing is sedate and drowsy. The Malos' singing combines with spontaneous dancing, stomping and leaping. Thus their group can also catch more of the raw sugar drops and spun candy thrown in baskets from the homes it passes by. It is so exhilarating! While the men and the older boys go out in the singing group from door to door and catch sweets thrown in the air, the women stay home and prepare various dishes with the many ingredients they bought for this occasion.

On a day of such plenty, with good things to eat in every home, who will be eager to come and eat the food offered in Ramkeshab's home? And yet his longing to invite and feed some people on that day grows irrepressible. He decides he will send offerings to the temple of Radha-Madhab, and for the meal at his home he will invite Ramprasad from Jatrabari, Mangala and his son Mohan, Subla's wife and parents-in-law, and another person who keeps coming to his mind, the new resident of this neighborhood, Ananta's mother. And the boy he longs so much to hold and caress. But will she come to his home? Maybe by now Kalo's Ma has already invited them, and they will eat better there!

After receiving the invitation, Subla's wife and her mother grind the rice from Ramkeshab's home and take it back along with the rice they have already ground for their own home. Let their celebration of the festival this time be held in his home instead of theirs.

The longing that Ramprasad has not even been able to put into words is also fulfilled by Subla's wife. After the preliminary steps of preparing the ground rice batter at Ramkeshab's home with the help of her mother, Subla's wife comes to Ananta's mother at dusk and pleads with her, "I need your help in making cakes and sweets. Come along."

"Where?"

"In that home where the lunatic lives."

Ananta's mother feels her heart jump. "No, no, sister, I can't. I don't know them well. They've never said anything to me and I've never been there. Please, sister, I can't go like that."

"Do you recall, sister, how I too was once a stranger to you and how I became your friend? People become related by seeing each other; cows become related by licking each other. Don't say no, sister. The man is old, may not live for long. He has this desire to feed some people. Who can be his guest tomorrow of all days? He's got only a few guests. One is Radha-Madhab in the temple; after that he'll feed my father, Mohan's father, and the big leader, and the other person is your Ananta. You and I are needed to make the sweet cakes, do you understand?''

Giving Ananta's mother no further chance to refuse, she takes Ananta with her to the kitchen of Ramkeshab. The first cake of the first batch from the new clay pan she sets aside for Radha-Madhab in the temple. The next one she hands to Ananta, seating him on a low stool. Between turning out the sweet cakes, she watches with pleasure as the boy enjoys it.

Ananta's mother lights the lamp for her darkened home and puts it out soon after, locks her door and goes to the host's kitchen. Ananta, now sitting right next to Subla's wife, is occupied with eating cakes in a way that warms her heart. After a while Mangala's wife joins them, having seen her husband and son off on their night fishing. Three pairs of hands work together now, deftly turning out the cakes. The two old women, Kishore's mother and Subla's mother-in-law, try to help but cannot keep up with them. Later in the evening, when they see both old women nodding, the three young women give them leave to go inside the hut and take Ananta with them to sleep. The three keep up their work at an even pace and with ease and assurance, as if they owned this home for the duration of the night.

The madman has no sleep at night. And tonight, his agitation increases. A little earlier he came near the door of the kitchen and aimlessly looked at the women. Then he went back to the porch and sat there singing, raving, and digging at the floor with a cleaver. Not pacified with all this activity, he starts toward the kitchen again. Seeing him, Mangala's wife closes the kitchen door. Once the door is closed, he goes back to the porch and sits quietly through the long hours of the night.

Deep into the night, Mangala's wife suddenly wants to hear stories and insists on Ananta's mother telling one. "Tell a story, sister. A new person from a different land, you must have stories we haven't heard.''

Ananta's mother thinks about her remark. So many elements of a story have accumulated in her own life and that story is so strange, so amazing, that if she pushes it aside and tries to tell a story she merely heard, it will not crystallize—it will move neither her nor her listeners, and she will be unable to put her heart into it. Next to the story of her life, all other stories seem utterly trite. But that story is not for telling here. Not here and not for anywhere else. Just as the story itself has no definite boundaries, the future of her story is also very indefinite, its resolution unpredictable. She cannot easily reveal it to anyone, but bearing it as a secret takes infinite patience and harsh self-control. In order to keep it absolutely hidden deep inside her mind, she has to apply a great deal of restraining force. Still, she has resolved to herself that she will reveal it only if and when a certain final moment comes. Until then, no matter how much her heart bends and twists and shatters to bits, she will keep it carefully hidden in there.

Mangala's wife mocks her preoccupied silence, saying, "Well? 'O poor woman of Brindaban, which black charmer hit you with his flute and went on!' Are you going to tell us a story? I don't like to wait forever. If you don't have a story, say so. If you have one, tell."

Pouring a ladle of batter into the oil simmering in the pot, Ananta's mother starts: "I know a story of how a certain young man went crazy about a girl after seeing her the very first time and said he wanted to have her as his wife."

"Did he marry her?"

"Yes," Ananta's mother says after thinking a little.

"Then what happened?"

"I don't know after that."

"Oh dear! Is this what you call a story? Who doesn't know that every man, not just one, goes crazy over some girl or other and absolutely insists on marrying her? But what happens after he marries her is the main part. You haven't told us that part, sister, you're hiding it."

"I don't know the rest of the story, sister. If I knew, I would've told it."

Subla's wife now opens her mouth. Ananta's mother's words startle her. How could she know that? "I know," she says. "I know how the one who was crazy for a girl later became really insane, and I also know how his friend died. But I won't tell."

She pauses and then proceeds. "When the lunatic man and his friend were young boys, someone's mother was very fond of them. That someone was then a girl of nine or ten. The two friends had made her Maghmandal float. On that day her mother decided she'd marry her daughter to one of those two boys; finally she decided the older one was nicer and she'd give her daughter to him. The day he—that boy turned young man—came home as a lunatic, the girl's parents changed their minds. The girl's father then constantly tried to avoid the lunatic's father. The lunatic's father called him and said, 'Why do you avoid me? To go to the market, you go around by Ramgati's yard instead of mine. Why? Don't I know that my forehead has cracked? Why would I ask you to marry your daughter to my lunatic?' Then one day, with the playing of drums, she was married. I know to whom, but I won't tell . . .

"I know more. Soon after the marriage, the lunatic's young friend went as a hired hand on a *jiyal* fishing trip in summer. In the middle of the big river, caught in a cyclone one night, the boat flew toward the shore, out of control. Employers are shrewd men; they make hired hands do all the dangerous tasks they'd never do themselves. The boat was going to hit the shore and shatter. Just before that, it was decided, all five in the boat were to jump off and try to brake the boat with their backs, shoulders, arms. They all got ready. But when the moment came, only the lunatic's friend jumped off the boat and tried to brake it with his shoulder. No one else joined him. They betrayed him. Alone he could not stop the boat. It knocked him down and crushed his chest to pulp. I know whose boat that was, who betrayed him, I know all that. But I won't tell."

"If you know, why won't you tell?" Ananta's mother asks.

"Because it brings tears to my eyes, sister, and chokes my voice."

"Who is the girl you talked about, that someone?"

"Her name was Basanti. She is no more. She died."

The air in the kitchen grows sad and heavy. Mangala's wife cannot stand this sort of atmosphere. Searching for something to say to lighten it, she suddenly remarks with an air of perspicacity, "I know too," and fixes her attention impenetrably on a particular cake in the pan as if she would not divulge what she knows even if the two of them begged together at her feet.

With the juicy story of Mangala's wife untold, the air returns to the heavy silence of sadness. Who can tell where inside the minds of these two women a thorn pricks tonight! Their awareness of the madman's silence presses even harder on their minds. Perhaps he is thinking. But what is he thinking? Imagining the lunatic actually capable of thought causes the waves from a long gone past to crash upon their hearts.

To cover an almost uncontrollable agitation, Ananta's mother pleads, "Please tell me the full story, dear sister. Let me hear it to my heart's content." But the courteous equivocation can't mask the pain in her heart. Her friend knows the whole story, but she does not know that its tragic heroine is the listener herself. Could anything be more strange than a storyteller unaware that her listener is the person central to the story's events?

At the earnest request of Ananta's mother, Subla's wife tells in detail the story of Kishore's gaining a wife during his journey and losing his mind after losing her. She ends formally: "That ends the legend of this rite, woman."

Hiding her tears, Ananta's mother says, "Yes."

"Then place a *bael* leaf upon the sacred urn."

The second part of the story that Ananta's mother did not know before is even sadder: the story of how Basanti was married, further depriving Kishore, and of how Subla was killed.

Subla's wife recounts the events.

Then the madman was brought home. His father had thought his son would bring money and with it would bring Basanti to their home. But on his plateful of served rice fell a heap of ashes. His son came back a raving lunatic.

Basanti's father Dinanath now began to avoid Ramkeshab. They were always on friendly terms and had become particularly close as word went around about the impending marriage of Basanti to Kishore. Now Dinanath would not pass by Ramkeshab's yard, and if chance brought them at the same time to the ghat by the river, he quickly walked past to avoid any question.

One day he could not bypass him like that, because Ramkeshab caught hold of his hand and said to him firmly, "Just as people know when the moon's up in the sky, they all know my Kishore's become a madman. Have I tried to hide it or mask it?"

Dinanath kept silent. Ramkeshab went on, "Am I swearing by my head and asking you to marry your Basanti to my madman?"

"Don't we know the kind of man you are, dada? You'd never say such a thing."

"Then why do you keep avoiding me like this, bhai?"

"I avoid you only because seeing your suffering makes my heart weep."

"I live with my sorrow. What good is your weeping over it?"

Dinanath's heart ached with sorrow. The only son has gone totally mad, destroys any part of the hut he can reach, messes up the household objects, screams and cries at the top of his voice. The old man has to deal with these troubles every day. Nearing the end of his own life, he now has this wound on top of that. Dinanath looked at his face and was appalled by how much he had aged in just a few months! And the old woman, she's almost impossible to look at, because the unshed tears turned her mute. It's easier to avoid them than try to console them.

"With whom do you now think of getting Basanti married?"

Dinanath guiltily said, "I was keeping quiet, trying to leave the matter alone for a while, but my wife's giving me trouble. She says Subal is a good match—better send for him and have Basanti married off to him now."

Then one night Basanti was married with Subal. Quite a night that was. The moon was in the sky, and the stars too. In Dinanath's yard, under the auspicious banana plant, Subal made Basanti his wife with her hand placed on his. Women sang and did the ululation from time to time. The music seemed so loud to Ramkeshab that he felt his eardrums would burst. But he remained seated inside his hut with a dim lantern before him, smoking his hookah, trying to obscure the sound of the music with the gurgle of the hubble-bubble. The old woman sat by him dozing. She no longer had in her the ability to understand or feel anything. Also unable to feel anything was the madman, who sat tearing up an old net meaninglessly.

That seemingly endless music went on late into the night. Then that, too, was over sometime. Perhaps the people in the festive household all fell asleep then. But the eyes of the old man and the old woman knew no sleep that night.

Since that night, five years have gone by one after another. Many things have happened in these five years. But who remembers them?

Still, one happening that many in the Malo neighborhood do remember is the death of Subal. A terrible death he died. He had gone in Kalobaran's big boat for the large-scale hauling of jiyal and other big fish. He wanted to go as a partner, but Kalobaran and his brothers refused. "The boat is ours, the capital is ours," they said. "We want you as a laborer on wage, not as a share partner." His wife did not want him to go as a hired hand. But he had little choice. He had just spent all his savings toward feasting the community on the occasion of his marriage, and the hard rainy month of Asarh lay ahead. Without a boat of his own, he could not expect to be able to feed himself and his wife in the hard time if he did not work for a wage over the summer.

The fact is, if you work for a wage for someone who owns all the capital and equipment, that owner treats you like a servant.

The boat of fish-trader Kalobaran was in the middle of the Meghna when the storm rose. The wind from the northeastern corner of the sky swept the boat off its course straight toward the bank. All the men got ready to jump off together moments before the boat would hit the bank and try to stop it with the joint resistance of their shoulders. Subal was ordered to jump off first and quickly shove his pole in the boat's way, assured that they were all going to follow him. A hired man feels a curiously strong sense of obligation to do his employer's bidding. That must be why Subal did not think of the consequence when he jumped as he was asked, but no one else did, fearing for their own lives. Subal aimed the end of his pole at the bottom of the rushing boat, and attempted to brace its middle with his shoulder. But the boat did not slow. With immense speed it ran aground up the bank. Subal was run over; he did not rise.

The conch-shell bangles on Basanti's wrists were shattered, the vermilion mark was removed from her forehead. But the inexpressible anger she felt stayed unabated.

Over these four or five years, she has forgotten many things. She no longer grieves for her husband; the pain she felt has subsided. The thought of the terrible death her husband died comes back to her from time to time. She tries to imagine the scene: the employer's callous order and the helpless employee jumping into the jaws of death to obey it.

The madman has been listening. Like a book read aloud, the history of his own madness has turned page after page across his mind. Maybe the memory calls him to himself for some time; maybe he temporarily regains the natural ability to look at himself and the world around him. Maybe not. The two women making sweet cakes in his kitchen and both deeply tied to his own life. Maybe their nearness fills his heart for a moment. Maybe not. What goes on inside a crazed mind is not for normal people to know. Still, it seems these two women's presence stirs something in his mind. Why else does he sit quietly and weep, instead of tearing nets and ropes and breaking clay pots?

Inside the kitchen, Subla's wife comes to the end of her story. From there they hear the lunatic sobbing outside. All the strength Ananta's mother calls up is not enough to check her sorrow, to stop the wringing pain in her heart. She fears she will break into tears any moment now. But the constant practice of restraint has become such a habit that she uses the power of her will to make herself still as stone.

Looking at her pallid face in the yellow light of the kerosene lamp, Subla's wife feels a shiver down her spine. In the stillness of the dead of night, the familiar face seems transformed into an unearthly strangeness. For one moment a suspicion peeps into her mind that this is the one the bandits took away on the new tributary!

What the light of day could show as genuine and concrete appears transformed into mysterious unreality by the dead of night. Subla's wife loses her practical common sense. The depth of night blurs the distance between imagination and reality. She thinks, yes, it's her, she must be the one. But not in flesh and blood. Sitting here is her spirit.

The presence of Mangala's wife by her side keeps Subla's wife from screaming with fear.

Mangala's wife notices the change in her and, thinking she is sleepy, says, "Go inside, Subla's wife, and lie down next to Ananta."

Only after lying down and holding the sleeping Ananta in her arms does she finally feel again the ground of reality.

In the morning, the lunatic becomes the same lunatic he was before. Ananta's mother has not closed her eyes throughout the night. Coming inside the hut, she finds Subla's wife, Mangala's wife, Ananta, all fast asleep. Also asleep are the two old women. The old man has gone for night fishing; it will be some time before he is back. The light of morning is all around but nobody there observes Ananta's mother. Her heart pounding like a hammer, and her mind tossing in waves of anxiety, she neatly arranges some cakes in a little wicker basket. The madman, too, has stayed up through the night. He is in the fenced cubicle on the porch, plowing up the floor around him with the cleaver in his hand. Ananta's mother stands before him. He looks up at her and comes out, raising the cleaver to hit her. She does not move. Extending to him the hand that holds the basket of cakes, with her other hand she touches his shoulder, his back, and his head. As a beauty would tame a wild beast. The madman slows the descent of the raised cleaver in his hand but does not stop it; he strikes her shoulder with its blunt side. She pays no attention. Trying to smile a little, she holds out a sweet to his lips. He turns his head away, gets down into the yard, and runs to its other end.

Ananta's mother is filled with hope. Maybe some day her madman will become well.

Later that day, she puts her arms around Subla's wife's neck and weeps for a long time. But Subla's wife cannot make sense of this sudden shedding of tears.

The cold of the month of Magh has given way to the fresh spring of Falgun. In the blooming *mandar* tree in the madman's yard, a koel comes and sings from time to time. Whenever she gets an opportunity, Ananta's mother goes there for a glimpse of him. But she goes like a thief, not letting herself be seen, not wanting the madman to see her as she tries to see him. Near the end of spring in Chaitra comes the full moon of Dol. Like the Malos up north in Shukdebpur, the Malos in this village too spend the day smearing one another with the powdered color abir and singing Holi songs. Subla's wife takes an early bath in the river and makes Ananta and his mother bathe. Then she gets Ananta to bring some abir from the market and says, "Come, sister, let's go to the north-end assembly to offer abir to Radha-Madhab."

Radha-Madhab are not alive. A temple image that is worshiped daily cannot return the touch of abir; in its silent immobility it only accepts all the abir placed at its feet. Still, there is novelty in placing abir on Radha-Madhab's feet today; it gives an opportunity to mingle with other women in a festive light mood. Ananta's mother says, "Let's go."

The way to the temple takes them by the lunatic's yard. He runs out from somewhere and blocks their way, demanding, "Oh milkmaids, give me some of your abir."

Subla's wife says with irritation, "Such a pampered madman! Why can't they keep their madman tied up? You know the saying: Clap at the antics of the other's lunatic, but first tie up your own lunatic. They leave their madman loose to give the neighbors trouble!" She somehow manages to sidestep him with her own plate of abir. Ananta's mother is a little behind her. Swayed by her feeling, she takes handfuls of abir from her plate and smears it all over the madman's bushy hair and beard. With a glint of mischief in the corners of his smiling eyes, he says, "Where's my abir to give you—hee hee hee!" And then he knocks the plate of red powder from her hand, runs into his hut, and closes the door.

"Why did you do such a thing?" Subla's wife asks, confounded.

But Ananta's mother says with a smile, "Today everyone receives color from someone. Nobody has touched the madman with color, sister. So I did."

"What if someone saw what you did?"

"I'd explain that the madman has made me a madwoman."

"Don't be flippant. I worry, sister, that the madman might one day catch hold of you and do something terrible. You don't know the reason he went mad."

"Yes, yes I know. He went mad after losing his beloved."

"You can't bring his beloved back to him."

"I can't do that. But I can try and see if I myself can become his beloved."

"Must be the springtime playing tricks on your mind. You want a man now."

She does not answer, to avoid prolonging this talk. Ananta stands quietly beside her, holding on to her sari. Pointing to the boy with her eyes, she whispers: "Watch what you say, sister. My son's with me, don't you see?"

But Ananta is fascinated by what just happened. The madman has the unreal look of a character in fairy tales. And his mother smeared him with handfuls of abir, and then the madman so oddly knocked the plate of abir from her hand and ran away. Mother lost so much of her abir. Bending, Ananta tries to retrieve some of it from the path. Subla's wife takes his hand and pulling him up, says, "I'm fed up. I'm not going to offer abir to Radha-Madhab. What good is giving abir to an image, anyway! Come, Ananta, let's go home."

Inside Ananta's hut, she smears him with her abir, kisses him, hugs him to her, and after releasing him, hugs him again. She looks at him, admiring the beauty of his face, his eyes, his child's body. When he speaks, his words are beautiful; when he looks into the distance wondering, he seems much, much older than his age.

"Try to quiet your mind, dear sister," Subla's wife says to his mother. "What good is it, having a man? They're like raindrops, nice when falling but soon over. They're like a tide—fills briefly with happiness but then leaves, taking away water from the river's heart. This Ananta is all our hopes and desires. Let the two of us together try to bring him up. Some day he'll be the one to put an end to our sorrows."

In the long hours of a hot afternoon of Baisakh, when Ananta's mother sits spinning thread, the restless gusts of wind set loose the dead leaves from the trees and bring them into her hut. She is not the only one these breaths of wind startle. But in her they also uncover the feeling of loss and emptiness she tries to keep at bay. Wanderer wind it may be, but it's quite bothersome. Pointlessly it litters her cleaned hut with scatterings of dry leaves. It doesn't even let her finish sweeping them out but whirls them back in even as she sweeps. Exasperated with the blown-in leaves, she gets up and closes the door. Then like another gust of the restless wind, Ananta is at the closed door. He was out looking for the green baby mangoes that the wind dislodges from trees along with leaves. Using his small chest and arms like a basket to hold the green mangoes he picked up this afternoon, he walks home and, finding the door closed, calls: "Ma, open the door, look at the mangoes I've gathered." She cannot but respond to this voice and opens the door. "Let me see. So many mangoes, Ananta! Go call your aunt to come and take a look." Ananta runs out and is soon back with Subla's wife, also unable to resist his excited call.

The rainy season brings the hardest time for Ananta's mother. They have nothing to eat. Fishing continues in earnest now, but all the net weaving that needed to be done has already been done, and no one wants to buy any more thread at this time. Though she wants to keep her hands busy with spinning, the hands seem unwilling, as no buyer comes now. With the scant meals, Ananta grows thinner by the day.

Whenever Subla's wife can evade her parents' eyes, she steals from their own kitchen and brings rice in a measuring basket hidden under her sari, a few vegetables or a fish, a bit of oil and salt, or a few pieces of turmeric root. That helps only a little, but even that she doesn't manage to keep up for very long. One day she is caught in the act. She lives in her parents' household; the kitchen is not really hers; she is like flotsam with no solid ground to stand on. What can she do! Silently she takes the scoldings of her mother and her father. They forbid her to visit Ananta's mother anymore. She has no choice but to obey their order.

Ananta's mother sees nothing around to help her stay afloat. The straw roof of the hut has holes through which water drips day and night. The wall panels have given way in places through which the rain-cold wind blows. The only sari she has is so worn that trying to cover her chest exposes her hips and trying to cover her waist leaves too little to cover her breasts. With Ananta she silently huddles in a small part of the hut where the roof doesn't leak. To save the pillows and the rag quilts from getting wet, she keeps those next to them all the time. Thus each day drags endlessly for her.

Lately the mother of Subla's wife has observed improper inclinations and actions in her daughter. One day near the refuse dump of their yard she notices a young fellow named Mynah with shoulder-length hair, who lives in the western neighborhood of the village and spends his days hunting birds with a bamboo slingshot and mud pellets. Mynah was aiming at a bird in the nearby thicket and, having missed it, sings:

> I had a parrot for a pet, a jaybird, and a mynah too.
> Got a goldfinch now, but my words it won't talk to.

The mother finds Subla's wife, gone there to dump refuse, smiling and talking to him. Shaking with anger, the mother goes home and reports it as soon as the father comes home.

After taking all the shouting and scolding from the two of them, the daughter also opens her mouth: "I'll talk to Mynah, I'll run away with him. How will you stop me? Take away my food and my clothes? I can do without food and clean clothes. But I'll still run away. Your face will get the lime-and-grime of shame, I won't care. I have no family of my own to worry about. I'll give my body away, I'll debase it, ruin it, do anything I want with it. You can't say anything about it. Try to remember how young I was when you married me off. He died. I knew nothing, understood nothing. From that innocent age, I had the life of a green widow forced on me by rules of virtue. Ever since, with my blasted luck I wander all alone crying in the forests. Yourselves, you've had a good life. How could you know how deep is the river of my sorrow? You think I've got no desires, no needs."

Furious, Dinanath says, "What's she's saying, the ill-begotten burned-face woman!" and proceeds to get his wooden clogs to beat her up. His wife stops him and persuades him to leave matters to her: "You go out of the house now. I'll try and bring my daughter back to her senses."

When the father is gone, the mother says in a consoling voice, "I know all about your misfortunes, but do you really want to force your father to apologize to everyone at the meeting of the notables? You know how well respected he is in the community."

"What good's that to me? Has it brought salvation to seven generations of my descendants? I wanted to soothe my sorrows by having Ananta's mother, my fellow sufferer, as my friend and by loving Ananta as the child I couldn't have. You denied me even that. If you won't let me go there, then I'll go after men. Let's see how long you can keep me locked in."

"Listen, you luckless girl, listen to me, go to her right now. Go to Ananta's mother now. Only keep your mind away from men."

"You know very well, Ma, that in the last two days you kept me from seeing her, she had nothing to eat."

"Take the food. Take two measuring-basketfuls of rice, take the catfish we have for cooking. Take whatever else you want and go see her. Hear me clearly, go to her right now with all the food."

"Ma, the only sari Ananta's mother has is so worn, it's shedding its fiber. I have three saris. Can I give her one?"

"You go to her with the food now. Let me ask your father about the sari. No, listen. Better not let him know. Go, give her one of your saris."

Subla's wife's need for male company vanishes that very instant.

In the month of Bhadra, fishing is in full swing. The price offered for reeled thread goes up; the butting and thrashing of large fish tear up even the fishermen's new nets. The men do not look at the price now, they are willing to buy all the thread available—fine, medium, or thick—all the women can reel. All the thread Ananta's mother managed to reel through the months of summer and rain sells out now in a single day. And day and night she is busy spinning and reeling thread. She doesn't have a moment to spare for talking; her spindler turns nonstop. One day she notices the dark calluses that have grown on the fair skin of her thigh with the constant turning of the spindle against it. So much thread she's been spinning! All that thread could have gone into making nets in her own home. After catching fish through the night with those nets, a man of her own could come home in the morning with a basketful of fish and money in the fold of his waistcloth! In all the other households, there is so much energetic life going on around work. The men say the kinds of thread they need, the women spin accordingly. When it's done well, how the men shower them with praise. When the thread breaks too often in spinning, how they scold them in sweet words. The women sulk and say, then let them bring home someone who's a more skilled spinner! The reconciliation following the argument fills their home with the sweetness of honey. In all those homes, so many other kinds of work go on along with the spinning of thread. And in her home only one kind of work goes on all the time, spinning and reeling thread to sell.

When she is alone with Subla's wife, Ananta's mother one day pours out her feelings. "Remember, sister, you once said I needed a man? Yes, you're right, I do need one. The life of a woman without her man isn't worth a damaged cowrie shell."

"Go for a man, then."

"If only I could find him."

"Catch the madman."

"I tried, but he didn't let me catch him."

"Stop joking, sister."

"I'm not, sister. I'm telling you the truth. If today the madman takes my hand, I'll go at once and live in his home as his woman. I can't go on like this anymore."

Subla's wife is confounded. "Why do you want the madman, of all men?" she asks. "If you feel so restless, all you need to do is look when you're at the ghat to fetch water and sign with your eyes to the one you like."

"Do I want a man just for that, sister? Look around. All the homes are steered by men and women are their companions. And all the irony of fate is on me."

"No, sister, I think you've become crazy for the crazed man. One day this man will devour you. Tell me the truth about this, sister, are you the one the madman lost?"

"How should I know who the madman lost where? All I know is, I can't live my life like this. If I can have the madman, I can live my life centered on him."

Subla's wife lets go a deep sighs and says, "Sometimes I too can't find the strength in my mind to go on. But I resolved long ago that I'll go on living like this to the very end."

Ananta's mother is quite different. As long as she was in Bhabanipur, her life was filled with the closeness of baby Ananta on one side and the two simple childlike old men on the other. Never for a moment did she feel distressed and disturbed. Even today her mind is not really disturbed, she only feels weary and exhausted. The distant pillar of light she aimed at always while treading her path is now beside her; but standing in the darkness at its foot, she finds she has no more strength left to go on. Let the madman himself come and take charge of her life or let him call her into his hut and kill her with his own hands. Inside Subla's wife lives a rebellious woman. Inside Ananta's mother has come to nest an all-consuming desire for family life. What she wants is: let him come and set up a home with her. But does a madman ever sense the desire of another person's heart?

Subla's wife once told her that three strangers—two men and a woman from a far-off place—came to their village one day three years ago. Her father was at the ghat slope by the river at that moment, and they asked him if the home of Ramkeshab's son Kishore was in that village. When he said yes, they asked to be taken there. They came to that home to find inside it a deathlike dark and grim old man, a skeletal old woman, and in the porch a madman sitting and wailing like a ghoul at night. They did not find the person they came to see. Finally one recognized the madman and begged him, earnestly holding his two hands: "Please, Kishore, tell us where is my daughter, where have you kept her hidden." Then the madman in a perfectly sane voice answered, "Near the mouth of the new tributary, bandits took her away." They did not stay for another second. In silence they left at once for the railroad station. After what her parents learned three years ago, they would never come back here.

There is the grim old man. She knows that if she goes to him and addresses him as father, he will welcome her to his home as his daughter; he'll say, "The goddess of my home's well-being has come." But afterwards, when he learns about everything, he'll say, "The bandits must have violated you; I can't have you in my home." If the madman ever becomes sane again, maybe he too will doubt and say, "The bandits let you go after taking your chastity. There's no proof you weren't violated."

Then there'll be no way left for my Ananta to live a normal life, no way at all.

Yet god is witness that they touched her just once when they were transferring her to their boat. As soon as they set her down and started the boat, she leaned over and dived into the water. A fisherman's daughter, grown up in a home by the river, she was a practiced swimmer from the time she was a small child. She knew how to go under water holding her breath and come up some distance away. The bandits could not catch her again. By the time she saw the bank and swam close to it, she felt her consciousness slipping. Fortunately, before anyone else found her, two kind souls came upon her: the two old brothers, Gaurango and Nityananda. Early that morning in their dinghy they were going toward the big river to buy fish from the fishing boats on the way back with their catch. When she regained consciousness in the two brothers' boat, they asked her if she was the daughter of a Brahman or a Kayastha family. She addressed them both as father and said she was a fisherman's daughter. They asked her where her home was and how they could send her back there. She asked them not to send her back but to take her with them to their home. This is her history.

With everything she ever wanted so close by, is she to have her life drained away in utter non-recognition? Even so, what about Ananta? He does not know who his father is; his father does not know him. This is too terrible. Subla's wife is aware of only one aspect of the problem and keeps turning only that in her mind. Even she has no idea of all the other aspects that Ananta's mother has to be mindful of.

One hope has taken root in her mind, she is not sure why: that the madman will someday become well. From seeing her every day, his brain will regain sanity. He will be fascinated with her though he doesn't remember her, grow emotionally attached to her from receiving her care and love without knowing who she is. He never did get the chance to see and know her that well. If she doesn't reveal her own identity, he'll never quite recognize her. Those who would have recognized her immediately were Subal and Tilak—both in heaven now. How nice those two persons were! They helped her in so many ways and treated her like a close relative. If they can see her from heaven, may their blessing for her be that the madman will fall in love with her without recognizing her. Holding on to the thread of that love, let her be able to become the madman's wife, start life with him totally anew, work out a new possibility. Some people will disapprove; they will speak ill of a widow's remarrying. But that won't be impossible for her to bear and live with. Besides, they've all been hearing the new talk going around that it is not improper for widows to be remarried. If widowers can remarry, then why can't widows? But is she really a widow, is her husband dead? Yes. In the sense of remembrance of feelings, her husband died indeed. She herself is also almost in a state of death, absolutely immobilized in spite of knowing everything. Both of them will be reborn when that happens. But—what about Ananta? As whose son will he be able to show his face in society? Maybe that problem, too, will be solved. She has sometimes wondered about that.

Maybe one day I'll tell him a fairy tale, that is, let him know the real story in the form of a fairy tale. Perhaps it will not only fascinate him but make him feel proud of his mother's courage and astounded when he learns about her ability to bear so much pain! Maybe one day I'll also recount to the madman such tales from memory, unknown to anyone else in the world, that in the depth of his mind he cannot but make room for the conviction that there is a curious identification between this woman of his mature love and that girl he wed by exchanging garlands. But before that I must fill his mind with my love and care, my smiles and capacity for joy, establish myself as indispensable in his life. Only after that I will convey to his mind a vivid, tangible impression of the truth that the bandits could not violate even my hair, that I dived into the river to save everything. My madman will surely become well again some day.

During the winter the madman's condition turns much worse. Even tied up, he is now hard to restrain. He has already broken everything in his hut. Now he takes to destroying other people's things, even calling in the passersby and assaulting them. This stage of insanity is most dreadful.

In utter hopelessness his father breaks down and cries out aloud or beats the madman when he cannot take it anymore. The madman's body is all covered with wounds, some healing, some raw, some made by his father in the effort to control him, some inflicted by himself.

One day another madman wanders in, no one knows from where, and the two lunatics laugh and smoke together and do all sorts of things in their strange amusement. Then that other madman, before leaving, brutally beats the already wounded body. Since then, Kishore seems possessed by the terrible idea and keeps inflicting wounds on his own body. His body bears so many wounds festering in various stages that he is now hard to look at.

Ananta's mother gets down to work, pushing aside the barriers of modesty and social custom. She steps out of her home, goes by herself to the Ayurvedic *kaviraj* to get herbal remedies for the wounds. She goes to his hut and washes his wounds with hot water and soap before applying the medication. At first he hits her too, hits her a lot as soon as she comes near. Finally he surrenders, exhausted. People notice a beautiful woman nursing with care and compassion a wounded wild animal. No one makes any adverse remark. Some stop at a good remark alone—she must be a rare woman of much kindness—and leave the rest of their thoughts unspoken. Subla's wife campaigns: a man is dying of his rotting wounds, and out of human compassion a woman not even related to him is nursing him back to life as if he were one of her own; how can that be improper? It pleases god; there is merit and virtue in this nursing and caring, a merit even if earned by one person brings benefit to the entire village. Thus she campaigns so forcefully through the community, in all circles she knows well or little, that no contradicting word comes from anyone's mouth.

Toward the end of the winter the madman seems quite transformed. Ananta's mother is filled with hope. Subla's wife privately stings her with a few pointed remarks, expresses her own irritation. But even so, her mind wants to understand a certain impenetrable mystery.

Spring comes again. Ananta's mother one day asks the madman's mother to help her take him to the slope of the river to give him a good bath. Together they soap him and scrub him and make him splash in the water and take a few dips. In broad daylight! Men and women, all the villagers who come to the ghat slope look at her doing this. But she is oblivious to their gaze. The only thought that stirs her mind while bathing the madman is this: if only the pathetic old woman knew, if she even once sensed that this person was none other than her son's wife!

Kishore gradually shows signs of delight at receiving the loving care of an unrelated woman. Ananta's mother's heart starts to tremble.

Although Kishore has tolerated and even cooperated with most of the impositions of her care, the thing he absolutely refuses to accept is her suggestion that the barber come and trim his hair and his beard. Her attempt at persuasion makes him react violently and she gives it up.

Then, once again, comes the day of Holi. To Ananta's mother this day is auspicious, one for the realization of good possibilities. In the page of her life, this day remains deeply inscribed. On this day the Malo fishermen retrieve their nets early in the morning after some minimal fishing and gather to warm up the singing session. Someone starts with the beat of tom-tom. "O Spring, you've come with joy, but my *lal*, my red one, has not come!"

The next singer cocks his head to one side, puts a hand over his ear in the manner of a virtuoso, and takes up the word, turning it into a lavish refrain: "Tale lale lale lale lale lale lale lal." As if to him the sky and the world are completely "lale lal," red with love's exultation. Reversing the usual order, he follows the refrain with the lyric: "Spri-ing is the time that gives me trouble, O, it does so make my patience crumble." Then the singer launches again his colorful refrain.

Ananta's mother's hut also glows, lale lal, with happiness and red color. Subla's wife brings a lot of red powder in a plate she arranged with much love and care. She's come to make Ananta lale lal all over. She'll surprise him and not give him any chance to resist, to demur. But as she smears him with red powder, she feels a tremor in her own heart, noticing how much the boy has grown in one year. While smearing his cheeks, she looks at his eyes and sees a change in his look. These are no longer a child's eyes that any woman may easily gaze into. But Subla's wife is disobedient, stubborn; she loves to disregard, to go on pushing hesitations aside. As in the year before, she hugs him to her breast and kisses him. But this time it does not feel like hugging a darling little boy, adoring the child-god Gopal. A different kind of feeling comes over her, changing the hearty simplicity of her maternal love. Her eyes close and her arms loosen. But Ananta's arms are still around his aunt's neck, held there like a garland of fresh flowers.

A different thought distracts Ananta's mother—how to make this day of enthronement of their love become meaningful again, bring it back to life. She'll put care and feeling into smearing the madman red so the memory of that other day will awaken in his mind and so, coming out of the insanity, he will place love-possessed eyes on his beloved as he once did. That will make her so happy. But will Ananta's mother be able to bear the happiness of that moment when it comes? Will her feet falter and her heart race as they did on that day?

Evading the notice of Ananta and Subla's wife, she steps out on the path. Elsewhere in the neighborhood, in the house where the festive revelers have gathered, the singing of Holi songs are going on and off beat, with too much spirit and too little control.

At first Kishore is thrilled with the touches of color from her hands. In Ananta's mother's eyes he looks so beautiful today. Will the true reflection of that day five years ago return today, bearing its sweet beauty? She has heard so many tales and legends about how grief over losing the beloved makes a person go mad, and how that insanity is dispelled after finding the beloved again. She has also heard that reawakening the memory of a happy moment can cure insanity. Insanity is not really a disease that requires medicine from physicians. It's not a disease, not at all, only a state of mind. If the momentum of that state of mind can be countered by another equally powerful emotion, then the insane ceases to be insane. She has thought it out. This is the only way the madman will be cured, if at all. May all the madmen of the world, not just her own, be cured in this very way! There is no other way. If there was one, all the lunatics would have recovered; but they do not.

Why doesn't he smear me with his two hands full of color—is he made of stone, can't he sense my heart's desire! she wonders. Yes, he can! He picks up a handful of color powder from her plate and smears her cheeks and her forehead! No one is around. The old woman is dozing on the other side of the wicker door; the old man, her father-in-law, has gone to the Holi singing. They are alone here. Ananta's mother puts all her strength into holding herself steady before him.

But Kishore changes drastically. His subdued insanity returns full force. He suddenly does something terrible.

With abrupt swiftness, his arms snatch the beloved; carrying her to his chest, he runs to the middle of the yard and starts screaming at the top of his voice: "Bring out the sticks, fellows, bring out those sticks. They've touched the chaste wife. They can't get away with it today. Hit them! Kill them! Not one must escape. Where's my stick, where's it gone—I say: hand me my stick!" Pausing to take a breath, he lets out another throat-rupturing scream. "Bring oil, bring water, over here, your daughter's fainted!"

The gathering at the Holi singing breaks up at the sound of his screaming. The men rush in. Kishore looks at the group of men standing in front of him and then at the young woman in his arms. He keeps looking at the one and at the other. His eyes grow even more dilated, redder. The young woman's hair escapes from its coiled bun and hangs down to the ground like a long snake. With her head hanging over his arm, her chest is raised high. So high that the breathing from Kishore's flared nostrils blows away its sari cover. She has fainted. Soon her breasts are bare. And Kishore, become totally insane, rubs his face into the softness of those bare breasts, which seem about to be uprooted by the rampage of the wild growth of beard.

Someone shouts, "What're you watching, Ramkanta, and you, Ganga-charan? Catch him. Rid the madman of his mad conduct."

Already keyed up with the excitement of Holi, the men now attack Kishore all together. They beat him savagely, not merely with their hands and legs, kicking, slapping, cuffing, punching, and shoving. But they go on doing many other things too! Some fetch their bamboo sticks and strike hard at his joints. Some heave him by his arms up in the air and slam him on a particular hard spot of the yard. Some do more: they pull him up by his long hair and beard, make his body fly in a few circles in the air before throwing him down. Finally, his beard torn off by the roots, Kishore's senseless body lands in a corner of the yard where it remains in a motionless heap. Then they stop, deciding that the crime of touching an unrelated woman has been punished adequately. They turn away from him and gather around the woman on the ground.

A moment before the mob attack, Kishore's startled senses came to the fore. Realizing what he was doing, he gently put down the unconscious young woman. She still lies where he put her down and where some women now try to revive her with oil, water, and a hand fan. She opens her eyes at this point and sees the crowd of people around her in the yard where she was alone with him. When some of the women try to help her to her feet, she slumps again. Through all this Subla's wife was absent— who knows where she was! Now she comes running, out of breath, pushing her way to her through the forest of men and women. Quickly gathering her up, supporting her to her feet, she somehow carries Ananta's mother, leaning limp on her shoulder, into her hut.

The crowd then leaves the place in batches. No one tries to revive Kishore, still lying unconscious in a corner of the yard. Later on his consciousness returns, and he tries to get up but fails. For the first time after so long, he speaks normally: "Father, bring me a little water." After drinking the water he says, "Father, carry me inside. I can't get up."

Kishore somehow clings to life that night. He dies before the dawn begins another day. His old mother, who has remained mute all these years, now breaks out in sorrow. Tears run like a stream from her eyes and her heart, once solid, swells with grief. She weeps, lamenting in so many words about how he died before drinking all the water he wanted to drink, before saying all the things he wanted to say.

Ananta's mother dies four days later. The high fever she developed the evening of the incident persists unrelenting, along with a strange burning sensation no one knows of what kind. Tossing and turning sleeplessly through her last night, she dies at daybreak when, with her head in the lap of Subla's wife, she becomes calm and her eyes quietly gaze at the slowly emerging light of day, the light that begins to paint warm red the morning sky, Ananta's morning sky.

Birth, death, marriage—on each of these three occasions Malos spend their money. With that money come forth the needed items: the wood, the bamboo, some oil and clarified butter, and an earthen pot. Energetically, with all the proper arrangements, they take her body away in a boat for cremation.

While lighting the pyre, someone remarks, "The madman knew he was right, he caught the right person. If she'd died four days ago, we could've put them together on the same pyre. They would've united in the other world."

Once three people went together on a fishing trip to a distant place. From there they started back with a fourth one. All four of them are now dead, some before and some after. What they saw and heard on that trip, the many ways in which they were elated and amused, the dangers and misfortunes that befell them, all this was like the stuff of a wondrous tale. Those whose experiences constituted that tale have now departed. Never again will they be seen in this world.

III

The Rainbow

The course of the river Titash curves here like a bow.

From one season to another the waterscape changes colors and shapes. Now, at the start of the rainy season, its misty soft colors resemble a rainbow. Green villages line the two sides of the whitish water. Rain falls continuously from the soft gray sky above and rainwater mixes with farmland soil to run in hundreds of brown streams into the white flow of Titash. Together, they create an atmosphere of enchantment, of sweet spiritual rapture, like the world inside a rainbow.

The rainy season advances. The sky disintegrates and the downpour goes on without end. The waters of Titash rise and keep rising, unbounded. Cool air blows briskly, pushes the opaque waters into waves that rock the fishermen's boats and rock even more the flatboats carrying potatoes.

One such boat that started from home some distance away, to sell sweet potatoes at the marketplace, now struggles in the windy rain and rocking waves. It is a small boat filled with large sweet potatoes, one to two pounds apiece. The boat's hull is weighted down by its cargo and seems ready to go under. The rain that falls on the boat's open top and collects at the bottom makes it grow heavier by the minute. If it isn't bailed at once, it'll go any second, with a tiny plop. But the bailer cannot get through the heaps of potatoes to scoop out the water from the bottom of the boat. Kadir Mian is at his wits' end. Woven bamboo leaves tied under his chin make a hat that shelters his head, but his body takes the full force of the slanting rain. Tilting his head sideways, he glances up at the sky, and Kadir's son looks at his father's helpless face. The river that surrounds them appears so empty of other human presence that their heads feel blank and produce no ideas at all. In a resigned voice the father says,

"Those sweet potatoes we grew with so much work, they're all on their way to the world under." The son says firmly, "Ba-jan, you swim across to Garibullah's banyan tree and save your life. I'll hang on—as long as there's breath there's hope. If I see the boat's sinking, I'll dump the potatoes in Titash's water, take the empty boat to the bank, and call you."

At that moment they notice the familiar shape of a fishing boat, moving fast through the wide expanse of the river like a water snake heading home at dusk. With two oars splashing and scull creaking, it cuts through the water and sends the waves higher. Afraid that the wash from one of those waves will sink his boat, Kadir Mian calls out, "Whose boat's that!"

From the tapered stern of the fishing boat, Dhananjay calls to one of the oarsmen. "Ho Banamali, quick, get the bailer out. I see a potato boat going under."

Instantly the two oars are pulled in. Dhananjay turns the scull up and pushes down its handle. As smoothly and swiftly as a snake moves its hooded head, the boat swerves left and comes to a dead stop alongside Kadir's boat. Dhananjay's timing is marvelous. A moment later would have been too late.

Then the hands of the five men, three in the fishing boat and two in the potato boat, work with the mechanical speed of a sewing machine needle. Soon the wide hold at the center of the fishing boat is filled with potatoes and the emptied hull of the potato carrier floats up.

Kadir's bamboo-leaf hat still does its job, keeping the ceaseless rain from his head. Overcome with the exhaustion that follows a frantic escape from danger, he sits on the fishing boat's platform and says over and over, "Malo's sons, you really saved us today, saved us in a big way."

The rain, which has been falling in a steady rhythm for some time, suddenly goes berserk and launches an all-out attack. Tearing open the sky, the water pelts down with a savage scream: Slash, slash! Kill, kill! The whipping of the wind and the drumming of the rain surround them with deafening noise. Banks, fields, villages all blur in the smoky whitish pall of the driving rain.

Banamali wants to take the boat to the bank to wait it out, but he cannot see any bank anymore. He knows it's not far from there, but he can't see it at all. Dhananjay, working to cover the back end of the dome with a wicker panel, ends his dilemma, "Banamali-bhai, on this wide curve of the river it's useless to move if you can't see. Stay put right here."

The two of them lower a thick heavy bamboo pole into the water and, by jointly pushing it again and again, drive it into the riverbed. After tying the boat to the pole with a strong rope, Dhananjay remarks in a decisive tone, "There! Let the boat turn here with the wind. Now, listen Mians, go sit inside the shed."

Noticing Kadir stop short as he heads inside, Banamali says, "Don't worry. There's no more cooked food in there. Finished eating all the rice and curry we cooked."

All five are thoroughly wet, and they have no other clothes with them to change into. In the tiny domed shed they sit huddled together, their wet bodies touching. Kadir's hair, now uncovered, is damp and disheveled. His wet white beard slowly drips onto Banamali's wet bare shoulder. Becoming aware of that, Kadir quietly wipes away with his palm the drops his beard has shed on Banamali. At this, Banamali turns his head and looks at Kadir's face. The sight gladdens his heart. The man looks somewhat like Ramprasad of Jatrabari village. A white-gold beard graces his face too, and the expression similarly mixes calm with alertness of mind. Ramprasad is like a descendant of one of those sages—maybe Valmiki— he heard described from the *Ramayana* and the *Mahabharata*. And this man, Kadir Mian? Yes, Banamali now remembers who Kadir Mian reminds him of. That time when during Muharrem stick players performed in the marketplace of Gokanghat, he went to watch; on his way back he ran into a Muslim man also from his village. Listening to his account of the heartrending story of Karbala, Banamali was on the verge of tears. Banamali also heard from him the story of their dear prophet, immensely heroic yet full of tender love for his near ones. Kadir strikes Banamali as if he wears a ray of that immense light of courage and love, quietly sitting here with his beard touching Banamali's bare shoulder. Sitting close to him makes Banamali feel happy. Indeed, Ramprasad of Jatrabari and Kadir Mian of Birampur too—each is that rare kind of person who gives you a helping hand if you stumble and holds your hand through a long briar-covered way; but then again, if in your sorrow you put your face on that calm chest underneath the beard, cling to him with both hands, and sob away, he doesn't scold you or sternly ask you to stop crying; he just strokes your back like a person who can't help any other way. Banamali's eyes fill with tears. His father, too, was that kind of person, but he is no more. Once on the way home after night fishing, with the wet net on his shoulder, he got caught in a gale and died underneath a tree that fell on him.

Outside the shed, large drops of rain fall on the bamboo panels of the boat's platform and shatter on impact into hundreds of bits. Outside the boat, as far as the eye can see is the river Titash. The countless raindrops pierce the surface of its water like stone chips and make tiny circles of water jump up around each of those points. The wind has dropped; there are no more waves. Yet the entire surface of the river is agitated. And all around them is the constant sound—*jha-jha jhim-jhim*—of rain coming down hard on the river's surface. The front of the domed shed is open, but no rain comes inside here. The wind blows from the back, and that opening has been covered. Kadir's gaze is outside the boat, where the raindrops like shafts of arrows shot from some great distance and at great speed pierce the immense chest of the river and trouble it. Banamali holds his towel out to wash in the rain and after wringing it out with care puts it into Kadir's hand. "Here, trader, wipe your body with this." Kadir looks affectionately at the young fisherman, at the fresh face and the well-muscled body, before he answers. "Son, no one in my family has ever been a trader. I've grown potatoes on the silt land. I go to the Saturday markets to sell them. I don't like selling to traders. They haggle too much and never pay if they can buy on credit."

"Fish traders are the same. Haggling with fishermen, they pay a quarter-rupee where one rupee is due. Then taking the catch to the city, they sell for a rupee what they bought for a quarter."

Peering ahead where everything is covered with the great round net of rain, Kadir mutters, "What a downpour! Can't even see if there's any village here." Of his increasing desire to have a smoke he says nothing. Just then the mind reader in the form of the youth called Banamali reaches for the hookah-lighting setup, which is a small length of bamboo tube with two hollow ends, one holding tobacco and the other a few pieces of pressed coal dust.

Banamali's move worries Kadir's son. He remembers how, when he was even younger, he often accompanied his father to sell milk to the Brahman and Kayastha homes in one village or another. Sometimes they would ask his father to come in and sit for a few words. While they themselves sat in chairs, they would get some kid to fetch a dusty old plank for him to sit on, pouring honey into their words. "Sit down, Kadir, sit down, have a smoke." Holding smooth polished hookahs in their hands, they would have a cheap coconut-shell thing brought out for him from under the porch shelf. Kadir enjoys listening as much as he likes talking. Once in conversation, he wouldn't notice where he was sitting and what he was smoking from. He'd simply blow the dust off the hookah they kept for the lowly folk and put his lips to it. So simple a man, he could do it and not mind. He knew they were rich and he was poor, as unmixable as oil and water.

But these are fishermen, they live with hard work and poverty as peasants do. You can't make a show of throwing the dust of respect at them the way you can at the rich higher-ups. No, what you want to do is put an arm around them as equals. Peasants and fishermen have a link nobody can cut even by hacking or erase even by scrubbing. Banamali here—he's busy trying to prepare the hookah. Suppose after smoking the full hookah himself, he detaches the chillum with the burning tobacco and offers it to his father? What would he do then? You can be angry at an insult from rich men but not at an insult from your equal. It just cuts through your heart with a knife of pain.

In the midst of this heavy downpour on the river, barely able to keep his head dry, Kadir might perhaps be happy to accept the clay top detached from Banamali's hookah. But when Banamali reaches into the bowl of embers, he finds that wet spray has put it all out.

After their boats have covered the river's arc and cleared the bend, the marketplace comes into view. The rain has stopped some time ago, and now daylight is out, clear on all sides, but not sunlight. Parts of the sky are still congested and somewhere in the distance rain continues. The cool air that blows in gusts from time to time feels like balm on their bodies now hard at work. Although they are not close to the bank they follow, the deep green shadows of its many large trees fall far into the water. Each distinct shadow trembles fearfully at the approach of Kadir's boat before the oars of Kadir's son strike and shatter it to smithereens.

This is the river's left bank. The right bank is almost empty here—no villages, no homes, few trees and shrubs—but just beyond the empty bank are the crop fields, in rows and patchwork that stretch far into the distance, ending at the blurred, shadowy presence of some villages. The wind from that direction, blowing across those fields and across the river, sways the tops of the trees on this bank.

Both boats, one long and one short, come aground together by the ghat of the marketplace. Here the river, after flowing a long way from west to east, turns a corner before flowing south. The ground of that sharp bend holds the marketplace. From the eastern end of the market a thin canal goes straight north. Looking out from that corner ground, you see that the river's sudden turn to face the south makes her long plait of hair fly up north.

On the eastern side of that canal is a village called Aminpur, a sparse village with some jute offices on one side and a few homes and trees on the other. While the market begins to gather on the canal's western side, a rainbow emerges above the trees in the opposite sky. The sun, finally out, hangs low in the western sky. Diagonally across from it in the eastern sky clings a large patch of deep, cool moisture-laden shadow with a hint of rain. The seven hidden colors of sunlight from the western horizon, trapped in the cloudy eastern sky, have produced this rainbow.

The prolonged fierceness of the downpour that occurred just two hours earlier is quite rare here. Those in the boat out on the river were not fully aware of the amount of rain that fell. Had they been at home, they would have heard the drumming on the roofs, even more deafening than the noise on the river; they would have seen the long furrows cut into the ground by the force of water rolling off the slopes of roofs. A blocked outlet somewhere has turned yards into pools, and in Hindu homes only the little altar of sacred basil remains above the water. Patches of grass that grew in neglect in the corners of the yards now swim happily.

The canal was dry all summer; it was just a trickle a bit earlier in the rainy season. In today's downpour, all the fields flooded. The chunks of earth in the plowed fields crumbled into the rainwater that rose within the ridge-bound fields; then the muddy water flowed over the ridges and on into the canal. From all directions the fields today extend a hundred arms to the canal, offering brimming bounty instead of the usual trickle, spectacular high tide instead of perpetual ebb. The canal that normally borrows from the river just to keep its throat wet today rolls in delight, surges and swells with pride. Celebrating this sudden plenitude, with splashing waves and flowing currents, it pours its excess into Titash. The rain stopped a while ago but the canal still goes on giving; its muddy water still runs in a stream into the river.

Kadir has been feeling thirsty but, scooping up water from the river in his cupped palms, notices half of it is mud. Banamali says to him sympathetically, "Leave it, you can't drink it. Canal water has ruined river water. I've got relatives in the Malo neighborhood here. I'll take you there after hauling the potatoes."

"What kind of relatives? You married from here?"

"No. Got a sister married here."

With Banamali's help, Kadir's potatoes are transferred in no time to the marketplace. To keep them from scattering, Kadir's son twists a bunch of water grass into a thick length and secures it around the pile like a dike. A few small potatoes roll off the pile, skip over the barrier, and run off this way and that. Several ragged small kids who are hanging around dive at them immediately and snatch up what they see as beyond the owner's claims. They are not the children of beggars, but their stunted bodies, scant and dirty clothing, and abnormal keenness make them seem even worse off than beggars. They are everywhere, in all places, all villages and all village markets. Peasants like Kadir who come to sell potatoes do not shout at them or go after them for a few potatoes. They feel sorry for these sad, destitute children and let them keep what they pick up, since they have no money to buy. But traders shout at them. If one of their potatoes is touched, the traders slap them, snatch it away, and confiscate even their little collections from spills elsewhere in the market. Such hard slaps on tender cheeks the children take without a sound; pressing a hand over mouth and cheek they quickly leave the spot, afraid of more beating. But when a trader takes away their little collections, when a plea for their return is rewarded only with obscene words abusing their parents, then they cry in muffled sobs. Many times Kadir has come to this market to sell his potatoes and seen these kids year after year at their pathetic collecting of stray potatoes. Some have died; some have grown up and started their own families; others waste away bit by bit slaving for some moneyed trader or some labor-hiring landed big farmer. They may no longer recognize Kadir, and Kadir may not quite recognize one of them in grown-up form. But he remembers well how, while unloading his potatoes in a pile on the ground of the market, he has deliberately pushed ten or twenty in the direction of these beggars for mercy. To this day he keeps up the covert giving. Seeing the first arrival of potatoes in the market, bands of these small robbers have all gathered here. They are ready, some with bags made of rag crudely sewn with thread pulled from the border of a worn-out sari, some with clay bowls, some simply gathering up an edge of their waistcloth.

A thought suddenly makes Kadir become the wish-tree. Perhaps he feels like giving away a large part of his pile. But his adult son is with him and might think it's foolish, senseless—bringing potatoes all the way to the market to sell and giving them away instead. Purposefully, in a happy mood, he keeps rearranging his pile of potatoes and sending a good many over the dike his son made. It does not escape his son's notice. "We haven't made the first sale, haven't opened shop properly, and Father, you're already giving like this!"

Kadir at once comes up with an excuse. "Buyers don't want any nicked potatoes. They just spend time sorting through the pile and then walk away without buying. Only those I gave away."

His son grumbles. "But we haven't even done the prayer before shop opening."

Kadir smiles openheartedly and replies, "I just did the shop opening by giving to these helpless orphans. They'll eat and pray for us. Today Allah saved us from a great danger."

Banamali has been watching Kadir's activities with amazement and delight. Kadir also looks at Banamali's eyes as he explains to his son: "They're all so unfortunate. Some without a father or mother and they get kicked and scolded. Some have a mother but she hasn't got a grain to feed them. Others, motherless, have a father. But, as they say, after the mother's death, father acts like cousin's father-in-law and brother like a wild beast."

Blowing into the coal of the hookah to light it, Banamali remarks, "I can see one whose mother just died."

Kadir's eyes fall on the boy. A tall but very thin boy, his ribs and bones showing, his child's face incongruously stamped with dark sadness. Standing apart from the band of urchins, he holds his large eyes steadily on Kadir's face. While the rest scramble to catch Kadir's rolled potatoes, the way village boys catch raw sugar drops thrown into the air in the name of Hari at festivals, he silently stands aside, perhaps hoping for something from old Kadir's heart. He waits as if he knows the moment the old man notices him, he'll direct toward him and him alone, apart from the other boys, a stream of his compassion. He looks on calmly, as if he's entitled to this gift of love. The expectation in his eyes shows an ever-confident trust; the world would do well to fulfill it—if it does not, he will simply walk away with a sigh.

Kadir picks up two handfuls of potatoes and looks at his eyes, signing to him to come closer, aside from the lot. A smile blossoms on his face, a transparent smile of satisfaction, but it is a pale smile. With the symbols of mourning a mother's death that he wears like a banner, he continues to stand silent rather than come forward promptly at Kadir's call, with the expression of politely turning down an extravagant gift.

"Come on and catch, or they'll take it all." Kadir now puts the offer into words.

Bashful before this warm generosity, the boy casts his eyes down to his feet, away to one side and the other, toward nothing in particular. Then raising his head he glances ahead once across the canal, at the eastern sky over Aminpur village; the unsolicited riches of Kadir's gift roll on the ground near his feet. And his eyes remain fixed on the sky where they came to rest. Looking steadily there, he is unable to lower his head and bring his eyes back. Kadir looks for the object of his intent gaze but cannot make out anything. Banamali follows his eyes and notices the rainbow in the sky above the trees of Aminpur. That's what holds the boy's gaze.

"Oh, the bow's out. He's watching it," Banamali says. He is a fisherman. Under the open sky fishermen and peasants go about plowing the water and the land. The sweetness of the coming of light and the sadness of its departure are never hidden from them. But do they ever really watch all those changes in the sky? They notice only the midday sun when it comes down like fire scorching their heads. So often in autumn and on winter mornings and afternoons, little clouds in beautiful shades of color float about in the sky. So many times between showers of rain, when the sun briefly opens its shining eye, a rainbow appears in the opposite sky. Do they ever look up and watch those? Maybe they do. But such things never strike their eyes as marvelous or uncommon; they appear and disappear. There is nothing in a rainbow to keep looking at in amazement. A baby in its mother's lap smiles at the sight of the moon and claps its tiny hands in delight. But grown-ups like Banamali never smile at the moon or clap their hands. Muslims like Kadir Mian, during their Ramadan fast, are so eager to see the moon of Id briefly peep from a corner of the sky to bring them messages of happiness and virtue. A thin, pale crescent of glowless moon it is then, what you might call a fragment of the moon. But when the same moon grows full and swims across the clear sky, then they hardly bother to spend time watching it. Similarly, a rainbow is for little ones to watch. It's for this stupid, immature beggar boy to watch. Let him do so, while from near his feet other boys pick up the potatoes meant for him. Banamali feels like picking some up for him. But like the immature boy, he too becomes immature. Yes, indeed, the rainbow is that beautiful to see!

He remembers when his sister was little, she too one day watched the rainbow in amazement. But she didn't watch it so stupidly, oblivious of all else. She had on a pair of glass bangles newly bought for her. She made those bangles tinkle to accompany the clapping of her hands and she chanted a rhyme: "Rama holds the bow, Lakshmana holds the string. Go rainbow, go back from where you spring." Little girls believe the chant makes the rainbow slowly fade before their eyes. It's been so long since he visited her last! She's married here, lives in this village. Her husband's place is not far from this market.

The rainbow in the sky is immense. Spanning two far corners of the sky, it arches high above with its seven colors, each so distinctly defined from the next with no blurring! Those colors seem to detach from the neutral gray sky behind and come forward. All shadowy indistinctness remains far behind, and the two corners of the sky from where this rainbow curves up are brightened by its glow. How luminous the colors are, how soothing and symmetrical the folds that join and delineate them—as if a master craftsman created them—so pleasing to the eyes, and how soothingly cool they feel! Where did the rainbow hide all this time that it couldn't be seen in the sky? Where did it come from now, all of a sudden, and how? This land belongs to the sun and the moon. They rise and set with daily regularity, going to sleep in the west and rising in the east. But from what land does the rainbow come, where does it usually rise? Doesn't show up very often here. After a long absence, one day it suddenly makes its appearance. How long it sleeps, like Kumbhakarna! And it wakes up following no rule at all, just rises when it chooses. But how immense it is! His little sister, in her rhyme she's right to call it the bow that belongs in Rama's hands. The bow that even the most powerful demon king, with his ten heads and twenty hands, couldn't lift—blood came out of his mouth when he tried to. Banamali heard this tale of Sita's marriage sung by roving singers. Finally Rama came along and picked up the bow with ease. That's how Hara's bow—or something like that, the singers said—became the bow in Rama's hand. But even before that, every day young Sita lifted the bow in her left hand and with her right hand wiped clean the spot where it was placed and worshiped in her home. Then Sita was married to Rama, who brought her over to Ayodhya. After that Sita never came back to her parents' home* . . . Banamali simply must see his sister today. It's been so long since he brought her home for a visit.

After some time the rainbow fades away in the sky. But it leaves its permanent imprint on Ananta's mind. He has never seen a rainbow before. He heard a story from his mother about a ship that once strayed and anchored by a distant sandbar inaccessible to humans. After the ship's people cooked and ate their meal, when they fell asleep in that island there were tremendous ground-shaking thuds of things falling heavily from great heights. Among those beings who dropped there out of the sky were quite a few spirits and demons, and also a great many other manifestations that weren't human and couldn't be seen in the world inhabited by humans—they never appeared before people. Spirits and demons may be scary, but many nice and great things also dwell in the skies. For example,

*Angry with King Daksha for slighting him at his ritual sacrifice, and with the other assembled gods for tolerating it, Hara (Shiva) strung his great bow to destroy them. Fearfully, the gods sang the lord's praise and pacified him. He handed the bow to the gods, who gave it to Hara's devotee, King Nimi, for safekeeping. Twenty generations of Nimi's descendants took care of Hara's bow, worshiping it daily, until King Janaka, the adoptive father of Sita (whom he found as a baby in a fold of the soil he was plowing), decided to give Sita in marriage to the greatest hero, one who could string Hara's bow. Many gods, demigods, demon kings, and even earthly kings tried to, but not one could even lift the bow. The sage Vishwamitra brought his young disciples Rama and Lakshmana to the court of Janaka, who ordered the divine bow be brought out. Five thousand strong men pulled out a gigantic eight-wheeled carriage that held the bow in a safe. Rama picked up the bow and strung it. When he pulled the string, the bow broke. Roving folk singers replaced the epic's original grandeur with familiar images, such as a daughter in her father's humble home innocently lifting the bow of Hara with one hand to clean the space where it is kept and worshiped. Poignantly, the singer notes that after her marriage Sita never went back to the home in which she grew up.

the sun and the moon and the stars. They too stay in the sky; they rise and set so regularly that human eyes have grown used to them. But the mysteries of even these he has not yet been able to penetrate. Ananta's sky-world is filled with magical mysteries. Today one of those unseen mysterious objects appeared before his eyes from the farthest region of the sky. From the lap of the unseen it came quite close today, almost near the top of that *jaam* tree of Aminpur.

The rainbow world of imagination disappears from Banamali's mind along with the rainbow from the sky, as if he's just been set down to face reality again. The boy's fair complexion is unscrubbed and dimmed by flaking and chapping. He has a tiny piece of unbleached white cloth around his waist and another across his shoulder; in his right fist is a palm-size roll of grass mat to sit on. A two-ended flat nail of the kind used for joining boards in boatmaking has been bent into a circle and hangs from a strand of cotton thread around his neck. These are the symbols of month-long mourning after a parent's death during which a son has one meal of boiled rice a day.

Moved with sympathy, Banamali asks, "What's your name?"

"Ananta."

"Ananta what? Jugi, Patni, Sau, or Poddar?" *

Ananta keeps silent as he does not know the answer to this question.

"Your mother died, or your father?"

"Mother."

"Where's your home?"

He points with his finger to the Malo neighborhood not far from there.

"You're a Malo then? Same caste as ours."

Ananta only vaguely understands the meaning of this statement: the man may be somehow related to him, like his aunt. Why else would he be asking him so many things?

"Will you take me to your home?"

Chewing on the cotton thread around his neck, Ananta silently makes a single sideways nod with his head to indicate that he will.

"The market's going on everywhere. Come with me, I'll take you for a look around."

The market is in full swing. Around Kadir and his pile, countless other potato sellers have set up shop. Countless buyers buzz around them, weave among them. They approach the stalls with empty sacks in their hands, haggle, and after making their purchases, with full sacks of potatoes on

---

*These common Bengali caste names relate to weavers, transport boatmen, pawn-brokers, and merchant-moneylenders respectively.

their heads, push through the crowd and go out of the market. A continuous din of people's voices rises all around. To be audible now to a person next to you, you have to talk loudly with your mouth close to his ear.

Kadir has found a wholesale customer. Selling in small quantities is a lot of work, though it brings a few more paisas per maund. But selling by the maund is much better, because it lets him finish sooner and leave. Ananta's companions left this area before the crowd thickened and the pushing of grown-ups and their sackfuls became too much. Ananta looks around and finds himself alone in a moving, restless ocean of people. The small boy Ananta wishes to hold the hand of Banamali.

Kadir holds up the large scales in his strong steady hand and, placing a quarter-maund weight on one side, scoops up sweet potatoes into the pan on the other side. His mouth recites nonstop a counting rhythm for the loading, unloading, reloading routine of bulk selling: "Comes one here, one here, one here one, and you've got one! Comes two here, two here, two here two, and you've got two! Comes three here, three here, three here three, and you've got three!"

When he finishes selling, Kadir says to Banamali: "Banamali, my son, come to Birampur sometime. Mention Kadir Mian's name and even a plow bullock will show you to my place. Come sometime."

Holding Ananta's hand, Banamali pulls him through the crowd as if he were pulling a boat against the current. Ananta is used to wandering in this marketplace every day but has never come in here during the peak hour on a market day. He is fascinated by what he sees today. One spot has a cluster of betel-leaf stalls. Wads of large-size betel leaves are arranged on flat cane baskets and each vendor frequently dips his hand in a clay vessel of water by his side and sprinkles the betel with water; each also puts the coins from selling in the same vessel. Banamali buys a good-size wad from one of them and hands it to Ananta. Looking at the wad in his hand, Ananta's eyes fill with tears. He wishes he could open his heart to Banamali and tell him why holding it makes him sad. In the morning of each weekly market day, this same vendor unloads betels from his boat and sits on a squat stool picking through them and throwing away the spotty and partly rotted leaves. So many times he collected those with the other boys. His mother could never afford to buy betel leaves; she was happy to have the spotty betels he salvaged for her from the dump. A few days ago, when Ananta brought the vendor water from the river in his vessel, the vendor threw him some very slightly spotty betel leaves. Out of habit Ananta picked them up, forgetting that his mother had died only a few days before such good betel leaves were thrown his way. Aunt isn't fond of chewing betel leaves—she isn't glad if he brings her some, doesn't mind if he doesn't bring any. Aunt's mother chews betel leaves—but she isn't glad if he brings her some, though she's mad if he doesn't, and then she hits him.

But such things he cannot tell this man, a man he met only today! And there's something else. The vendor can't fail to recognize him as one of those who hover near his stall for half-rotten betel leaves. He must have thought this boy would always simply pick up what's thrown away, never have a paisa to buy any good ones. Let him see that today this boy holds in his hand a large wad of the most expensive betel leaves from his basket—bought in exchange for money.

In the lane of vendors of betel nuts, Banamali buys some chopped-up betel nuts too. In another area are several stalls of cotton vests, each with a display of open boxes arranged on burlap spread on the ground. Banamali buys a vest with its button panel embroidered with a green flowery vine from neck down to mid-chest. In the new vest with the flowery green vine now covering his bare torso, Banamali looks like Ananta's mental image of a prince. And the vine's so pretty.

Soon they come to an even more fascinating part of the marketplace. On both sides of the walking space left in the middle people have set up stalls in dense rows. They are gypsies, commonly called snake catchers, which they mostly are not. Their displays are the most tempting. On one side are thick-corded amulets for waists and arms, laid out like tame snakes, some in black cord and some in red and yellow, each with a dazzling bright top. Elsewhere is an assortment of hand mirrors laid out in overlapping layers. Several vendors have soaps in many colors and shapes. Another has strings of colored beads and bangles made of shiny glass and strands of silk-thin metal wire. Banamali squats beside a display of soaps, sniffs two or three, and asks the shopkeeper if she has any floating soap. When handed one, he asks its price and sniffs it purposefully but puts it back. He picks up a few glass bangles and, inserting his three middle fingers in them, tries to gauge the diameter and compare it with the size of an imagined wrist, then he puts them back without buying. The only thing he buys is a set of fish hooks. Meanwhile, Ananta is drawn to a corner with books for children to learn the alphabet and arithmetic counting. Sitting beside the stall, he starts turning the pages of one. Just as his eyes are caught by the picture of a farmer plowing with a pair of cattle, the vendor woman yells at him in a ringing voice. Ananta cannot look at the book anymore.

Banamali tugs Ananta along by the hand through the market and says to Dhananjay, "The village barber cuts hair the way you'd chop a taro root.

The marketplace barber cuts hair smooth as if he used a carpenter's plane. I'm going to have a haircut. Wait for me in the boat."

At the raised ground with all the barbers, some have scissors in their hands that work briskly away over their combs, sounding *kachum-koochum kachum-koochum*. Others sit quietly, with shaving knife, scissors, comb, and nail chisel laid out before them. Seeing Banamali approach with a head of unkempt overgrown hair, they guess his purpose and from all sides compete for his attention. But though Ananta's hair has also grown long and untidy, none of them calls him, noticing the emblems of mourning he wears.

When the haircut is over, the afternoon is gone too. The barber puts a small mirror in Banamali's hand, but very little can be seen in it then. Banamali leaves the barbers' area feeling not too pleased and, again tugging Ananta by the hand through the sea of people still in the market, comes out near the boat landing. The market is dispersing. Dhananjay waits in the boat, ready with his purchases of a sackful of *gaab*, two bamboo poles, and a week's provision of turmeric, chilies, cumin, and salt.

Banamali says to himself that it's too late today to visit his sister in the Malo neighborhood—he'll visit her the next time he comes to this marketplace. And to Ananta he says, "Hey son, like to come with me in my boat? I roam the river and canals and ponds with my net, catch fish and sell fish, cook and eat in my boat, and go home once a week. Want to come with me in my boat?"

Ananta nods his head sideways to indicate his consent. When Banamali says, "Come along then," he immediately steps in the water to get into their boat.

"No. No. Not right now. If I take off with you without even asking your folks' permission, they'll be mad, they'll come after me and fight."

Ananta shakes his head, wanting to tell him no one will care and come after him.

"No, not yet. Go back home now."

Ananta clings to the stern of the boat with all his strength.

Dhananjay's gruff reminder makes Banamali get into the boat, but he feels very sorry to leave the boy behind. He should at least take him home, after dragging him along all this time.

While Banamali sadly considers this, Dhananjay lowers the pole and pushes off. Tearing itself away from the grasp of Ananta's two small hands, the tapered end swings out to the right, and soon the boat moves away and disappears in the growing darkness. Ananta lets out a deep heartbroken sigh, walks to the ground by the water, and keeps standing there.

It is dark all around, and not a thing is visible. But he knows his way home from the marketplace, and there's nothing to be afraid of. Yet he feels discouraged in every corner of his body and his mind. His legs do not want to move toward home. But Banamali's parting words resound in his ears now and then. "Go back home now. I know your neighborhood. My sister is married there. Don't you worry. I'll come again."

You said you'll come again, but when! My legs no longer want to go back home! When will you come and take me away! Preoccupied with this thought, he reaches the yard of his present home.

He pauses, dreading the sound of a familiar voice. Soon he hears it. "Dims like the flame from a sinking wick but doesn't die. Seeing him gone all day, I hoped the spirits got him. Now he's here, like the light of a late-rising moon! How I want to drive him away, hit him on the head with a half-burned log. But no, my burned-face daughter is my undoing there."

Subla's wife, Basanti, just back from looking for Ananta along the side of the river, tries to do her chores; but worry slows her hands. She comes out running and objects, "What're you saying, Ma? His mother just died, he's in mourning, the pyre torch still in his hand and a bit of boiled rice in his mouth. How can you say such things to him! Even an enemy doesn't say such cruel things!"

"Enemy, yes enemy. This one's my enemy. Let him die right now. I'll worship Subachani."*

At this, Subla's wife takes on her fighting goddess persona: "Why should he die? I'll die before he does—I'll go away from this home!"

Immediately her mother pipes down. "I'm not doing anything yet. But one day I'll hit him in the back with a split log, throw him out."

Lying down to sleep that night, his aunt tells Ananta some new things: people say when a mother is dead, she's no longer the same loving and caring mother she was before; she turns into an enemy; she keeps trying to take her son with her where she's gone after death; especially dangerous for the son is the month-long period until the *sraddha* rites are over. Till then her spirit always hovers around the son and if it finds him alone in the dark by the river or under a large shady banyan or *hijal* tree, with no one around to protect him, then it takes him away and kills him!

That night Ananta sees his mother in a dream. Wrapped in several torn rag quilts, she has come from somewhere and slumped on the ground by the side of the canal. Yes, there's no doubt, she's come to take Ananta. But not even the slightest trace of anger, cruelty, or anything showing a

*Colloquial name for Shubha-Chandi, the usually angry goddess Chandi in a welfare-granting form.

desire to harm him or kill him. She just looks at his face with immense sadness in her eyes, and her face is appallingly clouded with the pain of sorrow! Yes, his mother does want to take him away; but not to kill him, only to keep him near her. Ananta is moved to a deep compassion for his dead mother.

It takes Subla's wife well into the afternoon, despite her frantic efforts, before she can fix for Ananta a mourning day's first and only meal of rice from unparboiled paddy. The child goes limp with hunger. Subla's wife knows that, but she can do so little to help him! As a widow she herself is a dependent in her old parents' very poor household; on top of that, now she's brought in another dependent not even related by blood: a dead mother's boy in need of special provision for the mourning period. She has added to her own trouble, and her parents' troubles too. Her father comes home in the morning after his nightlong work with the net and the early morning work of trying to sell fish. First she must take care of the basket of fish he brings home; clean the fish, put some out to dry under a net, and cook some for his meal. All her old mother does is order her and remind her of the tasks. After doing all this, she manages to give her fiercely hungry father a meal, and he calms down a bit. Only then can she talk him into going out again to the marketplace to spend some of the little money he just earned to buy some unparboiled rice and a ripe banana or two. Subla's wife then cooks that rice in a new clay pan, cuts a strip of trunk off a banana plant to make seven little boats, sets them out under the altar of sacred basil in the yard, and puts some of the boiled rice and banana pieces in them. Back from bathing in the river, Ananta adds water to the food. After that they step aside and wait for the crows to come and eat the food. The day no crow comes to eat it, Ananta has to walk around with the containers in his hands and call the crows, *Aa-aa*. They told him his mother comes in the form of a crow to take his offering of gruel-like rice and banana pieces. Whatever Ananta hears, he does not disbelieve. Intently he watches the crows that come to eat his offering and wonders which one could be his mother. No longer a human being, she can't talk but keeps looking up at him while eating—maybe that one is his mother! But it doesn't seem to want to stay for long, flies off without finishing the contents of the container it ate from.

Then he goes to the ghat slope of the river to wash the banana trunk boats, and with those in his hand he takes another full dip. When one day he mentions his discovery to the women at their chores there, some of them sigh, some smile. When he is leaving the ghat with a small earthen pot filled with water from the river, one woman calls him and asks, "So, your mother comes back as a crow?"

"Yes."

"And leaves without finishing the food!"

"Yes."

"Why do you think she doesn't finish eating before flying off?"

"Doesn't stay very long for fear I'd want to talk to her. Those who've died can't talk to the living. That's why they don't even want to listen to a person talking, they leave after sensing a person's thought"—Ananta melts with compassion as he explains!

When his mother was alive Ananta always felt proud of her, confident because of her. He considered himself insignificant compared to his mother! By dying his mother somehow diminished him in people's eyes, left him hanging his head. If only he could remain in the sheltering shadow of a mother like his, he could accomplish many impossible things. Now, with his mother dead, he feels he has nothing, he's not worth a paisa to people. If he dies now it won't matter to anyone; no one will even mention him. But his mother? Even though it's almost a month since she died, has anyone been able to forget her? Whenever women come together on the ghat slope they talk about her, express sorrow for her, sigh for her. Especially when they see Ananta there, they start talking of his mother at once. Ananta feels immensely grateful to his mother.

The young wife who lingers longest at the ghat, talks most, and tosses in rhymes and riddles every now and then throughout her conversation, is known by one or the other of her two identities—the sister of Banamali of Sadakpur village; the wife of Labachandra of this village. But few here know the former; in this Malo neighborhood most know the latter. She enjoys some prestige among the women because of the nice way she mixes her talk with rhymes that roll off the tip of her tongue; she's the kind of woman who stands out in any gathering of ten. On the day of the sraddha several women come to attend. She is among them. The barber comes and shaves Ananta's head. The bunch of straw on which Ananta slept each night for one month, the roll of straw mat now half-torn that he constantly carried for sitting on, the two slips of unbleached white new cloth he wore around his waist and shoulders—all this he bundles together and buries in the mud beside the river away from the ghat, following the instruction of this other woman. Then he takes a bath in the river and comes back. After the priest chants the mantras over five clay bowls of uncooked rice and leaves with a quarter-rupee as his fee, this woman gets busy trying to hurry things up a bit: "How long will it take to have the food ready! Only a finger-long person, he's starving to death!"

To do all the necessary work by herself takes Subla's wife some time, but still she cooks five dishes with much care. Seeing Ananta slouched in one place, his aunt's mother snarls at him, "Master of laziness, you there, can't you even cut a strip of banana trunk!"

This woman objects. "Scold him all other days to eternity, Mother, but bear with him just this one day. Give me the chopper, I'll cut a strip of banana trunk."

On a long trough of banana trunk, Subla's wife arranges the rice and the vegetarian dishes she has cooked, remarking, "This is going to be the poor widow's last meal. Must do it well. Never again will she come back to eat."

In a corner of the food Subla's wife also puts a betel leaf with a betel nut on it, and next to it she even adds a bit of tobacco and charcoal. When it is ready, the other woman says to her, "Sister, you were so close to her! It'll be too painful for you. Let me take him down with the food."

Ananta picks up the trough of banana trunk filled with the carefully arranged meal and walks toward the river, and the other woman accompanies him. She directs: "Put it in a spot that's neither covered with water nor completely dry, then turn around and quickly come away. Don't look back anymore."

Leaving for his mother her very last meal in this world, Ananta walks back home behind this woman.

Sometimes a secret rite of death transference is performed: a sick person is taken by the family to the point where three paths join, bathed there, and brought back; a flower is left at the spot. Anyone stepping there will die. The old woman wonders aloud when their unwanted dependent will walk one such path. In the mourning month he ate once a day; now he eats three times. From where will all that food come?

She has a point. The old man worries; he is the only earner feeding three stomachs; on top of that is this unwanted dependent now. But what can he do?

One day the old woman gives him advice. "Now that the last rites are over, take him by the ear and put him in a fishing boat as an apprentice or take him in your own boat to help you."

The old man adds his own fuel. "Yes! Some day I'll pick him up by the ear and drop him into the deep swirls of the Jagtar *dahar*.* Then trouble will go."

The thought of floating in a boat on the river, catching fish, stirs a

Dahar is the deep part of a river where an obstruction makes currents swirl and deepen the riverbed.

feeling of happiness in Ananta's mind like a puff of fresh breeze, but it disappears when he notes the tone of the old couple's talk.

In spite of that, when one evening the old man picks up his net and orders him, "Hey Ananta, bring the hookah and the tobacco holder— you're coming with me to fish tonight," Ananta swiftly finds and picks up the items commanded and gratefully follows the commander.

But his aunt comes out running and stops him. She knows how quick-tempered her father is. If he gets angry for some reason and starts beating the boy in the boat, there will be no one to save him. "Don't, Father, don't take him yet, he's barely out of mourning. He's too little, who can say he won't fall in the water or get snakebite! Don't take him now, take him when he's a bit older."

Her pleading stops Ananta with a look of disappointment on his face, and the old couple with far more displeasure on theirs, and the hint of a violent storm coming in the near future.

Storms come often at this time of year. Sometimes during the day, some-times at night. Day storms are less worrisome than night storms, which shake the huts held by bamboo posts so hard that they seem about to crumple. Even such moments are less frightening than when a storm rampages throughout the night, sometimes night after night with unre-lenting fierceness. People do their work in the day, eat their food, and as the evening approaches brace themselves for the coming storm. The black clouds amassed in the northeastern corner quickly spread through the sky like billowing smoke and a strong wind blows. Then comes the storm. People stay up through the night, fearing their huts will collapse that very night. Even when the huts survive till the morning, they know the danger is not over. A collapse may occur in the coming night's storm or in to-morrow's! Those evenings Basanti is even more afraid of the old man's stubbornness. Some stormy night he may drag Ananta to his boat, ignor-ing all her pleading. How will she stop him by herself? The last treasure of a helpless woman entrusted to her will be destroyed. In some bend of the river, the old man's boat will capsize in the storm. No doubt he will die, and, taking the boy along, kill him too.

The daytime storms fascinate Ananta. One afternoon as he wanders aimlessly through the neighborhood a storm sweeps in. The children leave their play in the yards as their elders call them inside. No one calls Ananta in, and he wonders which hut he could seek shelter in, when he finds the woman who accompanied him to the river on the day of his mother's sraddha pulling him by the hand. Storm and rain start at once, joined by a swarm of hailstones. A few hail pellets strike Ananta's shaved head and wind-driven large raindrops sting like arrows the dry skin of his bare body. The next instant the wind flips the woman's sari off her head, exposing her carefully done hair and its line of parting marked brightly with vermilion. Several large hailstones punch down the neat hair bun, and large raindrops wash and fade the vermilion. Her other hand meanwhile covers Ananta's shaved head with the veiling part of her sari.

Without stopping for shelter at any other hut, she heads with Ananta for her own hut and stops under the eaves of her porch. By then the storm's fury is in full force. Ananta has never in his life seen a storm of such great ferocity. The roofs of the huts around them shake; the tops of the trees are twisted and pulled down to the ground one moment and thrown back up the next; the vines torn off their supports roll on the ground and are swept away by the ruthless wind in various directions. The storm is unquestionably powerful. But this woman is no less powerful. Competing with the roar of the storm, she shouts,

> In the name of Rama and Lakshmana, and of the lord of arrows; *
> In the name of the thirty million gods and goddesses!

The storm is unperturbed, blowing as hard as before, pushing aside all thirty million deities with the flick of one proud finger. Now the woman takes out another weapon.

> Your nephew's wife lives in this home.
> Don't touch it, don't, she's now at home.

But the storm does not respect this restriction either. Showing its will with brute force, it immediately shakes up her hut on its way. The woman won't cower. Pitching her voice at its highest note, she now shouts at the storm.

> Go away, fellow, go to the hills and the mountain tops!
> Go and fight on your way out with the big tree tops!

Perhaps unable to ignore this order, the storm slows a bit, grows more and more sleepy, and then its breath is still. Ananta looks at her face in amazement. So much force in her command! Even a storm this violent finally bowed down to this woman's words!

Storms often bring much loss to the Malos. Half of what they possess is in their homes, and half in their boats on the river. Those who have homes left intact sometimes find the boats tied up by the landing com-

* Local name for Shiva.

pletely smashed. Those who struggle all night with the storm in their boats out on the river sometimes come back in the morning to find their huts collapsed.

But today's big storm brought little damage to this Malo neighborhood. It hit only two families. Kalobaran's big boat, out in the big river to buy fish, was smashed up. Its men are back on foot next day with the news that not even one board could be retrieved.

And the hut of Ananta's aunt's father has damage—the room in which Ananta sleeps along with his aunt collapsed. Having the room raised again uses up the small savings the old man had. Now all they have to live on is what he can bring home from day to day. The day he catches little and comes home without rice from selling fish, they have to fast. Reduced to this state in the season of hardship, they can by no means keep an extra dependent. The old man says this almost like turning prayer beads. Even without a reminder Ananta's aunt is painfully aware of the situation; but his constantly repeated complaint makes her fear for Ananta's life. And the way her mother acts makes her worry that one day she'll really attack the boy with a hot cinder log.

In desperation she considers seeking the help of Kalo's Ma. Finally one day she goes to the woman she detests and appeals: "You were so kind to his mother. Living with me now means endless hardship for him. Take him in for a while so he can eat two handfuls of rice and live."

But Kalo's mother is glumly uncooperative. A big boat destroyed is a big loss. Anyone would be upset and not ready to listen to someone else's problem and appeal for help. Still Kalo's Ma does not flatly say no. She says that when the dry season comes, Kalobaran will have lumber brought from the north to get a new boat made, and when that boat goes out in the big river to catch jiyal and other big fish, he won't forget to take Ananta along. Hearing this makes Subla's wife twist within, in pain and anger. What she is reminded of happened so long ago, but it still revolts her.

Another day of heavy downpour clears up in the afternoon. Days of rain make betel leaves rot rapidly; the shopkeepers throw away rotting betels in wads without bothering to pick out the few good ones. Girls and boys of Ananta's age bring home handfuls of scrounged betel leaves. His aunt's mother goes on about seeing with her own eyes how the mothers of those enterprising kids chew paan in red mouthfuls, the good ones salvaged by washing the collection in a basket. She grumbles about Ananta's failure to collect any. Taking the old woman's hint, Ananta happily runs for the marketplace.

The rain stopped a short while back. Over the path to the marketplace water still streams from some pond that overflowed, carrying a hyacinth leaf or two along. Some boys of Ananta's age mimic the way their elders lower a large net into the canal, with four corners fastened to the ends of two long bamboo poles placed along both banks of the canal. Placing two lengths of bamboo strips on two sides of the path, the boys similarly lay a net of scraps of thread tied together. They use the pressure of their heels on this end of the strips, pull the strings like ropes, and arch their bodies back to lift the other ends of the strips. With the air of pulling up a netful of fish, they toss to one side all the unseen fish. They draw Ananta's attention by calling out to him all at once. Ananta runs to them and asks with curiosity, "What kind of fish are you getting?"

"The usual, you know, like *chanda, baicha, tit-punti,* so many of them came in today's flood."

Catching imaginary fish, Ananta too is carried away with them. They play for a while at fishing, absorbed. They just play, as little girls play at cooking rice with mud. Suddenly one of them discovers a real fish, a baby koi, trying to move up the stream thrashing with its gill covers. All the boys run to it with loud shouts and, like robbers, capture it. Soon they notice that other koi fish, both small and full-size, are following one another, pushing upstream along the path. Ananta and the other boys are overjoyed. Using the lap fold of whatever clothing they have, they happily catch the fish. While they are thus occupied, the afternoon ends. The thinning stream on the path comes to an end; the koi, too, end their gill-walking for the day. Without a thought of scrounging betel leaf in the market, Ananta cheerfully comes back with the fold of his cloth filled with live koi fish.

The head of the house is not in a good mood. Laying his net in the canal, he caught a boatful of small fish but sold none. No fish trader turned up because of the excessive rain and the market did not take place. Fish can't be set out to dry on a day like this. Some will be cooked for the meal, but the result of his day's work is mostly going to waste.

The old woman grumbles bitterly. "I wanted betel leaf, and he brings fish. Do I lack fish? What shall I do with more?"

Next day at noon the old woman remembers that she has not yet hit Ananta with a cinder log as she decided to do. She goes by the hearth but finds no cinder log there. Her fiery-mouthed daughter is cooking with straw, and Ananta sits by her eating something. The old woman snatches from the stove a bunch of the straw burning at one end. She can't use it to hit him on the back, but she's going to stuff the burning straw into his mouth. With this thought, she grabs Ananta with one hand and with her other hand brings the straw to his mouth. When her daughter tries to stop her, she lets go of Ananta and tries to stuff it into her daughter's mouth. Her daughter snatches the burning straw from her hand and throws it to the ground. The flame unexpectedly grazes the old woman's hand and burns a patch of skin. Shaking with anger and pain, she grabs her daughter's throat. Then a ferocious scuffle starts between mother and daughter. The daughter maneuvers her mother down onto the ground and sits on her chest. Grabbing her mother's hair she bangs her head on the floor a few times before letting go. The old woman somehow totters back up to her feet, grabs hold of the large pot of cooked rice, drags it into the main room, and bars the door.

In the middle of the fight Ananta runs out to fetch that woman at whose order the storm stopped the other day. Who else but she can stop this battle? Not finding her in her hut, Ananta comes back and finds his aunt sitting with a darkened face. Her hair and clothing are disheveled, her back is uncovered as she has not bothered to refix her sari. His aunt seems to have collapsed from exhaustion at winning the battle. When Ananta fearfully comes near her, her eyes look up at him and suddenly flare up. Roaring like thunder at him she says: "My enemy, get out of here. If you eat rice again in this home, then you eat the heads of seven generations of your ancestors. On account of you, I beat up my mother. Who are you to me? The bottom of my leg, the dust on my feet. Go away, go right now, go into the open mouth of death. Get eaten up by the Dakini-Jogini she-demons, walk into the mouth of Kali. Let virtue never bring you back. Lose sight and smell and go where Yama pulls you. Never again show your face before me. Go the same way your mother's gone."

But what's this? The pale sad face, always so endearing, turns hard with determination. The large eyes, so gentle and lovely, turn red and fierce as the morning sun. Or is this a dream that Subla's wife sees?

A mighty hero, victorious in battle, as if walking away from all he conquered, leaves everything without a moment's hesitation. Those thin legs hold so much power! Ananta's steps seem to make the ground tremble. He's not running, he's walking slowly, deliberately. But the sound those steps produce! Each footfall seems to come as a blow that strikes at her heart. He leaves the porch and then the yard. Crossing the tiny boundary of her love, Ananta is about to leap into an unknown world. Subla's wife cannot hold back anymore. Getting up and stretching her arms after him, she calls in a faltering voice: "Ananta!" Ananta does not turn back. Subla's wife is about to fall. Her mother comes running from somewhere and holds her. Laying her head on her mother's old chest, Subla's wife feels her body grow limp. Her eyes close.

Under the endless sky, Ananta is supremely free today. No more will he respond to calls and claims from behind him. First he goes to Titash and stands on its bank looking at the river to his heart's content. Waves follow on waves, like a wild dream, like a soaring song. The water rises. Boats move on. No barrier anywhere, no obstacle. Everywhere is activity, mobility. If only *he* would come along at this moment, today! He said he would. But days have passed, and he has not come. Ananta goes to the marketplace ghat, to the spot where his boat was the other day. Ananta will sit here and wait day after day. He's bound to come on one of the weekly market days.

At the mouth of the canal near the market Ananta finds a large broken boat left tied up and partly submerged. He climbs into it. It's extremely slippery. Cautiously holding on to the hull, he goes inside the shed and notices that the deep hold underneath is half filled with water and has no floorboards over that dark well. It looks so scary; one slip of his foot and he'll fall in and drown. He crawls toward the stern end of the shed and finds a few planks that are dry and smooth. This side is protected from rain and sun, and from human eyes—no one will spot him in here. Wonderful! Ananta could stay here forever. And he will stay here—until the day he comes.

From this point the river's flow is southward. He can look out far and see to the very end, the farthest of the distant lands in the south from where waves, as if pushed by someone, come all the way to touch Ananta's shelter in this boat. He gazes in that direction. But the one he waits for won't come from there but instead from the west.

From time to time he turns his gaze to the river's flow from the west and looks hard as far as he can see. He isn't coming. When Ananta's mind fills with the disappointment, he returns his gaze to the long flow down south from where he expects no one. This unbroken long flow fills his mind with hope again.

Feeling hungry in the afternoon, he steals out of the boat and walks up to that vendor of betel leaves. Today is not a weekly market day, but the man sorts and arranges betel leaves all the same. At his silent assent, Ananta takes his water pot and fetches river water. The man throws him a wad of betel leaves in return, but Ananta does not pick it up. The man thinks for a moment and gives him a paisa. Ananta buys a paisa of roasted chick-peas, and after eating it finds his hunger gone.

The darkness around him is deep black. Lying down on a board by the stern, he feels very scared but falls asleep after a while. Waking in the morning, he feels that his mother has been lying right next to him—the warmth of her body still clings to the floorboard. They lied to him. How can his mother ever harm him? She can't come to him in daylight, because she's dead, but she comes in the darkness of night. He won't be afraid of anything anymore.

With much fuss, much show of pride the boy went away! Wherever he may be, he won't be dead. No one dies so easily, right? What if he never comes back to this home, if someone finds him, takes him along and brings him up? How can he ever come back to this home? May God arrange it so he'll never have to come back here! For a motherless child, all the people in the world are the same. Let him find shelter in some other home.

Thus Subla's wife argues to herself, one afternoon four days later, sitting quietly in a gathering of women. As soon as the topic of Ananta comes up, she intervenes. "Just as well the trouble's gone," she says. "How much trouble can you take, sisters, carrying someone else's charge? Not born of my womb, not reared on my back. Why do I have to bother so much? When his mother was dying in her hut alone, I was the only one there. Seeing no one come forward to take him in, I brought him in and took care of him. Now the mourning rites are all over, he can go where he wants. I've got no obligation, no complaint."

She comes out with so many words in order to block all the things others may have to say about Ananta. Still, someone comes out and says her son Brindaban saw him in the market, selling some little fish off his thin towel.

Another, chewing her paan, says her son Nandalal saw him standing silently before the betel vendor without bothering to pick up any of the rotting wads thrown to him.

Subla's wife wants to hear no more. But a third one won't let go without making her hear this: "Last night with some betel leaves and betel nuts in his hands he came to Labachandra's wife in her hut. She fed him, made a bed for him, and asked him to sleep; but instead of lying down, he left in the dark—disappeared like a ghost. Next day Labachandra's wife made her husband look for him everywhere all morning, but no one knows where he stays. Some say he stays in the jungle; some say he stays in a foxhole; some say he stays inside the deserted monastery in the cremation ground of Jatrabari! God forbid, sisters, that the boy doesn't become a renouncer!"

Labachandra's wife seems to overflow with compassion! Made her husband look for him. For how long has she been related to him? Who looked after him all this time? When his mother died, where was Labachandra's wife? As for that ingrate, if he must come back, nobody barbed the way to this hut! If he has to come begging for rice to eat, why at Labachandra's place—alms like that I could give too! Subla's wife thinks these thoughts, but she does not express any of them.

That night when she is in bed with a full stomach for the first time in a while, Brinda's mother comes calling her, "Subla's wife, come out and see what's going on."

She scrambles to her feet, rushes out, and sees Ananta squatting by the refuse dump next door, washing his mouth after a meal. Labachandra's wife stands by him holding a kerosene lamp. Subla's wife had no intention of appearing so close, and she is flustered. But the boy, not the slightest bit startled to see her, puts the jug down on the ground and walks off confidently, leaving them all speechless.

On the way back, Subla's wife says bitterly, "I want to catch hold of him one day, Brinda's Ma, and give him the beating of his lifetime. What do you say?"

Brinda's mother says nothing.

A conspiracy of silence goes on for some time and nobody tells Subla's wife anything. Then one day the word is out that the brother of Labachandra's wife has come. His name is Banamali. He uncovered the mystery that no one could. He pulled Ananta out of a half-immersed broken boat at the mouth of the canal. The next day the three of them are seen together by the village ghat, leaving in his boat.

After hearing all this, Subla's wife feels no inclination to go out there. Brinda's mother knows where her pain is, and she persuades her to come. "You took care of him for so long, you fed him and washed him. Today he's going away with strangers. Who knows if you'll ever see him again. Come, take a last look."

Yes, she must see him for one last time! Silently Subla's wife starts for the ghat.

Many women have gathered by the landing. A woman from the Saha neighborhood swings up a filled water pot to her waist and, coming up the slope, asks a woman from the Malo neighborhood, "Who's being taken away by whom, sister?"

"Labachandra's wife, Udaitara—her brother Banamali came to take her for a visit back home; they're going. My parents' home is in the same village as hers, the homes are next to each other."

"Oh, I see."

Subla's wife joins the group of women standing by the ghat landing. She sees how very happy both of them are. Udaitara talks in rhymes from time to time and makes jokes, and the ungrateful dog looks happily this way and that.

Udaitara is no longer Labachandra's wife; now she is Banamali's sister. With proud eyes she looks at the women gathered on the ghat slope. A young wife gazes sadly at her; her parents' home in Nabinagar village is close to hers. To cheer her up Udaitara addresses her, "Chhabi of Nabinagar—isn't that you? Haven't seen you in a long time too!"

The women who know Udaitara well break out into laughter.

Even the sad young wife giggles a little. "What's the groom-teaser talking about, dear?"

Amid these sounds of women joking and laughing, Banamali's boat sets off in the swollen water of Titash.

The sky is weighted down, congested with masses of clouds. The sun has not shown its face through the day. This monsoon sky, bending low and heavy, compresses the space overhead. Expropriating much of the air that belongs to people for them to breathe freely, someone has covered the Malo neighborhood as if with a dingy rag quilt.

The wind blows damp and cold. Subla's wife sets out with a clay pot to fetch water from the river, covering her chest and back in two or three layers with the veiling part of her sari.

The yardlike wide stretch along the bank of the river has laid open until now. There fishermen spread their nets to dry, young Malo boys reel thread over a long swath, small children and elderly widows come out to sit and take the warmth of the sun on winter mornings, boys run around and play games in the afternoons, a cow or a goat or two stray in to nibble at the grass in corners of the trodden ground. With its steadily rising water level, Titash like an ogre has swallowed up most of that wide dry ground between the river and the Malo neighborhood, leaving no room to move freely along the bank. In the good season * the water was quite a walk away from the huts; bringing home a full water pot took a bit of work. Now the river has risen so close: the water is right up where you step out of your hut and come out of the neighborhood. The space that's still left will fill in a couple of days. The spot where Basanti bathed in the dry season is now part of the riverbed; even the long bamboo pole of a

* Roughly, the six dry and temperate months of autumn and winter from Ashwin through Falgun (October through February).

large net can't touch the ground in that spot. The black sky that hangs low overhead and the black waters of Titash that advance rapidly this way seem to be in a conspiracy to squeeze the Malo neighborhood from two sides.

The awesome change of scene, looking toward the south, makes a heart sink. The month of Asarh just ended. Earlier, when the farmlands and the ghat landings by the river were still visible, the rainwater washed them and carried a lot of their soil in pale beige and reddish brown streams to the river. Now all those fields and croplands are under chest-high, even swimming-depth water. All the silt and soil brought into the river have settled to the bottom, and now the water above is clear. Thus the water of Titash now is neither whitish nor ocher brown but absolutely transparent, and because it is transparent it looks so black under the dark sky. Over that expanse of black water, wave after wave breaks here. Those waves bring the water closer and closer.

The fishermen have a bothersome chore: they must often relocate the boat-tying posts. One day the prow of the boat is in knee-deep water and the stern in chest-deep water. In three days, the prow is in waist depth and the stern in swimming depth. Clothes get wet as the men get into the boats, and so they have to pull out the posts and drive them in closer. This pulling out and sticking in of posts goes on until the boats' prows touch the cluster of Malo huts.

The water's new height reaches the Malo neighborhood and announces the fullness of the river. Shrubs, cane clumps, the assorted wild growth in the corners of huts and yards and in between them are now halfway under water. They block the entry of the waves but not the flow of the current or the quiet journey of small fish upstream in the current that flows through the yards and bushes around Malo homes. All the small fish have spawned; the babies are out and they have learned to swim and move in a band upstream. When washing plates you can see groups of them swimming by so close you can catch them with the edge of your sari. Ananta could catch plenty of them in a small net right here! He could also take them to the market and sell them. The price of fish goes up now: in the rising water large nets can't pull in much fish. When the water starts going down, large nets haul up grown fish in plenty: the price of fish is low then. Now it's quite high.

When nobody works in the water and the ghat is quiet, shoals are visible just below the surface, coming across the landing. So many village ghats they must have crossed like this, and so many others they will cross in the coming days, going over obstacles that must be mountains for them; where do they go, where will they come to rest? Who knows where their journey will end? But they are determined to move on. If you stir the water with a plate and push a wave at them, they back up a little, fluttering and wavering, but as soon as the water quiets they move on again. If you try to grab them with your hand, they dart out a yard and, parallel to their previous course, resume their passage. If there are too many people in the water, bands of them hide in pockets of the submerged shrubbery and wait and wait. Small fish fear the deep water; they wait in the shallow water in bands of growing numbers, and as soon as the ghat becomes quiet, proceed again on their journey. Nothing can deter them.

Alone in the flooded work area, Subla's wife catches a batch of them by laying the end of her sari in their way. Caught there, a bunch of baby punti flutter. Not wanting to separate them from the water, she releases them and stays on watching the shoals of fry go by, some striped, like little girls in striped saris, some transparent with a slippery coat that leaves stickiness on fingers that touch them. Ananta could catch them all with a small-meshed little net!

When the ghat has been under water a while longer, clumps of miniature water forests develop at about a four-foot depth along the slope. Twisting, undulating, getting thick and thicker, they become fortresses for the small fish. Malo boys do not sit around now. When the men are out in their boats, lowering and lifting different kinds of net, little boys armed with small triangular scoopnets are busy in the water over the landing, ceaselessly poking and teasing those fish fortresses. After poking at them for some time, they drag their nets up to the ground, to expose countless little shrimps dancing and waving their antennae in the air. Doing this ten or twelve times is enough to fill a narrow-necked fish basket. She could easily knit a small-mesh net for Ananta and frame it with three sturdy strips of bamboo. He could catch a lot of the baby shrimps with it and sell them in the market! With Subla's wife making the thread and the net, and Ananta catching and selling the shrimps, the two of them could easily make a living for themselves! Subla's wife could then be free of her parents' rebukes and restrictions.

The time comes when the cloud-laden sky clears for brief periods. Pushing aside the dense growth of dark mane, the sun smiles. The late afternoon sunshine paints the tops of trees and shrubs golden yellow. Now most men are out on the river, and those at home sleep after the meal following nightlong fishing. Women bring their spinning work out into their yards. Each yard has a permanently driven post with a hollow tube top into which they put the base of the fiber-wound wheel. The spinner attaches one end of the distaff's shafts of flax to the spindle and stretches the length all the way around another post set in the far end of her yard. Then she starts the spindle by using her bared thigh: moving the sari over the right knee up to her waist and raising the knee, she uses her palm to roll the stick of the spindle down the length of the thigh to accelerate its spin. One move makes the spindle turn a thousand times. Ten moves finish twisting the entire length of the joined shafts of fiber. Then, her left hand holding up the neck of the spindle, her right palm rolls its handle against her partly bared chest as the woman walks the length of the yard reeling in the spun thread. In other communities, this is men's work. But Malo women do not like to leave the task only to men. They cannot afford to either, as the men have too little time for it after working on the river. So, at a time of day when few men are about in their neighborhood and the weather is good, women bring their reels and spindles out into the yards of their homes.

One day at such a time a fellow from the Teli neighborhood—on his way through the Malo neighborhood—glimpsed the immodest appearance of the work-absorbed young Malo wives. He grew tempted and took to walking the neighborhood at that time every day. If anyone asked, he said he was going to so-and-so's place or coming from so-and-so's place. At first the women ignored it and went about their work. But when he started leering and signing to them, the women pricked up their ears. Taking the initiative on their behalf, Subla's wife answered his signing and took him into her room one night. There selected strong Malo youths strangled him, took the body out in a boat, and dumped it in the outer stream of the river. The current took the body away and no one saw the fellow again.

In this Malo neighborhood Tamasi's father is the only householder who keeps in touch with those from the Brahman and Kayastha neighborhoods. His home is near the market. Young Kayastha men come to his home to practice the tabla, and he seems not to mind this sort of thing because they let him play the role of the king in their jatra performance. The Malos are upset with him for this. He, too, no longer likes the Malos; watching the ways of Brahmans and Kayasthas has made him snobbish.

A moneyed man from the Teli neighborhood disappeared—just like that. Yet his whereabouts could not be traced for lack of witnesses or proof. No penalty could be secured by recourse to the law courts, no justice dealt out. Through Tamasi's father the Telis came to know that Malos were behind it. But without proof it was not possible to drag them to court. The Telis fumed and fretted but could not decide what to do about it. Finally men from Brahman, Saha, Teli, and other upper castes held a secret meeting. Some proposed men be hired to cut the Malos' boats off their posts one night and take them away to stave in the bottoms and sink them, and other men be hired to steal their nets and burn them.

But this proposal did not satisfy all; the penalty seemed too light for so serious a crime. So they discussed a second proposal that came from Rajani Pal, known in the entire Teli neighborhood for his clear head and knack for shrewd tactics. It did not take him long to grasp the irrelevance of such crude reprisals. "Bidhubhusan Pal of Bishnupur town is my maternal uncle," he said. "He's the manager of the fisheries branch of the cooperative credit society. Tempted by the low interest, the Malos have all borrowed. Like fish they're hopelessly hooked to a bait they can't swallow or spit out. Now the interest and the principal are accumulating nicely at the compound rate. You know well what sort of methods can be used to recover the cooperative society loans. All I need to do is ask my uncle to make each Malo do the frog dance."

But this proposal also did not satisfy many. Who knew when his uncle would find the time to come here with his men? It seemed too long-term a proposal. Didn't offer the hot revenge they wanted. Finally Rajani Pal's brother made a proposal: abduct the slut who had taken the missing man into her room, buy a few bottles of liquor, then take her to the inner chamber of the ruined Kali temple. But the matter did not roll much beyond discussion of these proposals; for the time being they remained only proposals. However, that day the enmity between the Malo community and the other caste communities united against them took root, and was never to be uprooted.

Night descends on the three as they travel to Sadakpur. Throughout the afternoon the shadow of the cloud-filled sky crouches like a dark giant over the vastly expanded river of the rainy season. Ananta sits by himself watching for some time, until it grows too dark to see anything at all. From inside the open-ended dome Udaitara now calls him in.

Banamali, staying at the stern, uses enormous effort on the scull. The force causes the ropes and the rudderpost to creak and moan at their joints and fastenings, and the entire boat sways and shudders as it moves on. Steadying himself carefully in that swaying boat, stepping slowly along the bamboo framework, Ananta goes inside the cover. He cannot see Udaitara but guesses her location, goes near her, and sits down. He says nothing and, overcome with sleep, lets his body recline on the platform. The boat's swaying motion and a few mosquito bites lighten his sleep at some point. He is faintly aware that his head is on something soft like cotton fluff and cool like moonbeams. A sheer fold of starry sky, in a profusion of sparklers, has come all the way down to be held over his body! And he sees a brilliant bridge spanning that sky, end to end—maybe it's the string of that very rainbow he saw some time ago. The seven-hued rainbow now hides but holds out its bright string for Ananta to behold. The string radiates the brilliant color of unalloyed gold, and both its sides are strewn with millions of stars. It has come so close to Ananta that he can simply extend his arms to hold on to it and, hanging from it, journey into such a mysterious region of the sky, where he will see only unknown things. He will never finish seeing and marveling at them.

To keep mosquitoes away, Udaitara spread her sari's brightly dotted *anchal* over the sleeping Ananta's body; not wanting his head to roll and knock against the hard platform, she rested it in her lap; and to keep her sari from shifting, she arched her left arm over his chest, holding down the fabric. Thinking her arm disturbs the drowsy boy who fumbles at it, she gathers back the sari she held over him and lowers his head from her lap. "Ananta, wake up," she calls.

Ananta wakes up and sees the world transformed. Under the star-filled clear sky the river lies motionless. In the distant vault of the sky, stars in innumerable clusters form luminous pathways. How immense must be the beauty of those paths, and the joy of walking along them, treading on the star-flowers, and watching the countless other star-flowers on both sides and overhead! Those paths are so far above that Ananta will never reach them. But the gods are gracious. Onto the still waters of Titash they have dropped a clearly reflected likeness, quite close to where he is. If Banamali would edge the boat out into the stream, Ananta could step from the boat onto those paths. But those paths lie in water; only fish can travel there, and Ananta is not a fish. The surface of the water is misty white in the faint starlight, and occasional little bubbles released by a fish or two here and there make the reflected stars shiver. How the same stars tightly fixed in their places up in the sky seem so loose down here in the water! How the fish make them move and dance from time to time, playing with them as if with small brothers and sisters! Ananta's mind becomes a fish and dives into the water.

Banamali's boat meanwhile moves farther away from the broad surface of the river and glides close to the lap of a village, as the high water from the season's rains has not only reached the village but quietly filled it, covering the ground and the low shrubbery. The large trees that stand like guards at the edge of the village are up to their waists in water. Their massive branches, dense with leaves and tangled vines, spread at various angles over the water. Presently Banamali's boat glides under them, into the deeper darkness of one tree after another. Now it is farther away from the starry sky and the river's calm bosom that is like the sky's mirror.

What holds Ananta so intently? Noticing his gaze on the stars, a rhyme comes to Udaitara's mind. The prolonged quietness is not to her liking. But what could she chat about with a young boy? How can such a conversation engage her mind? For one used to brightening neighborhood gatherings with her talk, how can she feel her effervescent self on the silent river in the middle of the night! Where's her audience of appreciative listeners? But Ananta does seem more intelligent and responsive than all other boys. At this late hour of the night when other children are asleep with eyes closed, his eyes shine, he's awake like the stars and wonders about the mysteries of the unknown. And the riddle that just came to Udaitara is also about stars. "Ananta," she says, "tell me the meaning of this:

> Flowers in bloom everywhere, but no one's there to gather.
> A nice bed is waiting, but not a body to lie down here."

Ananta does not know the meaning, but his eyes shine with curiosity. Udaitara explains the first part. " 'Flowers in bloom everywhere, but no one's there to gather' means the stars in the sky, scattered like flowers in bloom, which no one can pick."

Yes, they really are strewn where human hands will never reach, Ananta muses, but the gods who live in heaven are there. "Why don't the gods pick them? Rama, Lakshmana, Krishna, Durga, Kali, the lord Shiva—even they can't pick those flowers?"

"The gods can pick them if they want to; but they don't want to. Why pick flowers they themselves have strewn? Every night they scatter the sky with flowers and call on human beings: 'Here, we've strewn the flowers, you may pick them if you can.' But no one can. What then would they use to worship the gods? Finally, the gods made copies of those flowers bloom on earth, bloom daily so people can pick them fresh for their worship. The ones left unpicked drop off before the next day, as day-old flowers can't be offered in worship."

"If the gods call to us and tell us they've strewn the stars in the sky for us, then why can't we hear their call?"

"Not all can understand the way the gods call us. The great sages can, those who meditate, do ascetic penance, and worship. They can hear the deities speak; they can wash and feed the deities. They understand the gods' words and the gods understand their words."

"The gods understood my mother's words, too. Once—on the night of Kali puja—she stood very close to the image of the goddess and said something to the deity! I was kept off at a distance. Standing far off, I only saw but couldn't hear what she said."

"No, I'm not talking about that, you see, the kind of worship we all do. I'm talking about sages, the great ones, how they can hear the gods. When the image of a god is before our eyes, the god keeps silent! When there's no image before our eyes, then conversation occurs between the minds of great sages and the minds of the gods. That's what I'm telling you about. Talking with someone we can see is our kind of talking. Only the words that can be heard inside, with the speaker unseen, only those are a god's words."

"The great sages who can hear the words of unseen gods, only they pick those star-flowers?"

"Yes they do, but not in this life. When they leave their earthly bodies on earth and go to the land of the gods, then they can pick those flowers. In heaven, every day at a certain time there is the ringing of bells and gongs, and the sages pick just one of those flowers to worship the gods. That flower returns to its spot and stays in bloom as before!"

A last question arises in Ananta's mind: "Why do I see no trees, no leaves, only flowers in the sky? Are those flowers then treeless flowers?"

Glancing at the still surface of the river, Udaitara explains the second part of her riddle. "And look, Ananta, see how this river is like a nice bed, with no dust and dirt on it, no bumps and dips, cool like a fine-woven mat! It could rest the body well, but there's no one to lie down on it."

Yes there is, there's one—Ananta. If he could find a bit of hard sheet to put on the water, he'd lie down on it, stretch out his arms and legs, lie on his chest and on his side and on his stomach. The river's current will take him to distant lands; the gentle waves will rock him; and there'll be no one else awake in the surrounding darkness. He'll stay awake along with the darkness around him and the stars in the sky above and the fish in the water. Thinking he's asleep, all the fish will swarm around him and swim along. Lying awake through the night, he'll be drowsy sometime and fall asleep. The night will be over, but not his sleep; the morning will come, the sun will rise. From the two banks throngs of people—young and old, men and women—will stand gaping, thinking Ananta fell in the water. "Oh, how terrible it is, what shall we do, Ananta's fallen in the water!" Then I'll wake up and look at them. Rubbing my eyes and smiling a little, I'll sit up on the water, and then I'll quietly walk past the amazed crowd to do my day's work.

Udaitara giggles at Ananta's racing imagination and says, "No one lies on a river while there's life in the body. When the bird of life has flown away, when the body's an empty cage, then those who can't afford to cremate entrust the body to the river and let it float away. Only a dead person lies in this bed of water. Why would you have that misfortune? Or are you Lakhai pandit?"

"Me Lakhai pandit? Haven't learned a single letter yet and you ask if I'm a pandit!"

"No, I don't mean a pandit of learning. I mean the merchant's son, Lakhai, the son of Chand Saudagar. * He died from the bite of the deadly cobra. They made a boat out of banana trunk, put his body in it, and floated it off. That float went upstream, and his wife, the beautiful Bhelaiya, with a bow in her hand, went walking with it along the bank of the river."

"But Lakhai pandit was dead, and the beautiful Bhelaiya went alone— how come no merchant tried to take her away in his boat?"

"Managoda, the brother of Dhanagoda, wanted to. But he left her alone when she addressed him as her husband's maternal uncle. Everyone leaves alone a sister's son's wife."

"Oh, I see. Where did they go, he floating upstream and she walking along?"

"They reached heaven. There in the gods' court the beautiful Bhelaiya danced, and with that she pleased Mahadeb and Chandi. At their command, Manasa then gave life back to Lakhai pandit."

"They brought a dead man back to life!"

"Yes, but when bringing him back to life, they found his heel was missing, eaten up by fish."

"The fish could eat his heel only because he was dead. If he was alive, Lakhai pandit would've caught all those fish on his way and sold them in the market! But is it possible to get all the way to heaven simply by going upstream along the river? The same heaven where the gods live?"

*Manasamangal recounts the battle of wills between Chand Saudagar and the goddess Manasa, whom the powerful maritime merchant refused to worship. The two texts from the thirteenth and fifteenth centuries (by Vipradas and Vijaygupta respectively) were written during the rule of the Sen dynasty in Bengal, at the peak of the region's mercantile power and prosperity. The vengeful goddess causes Chand endless personal and professional troubles, the worst of which is bringing about his son Lakhinder's death from cobra bite even in his iron-clad nuptial chamber. The bride, Behula, conducts her husband's body over the connected rivers all the way to heaven, where the greater gods reward the demonstration of her virtue and virtuosity as a dancer with the return of her husband's life. Behula brings about a truce between Manasa and the merchant, who finally offers his worship to Manasa and promotes it among merchants and other upper castes. Folk versions of this story abound in riverine Bengal and refer to Lakhinder as Lakhai and Behula as Beula, Bhelaiya and so on.

"Yes. Rivers are all created in the land of King Himail, the land that unites this world and the heaven. King Dudhisthir went to that land first and from there he walked all the way up into heaven." *

Then it's possible even for a human being to walk to the land of the moon and the stars, and the land of the rainbow! When he grows up a little more and is able to earn, and has saved a bit, Ananta will take a trip. He will set out for the land of King Himail by walking, following the river upstream all the way, and then from that land he will walk on foot to heaven.

Ananta's respect for her turns into reverence. "You know so much! Accept my respect."

The boat suddenly hits something and comes to a stop. The large trees with their thick trunks half-submerged hold out above the water many branches filled with leaves. Moving underneath those dense forestlike canopies, the boat has reached the landing area of its destination. Udaitara was dozing and now sits up with a start. Banamali is out of the boat, driving in the post tied at the stern—Udaitara knows this from the repeated tugs and shudders going through the boat. It was in a dry season that she was married and took leave from this very ghat. All this was dry ground at that time; the water of the river was a long way off, close to the riverbed. So many rainy seasons have come in her life since then, all spent in her husband's home. She's never been back here in the wet season! Yet the familiar trees almost glow in her mind even in the late night darkness. The dry ground under them used to light up every day with a fair of moonbeam children. Small boys ran around playing catch, and small girls played dolls' house. The air was nice and cool under these large shade trees. Now cold water swirls there. Like Udaitara, the girls now live in other homes in other places; and the boys, now grown up, bathe in the river here.

Gathering her triangular bag of betel leaves and betel nuts, and a change of sari and other little items in a small bundle, Udaitara holds Ananta by the hand and steps out of the boat, cautioning him, "Watch your steps, Ananta, or you'll slip and fall in the water. So slippery underneath."

Almost falling at each step, Ananta holds on to her hand and says, "I slip—but how come you don't?"

"That's because this is the home of my brother and father. Every bit of ground is familiar to me. I played games out here in the wet season as much as I played with dolls in the dry season."

---

*In the folk speech, King Himail refers to the Himalayas and King Dudhisthir to Yudhishthira, the eldest Pandava, who as virtue incarnate entered heaven in his earthly body.

"Were you always playing when you were a child?"

"Not as much as my elder sister Nayantara. And my little sister Asmantara, she liked to play just as much. We got a lot of scolding from our parents for that. Neighbors complained about us playing too much. Three sisters together: we played, we went around, we didn't bother about anyone. Then the three of us were married off to three different places."

"Haven't you seen each other since then?"

"No. It's easier for rivers to meet than for married sisters. They're really nice, my elder sister Nayantara and my younger sister Asmantara."

All taras, a set of stars! Ananta muses as he silently recites their names.

Banamali lives alone. When he went out he must have closed the door from the outside. Though it's very late now as he comes back home, there's a light inside. Quietly Udaitara nudges the door with her knee and, as it opens wide, sees to her surprise both Asmantara and Nayantara sitting there and talking—about nobody else but Udaitara, their middle sister. Seeing both her sisters together after so many years, Udaitara is at a loss for words. But her eyes shine with tears of joy. How did they manage to come together in the wet season at its height?

The tale of their being here together on this night is short: at a chance encounter on a fishing trip away from Titash, their two husbands decided to come here with their wives on a certain day of a certain month. Both kept their word.

"Where are those two?"

"They've gone to some neighbors'."

"You didn't want to go visiting the neighbors?"

"We don't go visiting neighbors at night. We finish visiting before daylight leaves, come back home, and bar the door. Do you women of Gokan village go about visiting neighbors at night?"

Her eyes dancing at her elder sister's words, Udaitara hums. "I know all about your ways, woman of Nayanpur. Don't you tease me in so many words."

At this point the two husbands come in. The older sisters pull their saris over their upper faces as they are supposed to in the presence of a younger sister's husband. The youngest one barely covers her head and smiles at her sisters' plight.

Whenever two Malo men from distant villages come together, the first thing they talk about is fish. The topic of personal and family well-being comes well after that. The eldest's husband lost some front teeth since the last time Udaitara saw him; he has bunches of gray hair and his untidy growth of beard and mustache is speckled with white. Youthfulness is leaving his body but his muscular form is still strong, used to constant hard work. Taking the hookah from the middle sister's hand, he asks her before he puts it to his mouth, "How's the fish catch over there in Titash these days?"

"Staying home with my housewife's work, what do I know of how the fishing goes? Why ask me; ask the man if you can find him."

"I've never seen your man, don't know what kind of person he is. Why don't you bring him along?"

"Is the man a load on my head to leave behind if I wish?"

"Never a load on your head. He's the bangle for your wrist and the five-strand necklace. Bring him along and look beautiful. Don't bring him and look unadorned."

"Save the soothing words, good man. You know well that bangles stay on the wrist and a necklace stays around the neck. The man leaves home to catch fish in Titash. And when he comes home, if I say, 'Haven't seen my brother for ages, let's go visit him one day,' he says: 'Go set up home with your brother; I don't want you here.' Did you ever hear such words!"

"You misunderstood the words, dear sister. Maybe he says 'don't want' only because he does want with all his heart."

Noticing the thick strand of beads from basil stem around his neck, Udaitara falls into a respectful silence, which grows as she sees the gentle look in his eyes and his devoted expression as he sings softly, his head swaying with the rhythm.

> O, my darling Gaur is my conch bangles and the sari I wear,
> O, moonlike Gaur is the vermilion in the parting of my hair,
> And he is the lace I use to braid my hair daily.
> Not knowing how to love Gaur I step ever so gently!

When the spiritual atmosphere lightens, Udaitara says, "I've got something to say to you, dear men. You're not doing anything for our brother. Is he to spend his life a bachelor like the god Kartik? Is the sola crown never ever to be put on his head?"

"Talking of Banamali? As you know, dear sister, who wants to give a daughter to a man without parents, brothers, and kinsmen, a man without land and money and jewelry to offer? If there were at least three hundred rupees in savings to spare, would he lack a bride?"

Three hundred rupees! The three sisters were married one after another when their father was still alive. For each daughter, he took three hundred rupees and gave a feast for the community on the occasion. Now Banamali, too, must offer three hundred rupees to a bride's father so the father can do the same. How terrible a problem it is! Udaitara falls silent, without a solution. After a few moments she says, "If you have an un-married sister of some sort, why don't you give her?"

"I don't have a sister of my own, only a cousin, my maternal uncle's daughter. But I've got no say there."

At this point Banamali returns with a gale's force. All kinds of bundles hang about his shoulders, around his waist, in his hands. Among the food provisions are the ingredients for sweet cakes: unparboiled rice, raw sugar molasses, oil, and so on.

Through all this Ananta sits quietly on a corner of the bed and, unnoticed by any of them, listens to their conversation. Now the eyes of Nayantara, the eldest, light on him. Avidly the boy swallows each word of their talk and observes every one with intense curiosity as if he's looking inside them, into their very veins and arteries.

"Where did you find this one?"

"This one is my wayside find! He lost his parents. Subla's widow took care of him for awhile. But without family ties, do people ever value another's feelings? One day she threw him out. I felt so attached to him. And I brought him along; maybe some day he'll become something to me."

How casually she says it—she's found and taken someone else's child, not a doll made of wood or clay, but a boy! Do the laws of the land allow it, does the world accept it? She didn't give birth to him, didn't bring him up, just found him by the wayside, and she says he's hers to keep! If another's child could become your own like this, then childless people'd have little reason for worry or sorrow. But that never happens. Someone else's son is sure to be disloyal, to betray your love.

Banamali and the two other men have already gone to the other room—talking about how much fish was caught in which canal or which marsh in which year, and now their energetic exchange of information and ar-gument grows loud and can be heard in this room. The voice of Asman-tara's husband tops the others'. Among the Malos in ten to twelve neigh-boring villages he has quite a name as a fisherman. Prompted by her pride in that, she says, "Give him to me, big sister, I'll feed him, tend him, and bring him up. Later on, when he flies away like a faithless bird, I won't grieve."

"But you have time, little sister. God will give you your own, but not me, never. If I can have this boy, I'll take him home dancing in joy." Nayantara smiles, to lighten the pain of her childless heart.

Why, am I a bar of soap or a piece of towel in a shop that I can be made to change hands? How can she dare wish to buy me? Ananta does not say his thought aloud, though.

After Ananta and the three men finish eating, the three sisters spend a long time eating together from the same plate. Then they make one large bed in the other room for the men and put Ananta in Banamali's bed, before settling down to make the sweet cakes.

It is very late in the night. The oil lamp casts patches of light on the three sisters' faces, hands, and clothing and makes long shadows on the wall behind them. Their unhurried manner tells that they plan to spend the night without sleep.

"What'll we do if we feel sleepy?" the youngest asks.

"Udaitara is a master of riddles. She'll tell riddles and we'll solve them—then sleep'll run away from us," the eldest assures her.

Kneading a lump of dough in her palm, Udaitara promptly starts. " 'Fireflies crowd in the *hijal* tree, but at nightfall they break free'—what does it mean?"

"It means marketplace," says Asmantara, the youngest.

"Good. And this—'The basil tree sparkles under a veil of water, at the nudge of a *hilsa* fish it breaks in a shower'?"

The eldest comes up with the answer: "Mist at dawn."

So it goes for a long time. Ananta is thoroughly entertained, but sleep catches up with him. In the midst of listening to the sisters play with riddles he falls asleep.

Sometime in the depth of night, he briefly comes out of sleep and hears the sisters still at it, tirelessly telling and solving riddles, their hands ceaselessly moving at their work. With his drowsy eyes closed, Ananta's ears hear, "Ginger slices of milk-white color; without it life's useless here!" to which another sister says, "Silver rupees," and shoots back another arrow . . .

As the gray of dawn fades, Ananta rouses. Outside is the sound of singing and finger cymbals as someone passes by the yard: "Wake up, my Rai,* wake up, my precious pride; Wake up, O Rai, Brindaban's divine bride." Ananta gets up. Sometime during their nightlong project the three sisters did lie down. They're fast asleep in one another's arms, their uncompleted production of sweet cakes scattered around them. The oil lamp still burns, but the tiny glowless flame is going out; the wick has not been advanced for some time. Ananta goes outside. The other room is empty of the three men who slept there. Banamali left before dawn to cast the net, and his two guests went with him to find out about fishing conditions here.

*One of Radha's pet names used in Vaishnava folk literature and devotional songs (*kirtans*).

The eastern sky slowly takes on a soft blue-tinged light. Crickets still drone all around, little birds chirp in the trees. The man with finger cymbals moves from this neighborhood to the next. The last part of his song with the tinkling of cymbals reaches Ananta's ears.

> Parrot says, "Dear parrot-wife, no more drowse.
> Say: 'Wake up, Radha, then your friend arouse.' "
> Wake up, my Rai, wake up, my precious pride,
> Wake up, O Rai, Brindaban's divine bride.

Ananta follows the path, walking past yard after yard of the huts in the neighborhood. Now the young men are out on the river. Still at home are the old men and the wives, daughters, and mothers—all awake and out in their yards. The old devotedly bow their heads to the sacred basil after getting up. At the center of each yard is a small smoothly mud-plastered altar of basil, with flowering plants on two sides, creating a sweet aroma of flowers and basil in the air. Each wife has already swept the yard and now sprinkles down the dust with a solution of cow dung. Ananta walks past all those yards and comes to one where both the path and the Malo neighborhood end. After that is a deep ravine, followed by a vast unbroken stretch of jute fields covered with plants the height of adult men, with their stalks in waist-deep water and their dark green leafy heads waving in the wind. The dark green extends from field on field to the horizon, turning lighter green and merging near the horizon with the soft blue of the sky. Ananta lowers his eyes in amazed reverence before this scene of the infinite within the finite revealed by the light of early morning. The sweetness of his intimate absorption with nature does not escape the eyes of one person. The man, after bowing to the sacred basil in his yard, hums the Vaishnava devotee's prayer. He comes closer and regards the boy—a beautiful little child of nature's own, looking at and worshiping that invisible Brindaji basil that grows of its own accord on the other side of the boundless vast ocean that is this world.* He puts an eager hand on the boy's shoulder and says in an anguished voice, "Nitai, my Nitai, where were you hiding all this time, son, deceiving this beggar of love! Come to my lap!"

Pushing with both hands against the enveloping arms, Ananta says, "I'm Ananta!"

"I know, son, I know, you're my Ananta. 'They named him Ananta, seeing he has no end.' Oh, dear god, I know no other path to reach you;

---

*The Vaishnava legend says that Brinda, who was Radha's closest friend and trusted messenger to and from Krishna, is eternally reincarnated as the basil plant, the sacred embodiment of Brinda's essence.

I've no riches to give away, no knowledge of austere meditation. All I know is I love you. As you've come for my love, I won't let you leave me again."

Ananta is struck dumb with astonishment. The man suddenly regains his senses and says, "Oh, Hari, what a trick you keep playing on me! Again and again I try to tear myself out of the net of attachment, but you won't let me. Jashoda got you as her son and she cried when you went away; Sachi Rani got you as her son and she cried when you left home; King Dasarath got you as his son and he died grieving your self-exile. Still, what joy and pleasure in having you as a son to love! Once you came as my son, and then you left, I couldn't keep you. Why have you awakened that memory again today? Please let me forget, Hari, let me forget! Go home, go back to your parents, I don't know whose son you are—mother's son, go back to your mother's lap. I've got a lot of work to do now. It's time for my god to go to the pasture ground with the other cowherd boys—I must go and get my little darling ready for his pasture play."

He hurries off to his temple, which is tiny, like a play house, with an image of Radha-Krishna and some palmyra-leaf texts wrapped in red cotton cloth. He goes in there and starts to sing: "O, what a beautiful sight it's now becoming! Cowherd boys of Brindaban restlessly calling." *

A little later, broad shafts of sunlight fall dazzlingly across the neighborhood. The pace of activities quickens in each home. Men are back from fishing and selling the catch in the market some distance from this village. There's no time off from work in any home now—out in the yard there's the work of spinning thread, making bamboo nets from thin strips, repairing torn nets, toughening nets with gaab resin; and for women inside the huts, the work of cooking fish dishes for the midday meal. The morning's hectic work takes them to noon in no time. Before the men went out on the river, all they had was leftover rice soaked in water. Now mothers send small children to tell fathers that the meal is almost ready and they may bathe and get ready to eat. Back from taking a few dips in the river, they sit down to eat. Then they lie down to nap, and in the evening they leave with nets and ropes on their shoulders for another round of fishing. The cycle of work goes on without a pause.

The guests who came on the surprise visit take their leave one day. Banamali's home has overflowed with laughter, singing, talking, and family enjoyment. Now it falls silent again.

It is the month of Sravan—a session of singing with the reading of

*From a prayer by Narottam Das, a fifteenth-century Vaishnava poet of Bengal.

verses from the Padmapuran takes place every evening of this month. *
Banamali no longer goes out at night to cast his net. He does all his fishing
during the day, and every evening he sings with the reading of Padmapuran. The recital is held in a different house each night. The melodious
reading is done by that sadhu, the man who walks every dawn through
the neighborhood with finger cymbals, singing the divine wakeup, the one
who the other day mistook Ananta for Nitai reincarnated. Banamali is the
lead singer. He has a powerful voice, and a pair of percussion cymbals in
his hands marks the rhythm. Two other men play the two-sided lap drum
khol. The group has several singers, but as Banamali's voice rises above
theirs, the sadhu tells him first when to start the singing before the verse
he will read. And Banamali asks him if it should be a vigorous *lachari* or
a somber *disha.*

On a low stool before the sadhu rests the old quill-written copy of
Padmapuran, opened on its red cloth wrap. Nobody in this age other than
a learned sadhu can read this kind of text. He advances the wick of the
mustard-oil lamp in front of him and checks the verse he will read. Glancing at the verse in three meters, he answers: "Lachari." †

Banamali's response is dramatic. Bracing his right cheek with his right
hand, raising his left hand in front of him to send his voice flying, he
opens the tenor melody at nearly crow-high pitch.

> Mother, you do as you please, who can blame thee!
> But, Mother, where do I go, there's no place for me.
> When it sees me coming, the ocean becomes dry.
> O Mother, if I go near, even the ocean goes dry.

One or two others try to sing along but soon stop, unable to keep up
with either the volume or the melody. Only Ananta doesn't give up. He
manages to find the tune and follow along the melody. But partway through
the song, when all the robust adult voices in the chorus waver and let go,
his thin child's voice, losing the ground support, quivers alone in the
ocean of air and drowns. Sadhu-babaji looks at Ananta with appreciation
and says to Banamali, "An old tune it is, and a solid one too. These days
singers are out of breath too soon. How can they sing a melody of this
kind? In the old days when the melody soared in the singers' full-throated

---

* Padmapuran is a set of Puranic scriptures centered on the worship of the goddess
Padma or Manasa, the controller of snakes and the guardian of babies and pro-
creation. Archaeological evidence indicates that worship of Manasa in Hindu Bengal dates from the eighth century and the early Pal dynasty (Nihar R. Roy: *Ban-
galir Itihas,* pt. 2, ch. 22). Padmapuran and Manasamangal are in part scriptural
accounts of the spread of the worship to higher socioeconomic strata.
† Lachari is a Bengali song form in an energetic poetical meter suitable for dancing.

voices, people on the other side of Titash woke up with their ears filled with its sweetness. These days singers prefer light tunes. Young people from fairly new families can't really sing the Haribangsha songs and songs in the *bhatiyali* tunes. * One or two old singers still around in some villages can sing those songs. The power of their voices startles even strong young men! Sing a simpler song in lachari, Banamali.''

Banamali now starts perhaps too simple a song.

> Two golden children of sparkling beauty,
> In Bharat's bazaar I saw them so pretty.

Sadhu-babaji interrupts him, "No, this lachari isn't suitable here. Yesterday, in the verse I read at Prahlad's house, Lakhinder was bitten by a cobra. In this verse, his body is placed on a banana-trunk boat, and the boat's set afloat; it will journey upstream, and Behula will walk along the river's banks with a bow in her hand. Open with a somber song. Make it close to disha.''

"Right. How about 'Sumantra leaves for the battle, saying Rama's name for the journey to go well'?''

"Recitative from the *Ramayana*. The commander leading his army into the battle. It may work.''

In the verse that follows, the little banana-trunk boat pushes upstream against the current; Behula walks along the bank, bow and arrow in hand; when a crow or a vulture tries to land in the boat, she makes the motion of shooting an arrow and it flies off. So many villages, towns, wetlands, fields, and forests does Behula pass in this way, as the boat with Lakhinder passes up the river. Here the three-meter verse ends; and a verse in pentameter starts.

"Now we're in Chand Saudagar's home, amidst the crying and grieving. Open it with a sorrowful one.''

Banamali thinks a moment and starts to sing.

> Fortunate are the mothers with sons five or seven,
> Most unfortunate, I've only Blue-jewel, my only one.
> You went to stay in Mathura and never came home again.

Listening to this song, Ananta's heart aches with the pain of loss and sorrow.

At the end of singing, the sadhu-babaji wraps his old manuscript in its red cloth and says to the audience: "This boy Ananta here is like a price-

---

*Bhatiyal (from *bhati* or *bhata*, that is ebbtide) songs of Bengal use tunes boatmen sing when going downstream or during ebbtide, when they do not have to work at the oars. The soaring melodies are tinged with sadness and yearning, and the lyrics philosophically consider the flow of life, its losses and mistakes.

less jewel. Krishna has given him intelligence, given him a conscience before sending him into this ocean of life. If he's sent to school, he could receive useful learning. If you raise no objection, I'll enroll him at Gopalkhali Minor School when the rainwater around here goes down and the paths through the fields reappear. His fee will be waived—and if I can live on alms from ten doors, then as Krishna's creature he too will not be left without food."

The Malo men present all appreciate this proposal. Approvingly they remark: "This Malo community hasn't got a single educated person. To have a letter written, a deed of mortgage prepared, or our fish trade accounts made, we've got to go clutch the feet of Haridas Saha of Gopalnagar and feed him our best fish. If this boy can grow learned in books, then it'll be a pride for the Malo community."

"In that case, don't send him back to Gokan village with Udaitara; keep him here. In three months' time, when the good season comes, he'll attend school."

Banamali comes home agreeing to this arrangement. But Udaitara is not at all happy with it.

A wedding took place in the neighborhood a few days ago. Now the groom is back for the ceremony of taking his bride away for the second time. The neighborhood young women and the distantly related older ones decide to treat the groom to some nasty teasing because he hasn't behaved well. This groom didn't bring them the expected gifts of betel leaves, betel-dressing spices, and raw sugar drops. When he comes out for the midday bath in the river, the women sing for him.

> The groom knows how to eat, how to take,
> Not how to give; don't say this groom's polite.
> If the groom knew manners,
> Then a pot of sugar drops first he'd give us.
> The groom knows how to eat, how to take, . . .

But it does not seem like enough. They want to give him stronger stuff. But how? Someone comes up with the answer, "Don't worry, we have a groom-teaser. Banamali's sister—she's a great groom-teaser." They all clamor: "Bring out the groom-teaser." Surprising the women who come to ask her, Udaitara refuses to play along.

With the end of Sravan, the Padmapuran reading sessions too come to a close. Now every home gets ready for the worship of the goddess Manasa. They are also ready with the arrangements for the "seedling-wedding" ceremony. Before going away with Lakhinder's dead body, the virtuous Behula gave some parboiled paddy seeds to her mother-in-law and sisters-in-law and told them, on the day her dead husband came back to life, those seeds would sprout. They did sprout at the exact time. This bit of history may be unknown to the authors of the Puranas, but not to the young married women of a Malo community. To commemorate the deathless marriage of Behula, they hold in their homes a novel form of wedding on the day of worship of Manasa. The central ingredient for this ritual is a bunch of paddy seedlings. Hence the name of the ceremony. One young woman stands upright like a groom on a low stool, and another walks around her seven times in the modest posture of a bride, with a holder for the lamp and the seedlings, which she waves before the face of the "groom" after each round, to ward off evil. In this manner, pairs of young women are wedded to the accompaniment of singing by another group of women.

On the morning of Manasa puja, a young woman proposes to Udaitara. "Two years ago you married me, remember? This year I'll marry you, all right, Udi?"

"No, sister."

"Then you marry me."

"No, sister. I don't enjoy that sort of stuff anymore."

Ananta's curiosity is stirred by the talk of a wedding and he pleads, "Why don't you do it, when she's really asking you to?"

"You want me to? Well, in that case I will do it."

How amusing! Udaitara marries another young woman, both with their heads covered with their saris! The singing of the women amuses Ananta even more. One song describes how Lakhai holds an umbrella over the head of an unmarried girl, who gives him no cowrie shell, nothing at all for his work. The song ends as the singer says, "Listen Lakhai, stop holding the umbrella over that girl's head, I'll give you the money." The next song goes: "There she goes to that store to buy a clay urn . . ."; then the song tells how in that clay urn the goddess is invoked and worshiped. Next Manasa has a problem as to how to go back across the river; seeing a fisherman sitting in his boat with his net cast out, Manasa calls him and says, "Give me your boat to go across, and I'll make you rich in wealth and sons."

The name of Udaitara's husband's elder sister was Manasa; just as she mustn't utter her husband's name to show respect for him, she's not supposed to utter that name. So she refers to Manasa puja as Shaonai puja, as it is held in Sravan or Shaon. After the seedling wedding, when all the other women have left, she says to her new bride, "The Shaonai puja is over; the boat race is next. I really like being in the excitement of all these pujas, festivals, and noisy events."

Her bride has flipped off her head cover in their privacy and is busy picking up on a brass plate the five-headed lamp, the seeds, and other items to store them. She adds, "After that come so many more before the year is over—Durga puja, Lakshmi puja, Kali puja, *bhai-fonta* . . ."*

"But those are far away. The month of Shaon is just ending. Then Bhadra has to pass before we're in the month for the puja of the Great Mother."

But that's only two months from now—not that long, really, if you think about it, Udaitara says to herself. In fifteen more days the water over the fields and farmlands will go down. In another fifteen days Titash will draw back the overflow and paths will reappear on its banks. By then the rainy season will be over. Looking out toward the river, you'll see everything so clean and clear. Looking in at the homes and yards, you'll see everything untidy, in disrepair. Time to do the work of cleaning and tidying. Already present in the balmy air and clear autumn skies is the atmosphere of Durga puja. You must start the cleanup, the annual renewal of your home. But how can you clean the home before it's repaired? Well, that's what the men are for. In the season just over, continuous battering by the rain has ruined the sides of the porch, broken parts of the raised hut base; frequent storms and strong winds have twisted the fences. The men will bring new straw for thatch, bamboo poles, and cane—and repair the structure inside and out. Then daughters and wives will bring from the side of Titash smooth, rain-softened clay to replaster the sides of the porch and the hut base, recoat the floors and the walls, and mop them all clean and smooth until they shine like mirrors. Doesn't that work easily take fifteen days? Of the fifteen days still left at that point, seven will go into washing clothes, quilts and bedding, grass mats and bamboo underlays. In the remaining seven days, you'll clean and groom your body with soap and oil until you look radiant like a reflection of the goddess, then finally sit down and enjoy it all—and wonder how the days fly!

"So, Udi dear, why so quiet? You think the days drag on?"

A short while ago this young woman walked seven circles around Udaitara, held the five-headed lamp first to Udaitara's forehead and then to her own, sprinkled popped rice and yellow linseed flowers over her head—acted just like a bride in a real wedding—though it's only a ritual that goes with the worship of a particular goddess, a ritual like many others without real significance. But such an amusing ritual! Reminds her of the

---

*In this last ceremony a married sister wishes her brother (*bhai*) well by putting a dot (*fonta*) of sandalwood paste on his forehead, before placing food and gifts before him.

real one years ago. On that evening, facing Udaitara sat an unknown young man—hair and beard nicely trimmed, hair oiled and combed in a side parting—who in new clothes looked beautiful like a god. Indeed, a man looks so incredibly nice on his wedding day! Did she also look very beautiful on that evening? Three or four women had worked on her hair, applying oil and vermilion, and decorating her face with sandalwood paste that dries to a luster. With the tip of a still unfurled banana leaf she brushed the man's cheek—she was only a small girl then and her heart was pounding. She had difficulty looking at the man's eyes, even as people around kept saying to her, "Look up, look up, you must look at his eyes at this moment"—and four persons lifted up her flat wooden seat and raised it so her eyes were level with his, he standing—then she took a little look at him, but only a little, and lowered her eyes at once. Even barely looking at his face seemed hard then. But now! She can easily look at his face so many times, but does it feel the way that short glance did? What she tasted in that little look, where did that go?

Still absorbed in thought, Udaitara breaks into a giggle at one point. Her new bride, now busy with combing her hair into a bun, asks: "So, Udi dear, why did you laugh?"

"I laughed because I felt like it. Tell me, when I was playing your groom, didn't you feel too shy to look at my face?"

"Listen to her! I didn't feel shy before the groom of my real wedding, and you're merely the groom of my seedling wedding."

"You didn't feel shy before your real groom? That's strange! Why not?"

"The reason is like a story! My groom worked for my father as a hired boy. He had no parents, no family. He reeled thread and wove net. When I was eight and he twelve, my father got us married. I had been playing with him, running with him all over the place, catching fish and cutting fish with him. Why should I fear him, of all people?"

"Oh mother! So that's why."

"Listen, I'll tell you something funny. During the wedding, I threw flowers so they fell on his head, but when he threw the flowers, none landed on my head. They fell to my right and to my left, on my shoulder and on my back, but not one on my head. I never spare anyone in words, and he was just a member of our household. I was getting upset and I shouted at him, 'Why can't you throw them right? Why don't the flowers land on my head? Why do they fall right and left? Hopeless worker, expert eater!'"

"You reproached your groom like that? That sharp a tongue you had? What did the groom do then?"

"He threw a fistful of flowers angrily at my face and my eyes—"

"What nerve! Did you just take it?"

"No."

"What did you do?"

"I made a nasty face at him."

"Give me a nasty face just the way you gave him!"

"Stop it! Are you my real groom? You're only a woman."

"Then let me make a nasty face at you."

"Don't be silly. We're not little kids anymore."

"Not that old either, are we? Married at twelve; nine years gone by since then—only twenty-one now. Already I'm a grown woman?"

"You'd know if you're a grown woman or not if you had a baby or two in your lap. Never had to clean the pee-poop of a little one—your mind's unripe, your body's unripe. That's why you feel as if you aren't grown up yet. If you had children, then you'd feel your age too."

"You can say that."

And then the light of day fades into darkness. The image of Manasa, seated on her snakes and decorated with white waterlilies, grows dim before the eyes of Ananta who still looks at it in the obscuring darkness. In this and also in the other homes holding Manasa puja, the sounds of singing and rejoicing gradually slow and end sometime.

On the last day of Sravan many Malo homes hold this Manasa puja. It costs much less than any other puja but brings a lot more enjoyment. Malo boys take their dinghies into the marsh, deep and full like a pond at this time, and stir up its water with their poles. There, the snake-slim stems of waterlilies pierce their way from the underworld to rise in tangled multitudes to the water's surface. The entire dark still surface is studded with lilies in bloom. As far as the eye can see are lilies and more lilies everywhere, strewn like milk-white gems. Grab the bunched shoulder just under the flowers and pull until you feel it snap somewhere. Then haul them up, stem by endless stem—pull up the enormous lengths and pile them high in the dinghy. Fish move about them, turning and returning, and watch the Malo boys pull out the waterlily stems. In between pulling waterlilies, the boys too watch the fish and ponder their fate. The water level will start going down, dams will be set up in the marsh to block their exit; and then they'll all perish helplessly . . . though they know this, the stupid fish stay on in the quiet water as if out of some curious attachment. They can still swim into the current-filled water of Titash. Then they may not get caught as soon, and even when they do, it will only be in a Malo fishermen's net that gives them a chance to leap out; but caught in the Namashudra pond-fishermen's enclosure, leaping even a thousand times brings no escape for any of them.

By the time the decoration of the image with lilies is done, the priest comes. Among Malos a priest is as little seen as a fig flower; one priest goes around to ten or twelve villages on the day Manasa puja is held. With a wrap around his neck and a priest's handbook in his hand, he appears and at once orders, "Quickly, now!" Then with a muttered *Namo-namah* and a few bows to the image, he finishes puja in a home, takes his fee, and leaves. And within half an hour he finishes one village, hurries back to the ghat slope by the river, and hails a Malo man with the same air of urgency. "Ho Brindaban, take me down to Bhati-Sadakpur in your boat."

Although the reading of Padmapuran goes on until the last day of Sravan, it is not over then—the last two sections about Lakhinder's reunion and the salutation of Manasa remain, for the morning after Manasa puja. On this morning Malo men, rather than go out to the river to work with their nets, gather to be part of hearty Padmapuran singing and playing lap drums and cymbals.

For this last session of singing, Banamali has no voice left. Pressing a hand to one cheek and opening his eyes to their widest, he concentrates on coaxing out the last bit of strength left in his vocal chords for a final deep song.

> Palmyra fans in arm, Behula calls out to all,
> Who wants for a hundred thousand a fan invaluable?

But his voice can no longer gather the strength to carry the melody. It sounds off-key like a bamboo flute that has a crack in it. Of the other singers who are to back him up and sing the chorus, most have lost their voices even earlier. After attempting and failing to produce any melody, they too fall silent and sit listening. The final verses are read. Behula is secretly back, selling palmyra fans to her sisters-in-law in the guise of a cremator-caste woman. In the end she reveals her identity and Chand Saudagar's vow is defeated, and by offering his worship to Manasa he makes way for the goddess to eat offerings in all other homes in the land.

After the reading of the salutation, the old manuscript is carefully wrapped up to be stored over yet another year and reopened when Sravan returns again. A man distributes popped rice and raw sugar drops, and people leave one after another with a handful of the treats. Only those who wish to smoke tobacco linger. The site of the worship at the far end of the gathering is a sad sight today. Yesterday, the very same spot was bright and alive: the glow of oil lamps, the fragrance of incense, the fresh offerings of fruit and other food beautifully arranged on ten or twelve low stools. The freshly painted image of the goddess then looked alive and smiling; and her two snakes glistened and seemed poised to strike out at Ananta any moment. Today their colors are faded and dull. The unskilled craftsman's cheap dazzler for a day is already chipped and tarnished. The tongue of one snake and the tip of the other's tail are broken, caught in some clumsy worshiper's clothing, and their appearance now brings only pity. Coils of waterlilies with stems were neatly arranged on both sides of the image. Now children all over the place have got those, peeling the stems, eating the cores, picking out unbroken skins and blowing them into bottles. Some make garlands out of the stems and wear them around their necks. Ananta sits quietly and watches. A little girl who just finished making several such stem garlands looks up for someone to offer her work to. Her eyes fall on Ananta and she puts a garland around his neck. Ananta quickly takes it off and puts it around the girl's hair bun. The exchange takes an instant. The first thing he notices about her is the hair bun, huge in proportion to the little girl, as if her mother made it with hair from seven heads.

Happily she asks, "How come I've never seen you before? What's your name?"

"Ananta. My name's Ananta."

"No, that can't be! Be truthful, what really is your name?"

"I'm being truthful. My name is Ananta."

"Then why don't you have your hair in a bun like I do? Why aren't you wearing a sari the way I am? Why aren't your ears and your nose pierced? Where're your anklets and your bangles?"

"Silly! I'm male. You're a girl."

"Then your name is not Ananta."

"It is! Why not?"

"Because Ananta is my name. It can't be yours."

"Why? I don't understand."

"You're male. How can my name be yours too?"

"If it can't be, then how come I'm called by that name? My mother herself named me Ananta. My aunt, too, knows it."

"Only your aunt knows it? No one else?"

"The house I'm staying in now, the two of them, brother and sister, also know my name."

"That's all? No one else! Oh mother! Then listen to this. I was named by the astrologer-*thakur*. My parents know it; my seven uncles and five aunts know it too. And my six older brothers and five older sisters know it and also four aunts on my mother's side and two on my father's side."

"Oh father!"

"So many other people know my name, and they all love me so much! Nobody hits me."

"Nobody hits me either. A crone tried to, but my aunt stopped her from hitting me."

"Your aunt stopped her, but why not your mother?"

"Because I don't have my mother anymore!"

The girl now melts in sympathy, "No! What a sad fate! They say, 'The motherless are always luckless.' "

Feeling thoroughly belittled, Ananta promptly says, "I've got an aunt."

Frowning and letting out a sigh, she solemnly says, "That's better, you've a *mashi*. They say,

> Highest of the holy places is Kashi,
> Best of the well-wishers is mashi.
> The best kind of paddy is khama,
> The best of all relatives is *mama*." *

With this, the girl suddenly goes away somewhere. Ananta says to himself, Oh, how she drops proverbs and sayings at every turn! Wouldn't be bad to get her together with Udaitara.

A bit later he runs into the little girl again near the puja site. Thoughtfully, she asks him, "Listen, will you take me for a visit to your aunt?"

"How can I? That's far from here—half a day by boat."

"Don't people ever take someone else along to a distant village?"

"People do, but not now. In Baisakh, when the big fair is held beside Titash, people from faroff places come to visit and bring others along."

"Take me along at that time. Will you?"

"I don't have a boat, but I'll tell Banamali so you can go in his boat."

"But my father won't let me go in a stranger's boat."

"How can you call him a stranger? He brought me out from the hold of a broken boat near the mouth of the canal where I was starving for a week. You don't know what you're talking about."

The girl's face and eyes light up at this. "You stayed alone in the hold of a broken boat near the mouth of a canal? You weren't scared? You weren't worried spirits and ghosts might appear at night? Tell me how you managed to stay there all by yourself—"

"That's a long story. It'd take three days to tell."

"Will you take me to your village? And show me that boat?"

"All right, I will."

"When you take me there, will your aunt love me as she loves you?"

---

* *Mama* is the Bengali word for maternal uncle.

"Sure, she'll love you! She blasted me and threw me out."

"She threw you out and she never called you back in again?"

"No."

"Then let's not go there. You come to our home instead. No one will throw you out. Even if anyone does, I'll call you back in again."

These words sound very attractive to Ananta. He'd enjoy being in a houseful of people. Ten people talking in ten different ways; twenty skilled hands working while their ten mouths carry on lively conversation— the home resonating with their sounds. In the middle of all this, this lively girl would play with him; they'd play at weaving nets and catching fish. After all, before Ananta can climb into a boat as a real fisherman he'll need to practice casting and gathering nets through playing this way.

A melancholy strain threads through his thoughts at the same time. His world within holds only pain—no laughter, no amusement. It has the dark pain of existence without anyone close and loved. Its darkness seeps into the world outside, despite all the world's delirious beauty, of stars in the sky, flowers in the gardens, pastel clouds and play of colors in the waves of Titash. Gray ocean waves crash over him one after another, filling even the smallest crevices of his mind. He looks around and sees nothing but gray water—no bank, no end anywhere. The river Titash, held between two banks, just cannot keep that gray water away. It is like the saltwater expanse of the ocean, its constant wail of desolation drowns the light pleasures of the little river's dance.

Ananta wants to analyze the cause of this feeling. He sees himself as weak, a bit of straw moving in the great current of the immense and endless ocean of time. A short time ago, he had only his mother as his very own. Then there was his aunt; but Ananta senses she isn't really his. Banamali and Udaitara, too, are temporary companions on the way. When like his aunt they too move away from him, where will he go?

Where else but to a travelers' inn—he'll find one, somewhere along the way. Leave one shelter, you're sure to find another soon. Why not go to this girl's household, as if to a wayside inn?

Three women appear in his mind. His aunt, utterly helpless in the unsympathetic environment of her bitter old parents. She is the link between his past and his present, a link now torn apart by his step toward the future. She, too, is like an insignificant straw in the gigantic current of time. A thousand bits of flotsam go with the waters of Titash and will cling to one Malo fisherman's net or another's. But his aunt's future will hold on to no shelter. And Udaitara? Much pain has accumulated in her mind, but she's not one to crack easily. Constantly laughing and joking, telling riddles and proverbs, this woman covers her sorrows with a smile on her face. Maybe even the almighty controller of destiny can't design a pain that will subdue her. Why doesn't his aunt have this woman's ability to move on, ignore and sidestep what's painful? If she did, Ananta's mind would be relieved of much anxiety. And now this happy, lively girl here, she has barely started her life—like the beaming moon, she has the ability to make even the stars obscured by a clouded sky bloom and scatter, smile and stir, as easily as she can shower flowers in the garden by tapping at their stems. If she could be with him all the time, then the gloom within him might go away bit by bit.

The sudden peal of the girl's laughter startles Ananta.

"Why're you laughing?"

Eyes sparkling, she says, "Don't tell anyone I put my garland around your neck."

"What'll happen if I tell?"

"They'll tease you, calling you the groom."

"Rubbish. Am I trader Shyamsundar, do I have a beard like his, that they'll call me the groom?"

"Does the groom have to have a beard? Liar!"

"I saw with my own eyes. My mother took me along to watch the wedding. Lots of other people went to watch, too. Many of them said that after a long time here was an eye-satisfying real groom."

"Oh, I know—that groom was an old man. He may be old, but you're not."

Pondering this issue of whether or not he's old, Ananta loses track. At this point comes a call, "Anantabala, where're you, my golden mother?"

A mother calling her darling little daughter. It's almost time to eat; she's being called to bathe first.

Another little girl nearby ties a knot around a bottle she just made out of the skin of waterlily stem. Without looking up from it, she rhymes, "Anantabala, string of gold—wear any time, it's never old."

"See how many know my name? They've even made rhymes with my name. Ma's calling. I must go now. Don't tell anyone what I told you. All right?"

"All right."

"But I'll tell just my mother one thing."

"What?"

"That you put a garland around my hair bun."

Seeing Ananta is upset, she says, "Don't worry. She won't scold you; she'll love you. You too come with me to our place!"

Ananta says no. At this moment his heart suddenly fills with pain, remembering his aunt.

All of a sudden then, the sound of festive playing of musical instruments comes from the side of Titash. The boys at once leave the puja site in a bunch and run toward the river, all shouting: "Race boat, race boat."

The description stirs Ananta's curiosity. He has seen many boats, but not one by this name. He follows them to the ghat and sees something wonderful, truly wonderful to look at. A colorful boat on the river! The inundation from the monsoon is everywhere, enveloping everything. A few villages here and there in the floodplain stand still, as if freshly emerged from bathing. The surface of the river is whitish in the hazy sunlight. Beyond its inundated banks are the dark habitats of waterlilies, and even farther away the green fields of wet paddy and jute, also floating over water. The boat has crossed to the other side of the river and heads for a certain village in the distance. The prow of the boat is so low that it is almost level with the water; but the thin and greatly elongated stern, starting from the boat's middle, arches upward. The long pole of its steering oar rises up obliquely as if it wants to pierce the sky. Holding that pole, a man dances and stamps his feet on the deck, looking tiny and brisk like a bird. A group of men stand in the middle of its hold, playing cymbals and khol drums hung from their necks and singing a *shari* song. *

Scores of oars rise and fall on both sides with the rhythm of the music and make mists of sprayed water.

The colorful boat disappears behind the huts and trees of the village, and it remains hidden there for a long time. The boys console Ananta by saying it will reappear after clearing the back of the village. But it does not come out again!

When Ananta asks the boys why it's not coming out, they tell him that maybe the men in the boat have homes on that side of that village. After preparing the boat and painting it, they took it out with the crew and performers to rehearse for the big boat race that's coming up. Maybe they just took a round to try it out on the water and now they have tied it at their landing and gone home to eat.

Or maybe there's a waterway from behind that village that joins up with some wide stretch of water much farther away and the boat has gone out that way to take part in a faraway race.

* Shari singing is a genre of workmen's songs with vigorous rhythms, folk dialect, and themes from everyday life. There are shari songs for harvesting paddy and for rowing boats.

This last explanation seems more likely to Ananta. The way the boat was hissing along like a snake, it could not abruptly stop behind that village. With its colorful body decorated with drawings of vines and leaves, snakes and peacocks, it still races on, past village after village, drawing thousands of other children to the edge of the water and tripping up their minds! After racing on through the whole day, where will it be when the darkness of night falls?

The Colorful Boat

Four months ago the dry heat of Chaitra baked the fields and the paths. Then the water of Titash was some distance away from the edge of Birampur village, and several paths that cut through the heart of the village from the neighborhoods down to the water were the length of one full sprint. Around noon every day Kadir's son Chhadir took his five-year-old son Romu down one of those paths to bathe in the river.

First Chhadir massages him with oil; as he carries the child down to the ghat, the boy's oiled belly and face put little oily patches on his father's waist and shoulder. One small hand grasping his father's shoulder and the other rubbing that oil into his skin, Romu insists halfway down the path, "Let me down, Ba-jan, let me down." But his father absolutely does not. Instead Chhadir holds his soft little body tighter, rubbing it against his own hard muscular body and saying to himself, oh, that feels so good!

After reaching the shallow water at the ghat, he sets him down and with a handful of wet sand cleans his own teeth as well as the boy's, rubs clean both their bodies with his wet towel, and then walks into the water up to his neck with the child in his arms, and takes a few dips. Occasionally he loosens his grip a little and asks, "Want me to let go?" Quickly clasping his father's shoulders with both hands, Romu says, "Yes, let go."

The clear water is transparent in the sunlight and the current is gentle. Bands of *katari* fish float up to the surface and play. Other small fish gather under the film of oil from the bodies of father and son; they prick the film with tiny bubbles. The fish come so close that Romu extends his hand to catch one but can't—they are always too quick.

The entire body of Dharitree, the mother earth, is feverishly hot in Chaitra; only underneath the water of Titash it remains cool. With its

193

surface the water holds off Dharitree's feverish state, to keep its inside cool for the father and son. But even dipping and splashing for a long time are not enough to bring contentment. As soon as they come out of the water, the air on the ground feels as hot as before and they retreat to the water. To cool them all the way through, Chhadir squats before his son and says, "Come on, climb up now and stand on my shoulders—I'll go down to the underworld with you." Romu remembers a story he heard from someone about the snake queen of the underworld who lives at the bottom of the water. He is reluctant. "No Ba-jan, let's not go to the underworld. If the snake bites you, tell me, what can I do then?"

Little children's fears should be dealt with, Chhadir decides, and cheers him. "I bring death to the whole clan of snakes. Come on then, stand up on my shoulders." Holding on to his father's hands, Romu sets his feet on his father's shoulders and unsteadily hauls himself up, wobbles until he finds his balance and finally stands up straight. Happy with the achievement and the height he reaches, he claps his hands and says, "Now Ba-jan—now take me to the underworld."

Brimming with the delight and excitement of his son, Chhadir too holds his hands above his head and claps, chanting: "Thump-thump clap-clap! To the east we carry the deity up."

On the ghat slope are women of different ages, who have come for their own washing and bathing. Some of them remark, "Look at him— so carried away with playing."

"Of course. Getting a son at this young age, he really can't decide what to do with him, put him on his back or in his lap."

Coming out of the water, Chhadir wipes his son's body, puts the short two-cubit sarong around his waist, and says, "Now you can walk back."

A few steps up from the ghat, Romu tests the surface of the beaten path with his foot and, finding it burning hot, turns sad eyes to his father. "Ba-jan, carry me. I can't walk now."

In his father's arms, absently rubbing a soft cheek against the hairy chest, Romu says, "Ba-jan, buy me a pair of light clogs—just this size— then I'll never ask you to carry me again."

"His feet can't take the heat! As if he's the son of a *munshi!* * If your feet can't take the heat, how're you going to work in the fields?"

The yard of their home is still a short walk away as they pass a narrow canal from the river that skirts the village and goes away north. A boat loaded with clay pots and urns came into the canal during the high tide and stays there, caught in the ebb. Its heap of red and black pots rises

---

*Munshi is either a clerk or an Urdu teacher.

moundlike over the canal's bank and bits of sand in the clay glisten in the sun. Pointing his finger toward it, Romu says he won't work in the fields, he'll sell clay pots.

"Loaded with breakable things they travel from river to river. In any little bump or brush with another boat, clay things shatter to bits. A camel-faced chap like you, can you do the work of a clay-pot trader?"

"Then . . . I'll be a trader of mangoes and jackfruits."

"Stored in a boat, mangoes and jackfruits rot easily. If one or two go bad, rot can quickly go through the lot. Then a whole boatload has to be dumped in the water. Capital, profit, all is ruined. The sort of unmindful chap you are, how'll you know in time which one's going bad? You'll end up draining my father's savings and turning my father into a fakir."

"Then I don't want to be a trader."

"Right, Ba-ji. Traders tell too many lies. They cheat people by distracting them with their talk of five-seven-twelve irrelevant things; they want credit when they buy and cash when they sell! And the scales they use to weigh things they keep tilted when they sell and upright when they buy! That's why your Nana can't stand traders. When you grow up, if you leave your forefathers' work of plow farming and take to trading, then your Nana will call you, too, a thief and . . ."

"And what?"

"And he'll call you *shala*." *

Romu smiles but then stung by the teasing, he says, "Let me down now," with an offended expression on his face.

There is a lot of work to do in the fields now. Chhadir can't stay home in the afternoon to rest and be with his son. His son's mother, too, has so much work now that two of the ten bangles on her wrists broke in a single day. Her position in the household went up after she became the mother of a son. Her father-in-law Kadir Mian may spare her a scolding, but not his son; he would give his son the scolding meant for her. If he notices the deficit in his daughter-in-law's bangle-filled wrists, as she serves him a meal, he will scold her by using the phrase, "shala's daughter"—no one can stop him. When the gypsy vendor woman comes at dusk, she could buy a pair for two paisas to replace the broken ones. If only Chhadir

* The term *shala* literally means wife's brother—as Ramprasad uses it for Kishore, his dead wife's cousin. But it often conveys abuse of varying shades, from mild dislike to hate. It also occurs in mock-angry forms of friendly address: Kadir Mian expresses dislike for his son's clerk father-in-law, who replies in friendly protestation; Kadir uses it jokingly to address his grandson. Understandably, little boys find the term confusing, since they often hear it used abusively.

would give her money without asking the reason! A feeling of helplessness comes over her. When from time to time she feels this way, she looks at Romu, she hugs and holds him and tries to imagine how things will be when he grows up to share the financial responsibilities. Then his mother will have more independence in this household, won't she? Once again her eyes grow thirsty for the sight of Romu. But where is he?

By now Romu is beside the canal. Curiosity about that clayware-loaded boat has been building inside him, but he waited until afternoon. Seeing his father leave and his mother busy with work, he came to take a good look.

It looks as if a hill of piled pots pushed its way through the ground and raised its head high. The boat is a big one. With posts nailed to four sides of the boat's platform, they made a pen and stacked the pots in layers on top of layers. Taking some out of the stack in large baskets, the men spent all morning selling pots to the village homes. After returning with money and paddy, they cooked and ate, and now they are busy just taking it easy.

The boat looks like a giant stranded in the nearly dry channel, unable to move. But the men in it do not seem worried at all. They look as if they'll spend many days here, selling pots in basketfuls, walking through the village. When the high tide comes and pushes enough water into the canal, then the giant will move, and nobody'll ever see those men here again. They'll go to a different village each time, and do business like this in those new places. Is that why they're so happy?

As a cool breeze picks up, one of them starts to sing baromasi, the lyrics about a young woman's lamentation in her loneliness, month by month.

> Alas, here is Chaitra when farmers sow the seeds,
> bring me a bowl full of poison to end my miseries.
> When I'm dead from poison my parents will moan,
> never again marry me off to a man who's away from home.

Standing beside the canal, Romu listens, absorbed and fascinated.

On the other side of the canal, shears in hand, another person stands and listens too. Remembering some work to be done at home, Chhadir has quickly finished his day's work in the fields and is on the way back.

The singing goes on—stanza after poignant stanza, line after sad-sweet line. The tender melody, suffused with the pain of separation, makes the cool afternoon breeze heavy with sadness. The innermost discontent of a lonesome woman's heartache is revealed in the voice of a trader in pots. The woman lightens the weight of her sorrow of separation, month after month, from her family, her beloved, pouring it out into the melody:

The giving month of Asarh has come, alas,
when rain clouds renew all the rivers.
Back home is the traveler who left the last.
Did a tiger eat the man of this woman's heart?

Toward the end comes the month of Paush:

Alas, here's the chill of Paush to wilt autumn flowers,
I cannot keep forever my cherished youthful bowers.
Some glance at me sideways, others linger and stare;
how long can I guard my youth, as people's enmity I dare!

The shadow of dusk is not far off. Wives and daughters carry water pots down the path near the canal's other side toward the river, and others come back along that path. Upset at the song's words, Chhadir calls out, "Ho, pot boatman, don't sing this song in such an open manner here! Don't, I tell you."

Instantly the singing stops. The singer's face darkens with pain at the interruption. He casts his eyes down and says nothing at all.

Chhadir feels extremely sorry for the man, realizing that he was preoccupied only with singing, that he was not paying attention to the propriety or otherwise of any particular word in the lyrics. Enraptured with the melody in his own voice, he only poured over the fields into this balmy afternoon breeze the expression of loneliness of some young woman of some forgotten time. How can he be accused of indecency? Wading across the canal's knee-level water and taking his son's hand on the way home, Chhadir turns back his head and says, "Why did you stop singing? Sing in a lower voice, just a little lower voice."

Their yard is slightly raised in the middle and gently sloped on all sides. It is always dry, never lets any water collect. Ducks and chickens spent the whole afternoon here with their ducklings and chicks, and droppings litter the yard. The storebin is filled with the newly harvested paddy, plenty to eat throughout the year, distribute, and exchange for all the clay pots and caramel popped rice they need. In the room with the husking pedal a snake hole has been found; the room cannot be used until its floor is dug up to make sure it is secure. Some husking will have to be done with the help of a neighbor's daughters, out at one side of the yard in the moonlight. Grasping an enormous broom in both hands, Romu's mother watches the growing dusk as she sweeps this large yard, bending at the waist, her body moving with the broom. By the time she finishes, the day is gone and the clean yard shines in the pale light of the ninth night of the waxing moon. At this moment a man comes up the side of the canal, walks up the cow path, and steps into a corner of the yard. Four large rooms on four raised foundations, with small rooms tucked in between, surround the yard. He comes along the southeastern corner of the yard, stands at the dark angle of two rooms, and calls in a whisper, "Khushi! Oh bench clerk's mother!"

Putting the broom down, Khushi comes forward. "Ba-jan, is that you?"

"Yes. It's me."

"Come inside."

"Yes, I'll come inside this time. I've come with my back padded in quilts. If he calls me names, I'll call him names. If he fights and hits, I'll hit back. Ready for anything."

Khushi hangs her head in embarrassment. Her father comes to see her like a thief, because he has not been able to come up with the jewelry he promised as dowry.

"Where's your little clerk?"

"With his father in the north room, listening to stories."

"Where's the old clerk?"

Khushi smiles a little. "You mean my father-in-law! He's gone to the market."

Three members of Kadir's family wait with their minds made up to approach him tonight, when he comes home from the market, with three sets of complaints and appeals. Khushi, into whose womb has come a little brother or sister for Romu, wants some leave from the work of running this large household to go for a stay at her father's home. Her father is a court clerk; there's no plow, no farm to take care of at his home, not as much work throughout the day as in a farmer's home. She wants to rest, catch her breath for a few days away from this household's thousand daily chores. Her father too has come with this proposal, but he doesn't have the courage to tell Kadir himself. This is no courthouse where a client can be rebuked and made to behave. This is the household of Kadir Mian where he alone reigns. Her father's hesitation makes Khushi rebellious. She herself will tell her father-in-law what her father can't say himself even after coming here to say it—instead he hides like a thief in a corner of the room.

Chhadir has another appeal, and another complaint to back it. He wants the four hundred rupees from the selling of last year's jute crop; he'll use them to have a race boat made. From the time he was a child, he has done nothing but work all day in the fields with his father. He has never complained, never asked him for anything to fulfill some cherished desire of his own. Tonight he is determined to tell his father this, no matter if it makes him angry or whatever.

Romu waits for his grandfather with a third complaint. His father often insults him by saying his Nana will call him *shala* if he does this or that. Tonight he's going to settle this problem once and for all.

A small-scale storm seems likely to break out inside this home tonight. When Kadir Mian comes in, they feel panic as if the storm is already on. Almost immediately all three complainants come to him, but at first none can find any words to start with. Taking a deep breath, Chhadir comes forward to speak; otherwise he loses his position in the eyes of his wife and son.

"Ba-ji, what's that you have in your hand?"

"It's an eat-it-and-dance thing I have in my hand."

Clear words of displeasure. Chhadir quietly goes out of the room. Khushi covers her head with her sari and retreats into a corner. Romu sits nearby and watches in the light of the oil lamp as his Nana's lips tremble with anger behind the shiny strands of his beard.

Slipping his feet into his clogs, and after washing his face and hands, Kadir Mian picks up his hookah and calls: "Chhadir, O Chhadir Mian!"

Chhadir puts down near his wife the basket of paddy he fetched from the storage and comes promptly. "Calling me, Ba-ji?"

"Yes. I want to tell you we're in trouble. Magan Sarkar of Ujanchar has brought a false suit against me."

"Suit against you?"

"Yes. On a false charge. The land I have is from my father and brothers. I live rightfully by farming it. When I need to take a loan, I repay it after selling jute. I never stepped on anyone's crop fields. Nobody ever stepped on mine. Even so I face such tyranny!"

"Brought suit about what?"

"When the large room fell in the storm three years ago, I borrowed two hundred rupees from him. The next year I sold jute at twelve rupees a maund, got the cash in hand. When he was walking to his daughter's place along the cow path by my house, I called him and paid him all I owed him in principal and interest. He took the money and left, saying, 'I'll tear up the loan deed as soon as I return home, don't worry about it.' Now after all this time he's used the loan deed to file a suit against me."

"Ba-jan, you always do things in such a childish way!"

They have never brought a lawsuit against anyone, nor has anyone ever brought one against them. That is why the bad news drops a pall of sorrow over the whole family. The three of them stand around Kadir Mian with worried faces, oblivious of the guest who hides in a corner of

the room, himself a seasoned expert on lawsuits. Even Khushi forgets
that. But he is not one to go on hiding after he hears about a lawsuit.
From an invisible corner he springs into their midst: "Tell me which date,
in whose court he filed it!"

Startled, Kadir asks: "Who are you?"

"*Behai*, I'm Nijamat Muhuri!"*

"Behai! At first I thought you were a *bahurupi*."†

"Whatever you like to think. In this life I made so many bahurupis do
their dances. Finally, I've got to approach you by appearing to be a bahurupi!"

"That's not a right thing to say!"

"It is right. You never fought a single lawsuit in your life, how'd you
know what a *muhuri* is able to do? I let a kite go up into the sky, but the
spool of its string stays in my hand. All its rising and falling you can see
in the sky—that's my doing. The judge-magistrates are only like the tree's
branches. We muhuris are the roots. What's the name? Didn't you say
Magan Sarkar of Ujanchar? Don't worry about anything. Just get two to
four witnesses, and I'll make you win this case. You have my word."

Chhadir speaks up for him. "Ba-jan, don't worry. When my father-
in-law gives his assurance, you're sure to win the lawsuit, Ba-jan."

Old Kadir's face hardens, the veins stand out.

"Nothing to fear, Behai! Just watch what I can do. He pressed false
charges; now I'll bring false witnesses. Not only will I make him lose the
case, but I'll get a few people to bring against him charges of stealing their
cows or paddy from barns. You don't need to say anything, just stand and
watch."

Kadir's jaw tightens even more.

Chhadir tries one last time. "Ba-jan . . ."

"No. No. I'm not afraid."

"Then come with me. Let's find out what he's done where, if the suit
can be nullified before the hearing starts. Come with me tomorrow morning."

"Yes. I'll certainly go tomorrow morning. But not with you, nor to
that court of yours. I will go, just this once, to him."

"What'll you do with him?"

"I will look straight in his eyes and ask him. I'll ask his conscience if
he remembers or not about when he went by my home along the path
and I called him and returned the money without taking back the deed. . . ."

*Behai is the father-in-law of a son or a daughter; Muhuri is a court clerk or
lawyer's assistant.
†An itinerant showman adept at assuming many forms (human or animal) by
minimal costume change and clever mimicry of mannerisms and appearance.

"What if he says he doesn't remember?"

"He can't say that, muhuri, he can't. Through my eyes the anger of Allah will burn his insides to cinder. How can he be able to rob in daylight, act like a river pirate?

In disappointment, his son says, "Ba-jan, you do such childish things."

In even greater disappointment, the muhuri frets. "You live in a village and think like villagers. Giving you advice is like talking to a paddy field! Spending all day as you do with cattle in the fields, it's not surprising your intelligence is like that of cattle."

Both father and son take offense at this insult to their intelligence.

"So many people come to me for advice on litigation. You, shala, did you ever come to me? You've got so much land in farm and homestead, and you never had even a couple of litigations in your whole life—what kind of landowner and homeowner are you? Your heart is faint like that of punti fish. Otherwise you'd see how I could knock Magan Sarkar off."

So a pointless quarrel comes about. The muhuri was already fuming when he came here. Now, when Kadir tells him openly that he cannot stand the kind of creature known as muhuri, it comes to him as an intolerable blow to his self-respect. Enraged, he says, "I live in a village of gentlefolk, I mix with educated landowners. Would I ever tell anyone I've married my daughter into the family of a peasant like you?"

"And we don't like, Ba-ji, to have an elephant set foot in the home of poor people like us." Chhadir answers on his father's behalf.

Watching her father being insulted breaks Khushi's heart. Keeping herself out of sight, she says loudly enough for all to hear, "Why do you come to this village, Ba-ji, to be so insulted!"

The muhuri declares, "I made a mistake coming here. I'll leave now, and from now on I'll visit all other homes except a farmer's."

Angrily Kadir taunts him, "Want to go away in the middle of the night! How brave! Go if you're up to it."

When the muhuri starts to leave, Kadir suddenly brings out two sticks. The muhuri is dumbfounded. Kadir points one stick toward him and hands the other to his grandson. "Take it, shala, hit your grandfather."

Romu takes the stick but stands confused, looking alternately at the heads of his two grandfathers, unsure which head to hit.

In the afternoon before that evening, Magan Sarkar was returning home from Brahmanbaria after filing the suit against Kadir.

His path lies alongside Titash. The sun hangs low; it will soon set over the faint smudged line of villages beyond the open fields on the other side of the river. Warm red pools in the western horizon and sprays the layers of cloud above with many hues, as in Holi festivals; the clouds change color from one minute to the next. A cool breeze is blowing. There is a quiet serenity in the atmosphere. Cattle walk slowly and surely to their homes nearby, and the boys tending them have no need to prod. On his left is the line of the river bank, and on his right little fences that protect planted patches. The silk wrap on his shoulder, blowing in the breeze, catches from time to time in the bamboo slats of the fences; the smooth leather shoes on his feet collect the dust of the fields. As he takes care of his fine clothes on that path, anxiety suddenly seizes Magan Sarkar's mind. Even in these fields there are many plots he owns, but how many—sometimes he himself isn't sure. He loses track of how much land he acquired in all. But the ways he acquired them—this account suddenly glows before his eyes a couple of times as if flames light it.

On the path he runs into Rashid Modal. Rashid Modal is barefoot and wears only a sarong and a loose vest. He is advanced in years just like Magan Sarkar.

"Rashid-bhai! Have you heard the news of Dolgobinda Sa'?"

"How could I not? It came in a letter from Calcutta to his nephew."

"I hear his condition is bad."

"Yes. He's in a ready-to-depart condition."

"What's going to happen?"

"He'll die, I suppose. What else?"

"And what'll happen after that?"

Rashid smiles a little but does not notice the ripple of Magan's sigh in the air!

Next morning, Kadir Mian is at his door and calls for him. Magan is indeed startled, frightened to see Kadir's eyes, hibiscus red. Kadir didn't sleep the whole night. He was awake, asking why human beings become so treacherous. Why, Allah? Why is a man not able to believe another man even a little? Why do people have to smash, with clubs they hold in their own hands, whatever trust others have in them? Why? Isn't man the highest creature in the universe?

Magan Sarkar, too, didn't sleep last night. After returning home, he learned that Dolgobinda Sa' was dead; his nephew got a telegram saying just that. "Alas, Dolgobinda! You, Rashid-bhai, and I rode the same boat, we made our money from bribes in the same occupation, we used the same methods to trap people in our nets of debt, evict them from their ancestral homes, and auction their land in the name of unpaid loans. Today you're dead, Dolgobinda. And some day, I too will be dead. Oh Dolgobinda, you're dead now!"

Kadir is surprised to see Magan's eyes, tinged as they are still with the red of the setting sun. Kadir says nothing. Silently he stands before Magan.

Magan shudders at this specter and says, "I beg you, Kadir Mian. Forgive me just this once. I've ruined many lives in my time, but I'll stop. Let me do this one last act of ruining you. Don't obstruct me, don't object, just bear with it. This is my last job. You'll see—after I cheat you, I'll turn into a good man, never cheat anyone again! For my last trick, let me cheat you, you alone."

Perplexed, Kadir replies without comprehending anything at all. "So be it, Magan-babu. I'll just bear with it. Do not fear—go on with your lawsuit without worry. I won't put up any witness. I'll silently accept your charges. When the amount of money is decreed, if I don't have the cash, I'll sell my land to pay you. Let it be, if it helps you become a good man."

Next day the word goes around that Magan Sarkar died a terrible death. Apparently he climbed up a coconut tree and from there he leaped to the ground.

After hearing this, Kadir is overcome by a feeling of detachment. Hence, one day soon after that, when Chhadir comes up and tells him he wants to take part in the boat race at the close of Sravan and needs some money to have a race boat made, Kadir calmly opens his cane chest, takes out the four hundred rupees there, and hands it to his son. "Here. Build a boat, build a room, throw it away in the water. Do anything you like with it." His son is overjoyed at the unexpected ease with which he gets his wish.

One evening at home Chhadir is all excitement on the topic of his buying of lumber. "It's like a story," he says. At the hint of a story, Romu comes and sits close to his father's lap, looking at his face, eyes huge with curiosity and wonder.

There are two Malo men whose bodies have the strength of elephants. Their names are just as spectacular—Ichha Ram Malo and Iswar Malo—their home is the village of Nabinagar. What do they do? They go up to the place where the hill streams come down in strong currents. There, they tie enormous logs cut from tall trees to their own waists with long thick ropes and bring them downstream and into the river those streams join up with. One of those large trunks is to be sawed into boards, and those boards will go into making Chhadir's race boat, which he will make fly on a thousand oars when it competes with ten or twenty other race boats. And leaving all those other race boats behind, his will win the race. And then he will receive a medal, a large brass water pitcher, and a fattened goat.

"Useless—totally useless!" Kadir remarks even as he counts out the money and gives it to his son. "You'll go through so much trouble just for that?"

Chhadir's enthusiasm is undiminished. "These things seem too little to you, right? But if I win, the real reward is the honor not only for you and me, but for the whole of Birampur village."

"You'll have one day of hectic activities and fun, perhaps you'll win, and get that brass pitcher, I agree. But afterwards, what're you going to do with that boat? What use can it be put to, a thin boat one hundred and fifty cubits long, with its hull at water level?"

"We can use it for many kinds of work. In the months of the rainy season, when water stands on the land and the fields, we can take it to the marsh and bring it back loaded with water grass for the cattle."

"For cutting water grass, the flatboat is enough."

"Yes, but the flatboat for cutting water grass can't do the racing. And this boat works for both racing and cutting water grass."

"When the flatlands dry, and we can't take it to the marsh, what are you going to do with it? It'll dry in the sun and keep cracking."

"No, it won't. I'll *gerapi* it, let water in its hull, keep it partly under the water of Titash. In its belly I'll put branches; the fish will gather there for shelter. From time to time I'll bail the water and bring home a basketful of fish."

Kadir is finally impressed and says with surprise, "Mian, that's marvelous thinking."

Several nights in a row, Romu dreams about those two Malos who, with thick ropes tied around their waists, are bringing for his father the trunk of a tall tree all the way down from the hill, through streams and canals, and long stretches of the river.

He keeps going to the side of Titash, and one day he spots in the distance a *chali* float, a row of tied logs, like a tiny dinghy with a tiny shed on it. He also sees those two men, Ichha Ram Malo and Iswar Malo, from the land of fairy tales, working thick poles on its two sides. Crossing hills and mountains, cutting across canals and streams, passing through so many distant and different lands, they come with a load of stories, not just logs. Inside the little shed is their tiny household. With only a thin towel on them as a brief loincloth, their bodies are smooth shiny black. Romu imagines they emerged like porpoises out of the water somewhere along the way and picked up the poles to push the log chali, and when they sell all the logs, they will dive under water and disappear again like porpoises, leaving no trace at all of their existence in this world outside the water.

After a few brief words with Chhadir, they release one of the logs tied in the chali and, leaving it there, move on. Chhadir had asked them, "Malo's sons, stay here awhile, cook your lunch here, eat and rest; go tomorrow at dawn." Briefly they declined. "No, sheikh's son, can't stop here, must push on until we get near the ghat of Gokan. Then we'll cook."

Immediately they push off with their poles. They sounded so hurried in their words, yet how slowly the chali moves! It looks like a vehicle from some prehistoric age, with no connection whatsoever to the fast pace of this age. It moves so slowly but wastes so little time for the stop. Romu thought that once he managed to gather the courage to sit close to those two men, he'd find out about many things from them. But they move slowly away, so slowly he could walk along the bank and easily leave them behind, but what deep grace in their slow movement! You couldn't imagine such important seriousness in a fast pace.

Romu consoles himself with this thought—people who carry many kinds of news from distant lands don't stop anywhere for long; they move on, just this slowly and firmly, just this slowly and cruelly.

Next morning four saw men arrive, carrying a huge saw on their shoulders. In a plot of uncultivated field beside Titash they set up cross-beams and, calling on more men from the neighborhood, all work to haul the long tree trunk and place it horizontally on the structure. Then two saw men position themselves above it and two under, and they start sawing—*chan-chun, chan-chun!*

In two days they finish sawing the trunk into long boards. They stack the boards, take their wages, and leave. And all the children of Romu's age, who quietly watched the saw men at work, now plunge into the pile of sawdust left behind, and go wild jumping and playing in it. Romu goes on turning over the thought of this most entertaining event that his father started, something no one in this village ever did before.

Then one day a temporary thatched shed goes up on the bank of Titash. A few days after that, those who are going to stay in that shed also appear carrying several small wooden boxes on their heads. They are carpenters, four of them; they settle down in the work shed with all the equipment needed for boat making. The day they finish measuring the position of the prow and the stern and put together the connecting frame, Romu's amazement knows no bounds. Only the boat's spine begins to show. The tip of that spine pushes away at the sky at an odd angle, rising to such a height that Romu's eyes cannot gauge! But two carpenters climb to the tip and sit up there hammering nails!

A few more days pass with a lot of careful measuring, aligning, and fixing of the spine. Then the work of constructing the boat starts full blast. One at a time they take each long board, coat it with mud, bake it in a fire, and stretch, bend, twist, and crease it; then they add it to the frame. They take two-ended flat nails, one at a time, lightly tap them with a hammer into a board, then turn the board and align it with the crease of another. Then the hammering goes on in a clear, distinct, uniform rhythm—*doom-doom, takur-takur doom!*

Steadily the bones and the flesh of the boat get added to the spine, although the complete body is still many days away.

Chhadir says to him, "Romu, Ba-ji, you've some work to do. While I'm gone to the fields, you'll light tobacco for the carpenters when they want it."

Romu feels privileged to have a job to do. From then on he spends all day there except around noon, when the carpenters stop their work to cook their meal and, suddenly aware of his own hunger, he comes home to eat. But even then his mind stays with the carpenters, their little household in the open air. There, the skillful use of only a few hammers and chisels brings into existence such a long and thin, fantastical boat.

Romu's father and grandfather get into a heated argument one day about his future. Chhadir announces he wants to send Romu with books to the maqtab, the primary school at the village mosque. Kadir smiles at this and says he wants to send Romu with a little stick to follow the cattle to the grazing fields.

"Sent to the fields, he'll become an illiterate farmer just like me, and stay ignorant all his life of the knowledge of the world and its goings-on. He'll never be really brought up."

"Sent to school, he'll become a muhuri like your father-in-law, so he can make mothers-in-law and daughters-in-law change places in bed, and step aside to count his bribe money. No need for that kind of education."

Romu's mother interjects, "As if my father is to blame for all the bad things done in the world. My father takes bribes, my father steals, my father cheats, my father does this and he does that—what doesn't he do!"

"You keep quiet!" Chhadir shouts at her.

"No, I won't. If my father's guilty of so many offenses, then why did you knowingly bring home the daughter of such a thief? And even after bringing me in, why didn't you throw me out?"

"Thrown out of here, you think you'd live more happily in some other home?'

"Oh, what happiness I roll in here!"

"Will you stop, poison-mouthed woman, or will you keep those jaws going?"

"Calls me poison-mouthed woman, calls my father a thief, and expects me to keep quiet!"

Chhadir moves toward her angrily, as if to hit her, but Kadir grasps his shoulder and makes him sit down. For the first time the girl shows her face of rebellion. It hits a soft spot somewhere in Kadir's being. The muhuri's daughter continues in her forceful new voice. "Thief or swindler, he's the one whose daughter I am. Even though he's a father, he brought me up like a mother, he fed me, washed me, held me—even with a thousand faults he's my father. Even if he is a thief, he's still my father, not anyone else's here. If I die, the bosom of my father will be empty, not the bosom of anyone else's father."

"No, it won't! Big words come so easily to the daughter of a thief. Who told you no other bosom will be empty!" Kadir's eyes glisten with tears. And his chest aches with pain, remembering Jamila. By piling up more faults on the muhuri than he deserves, together we torment his helpless daughter, he says to himself. When they torment my Jamila in the same way, by piling up more faults on me than I deserve, does she listen silently, staying still like stone, and shed tears? Does she make no attempt to protest? Maybe if she does, that could save her by lessening her pain. But if instead she slowly wastes away thinking she has to bear it helplessly in silence, then would someone give her a few words of consolation? Jamila, too, is a motherless daughter. Just as this one is the treasure of the muhuri's heart, so is Jamila to Kadir. As fathers, is there any difference between the muhuri and Kadir? The only difference is that the muhuri remarried. Out of consideration for his son, Kadir hasn't done that. If the muhuri hasn't been able to forget his daughter even after remarrying, then how could Kadir, having poured out his love to his son and daughter all these years, forget his Jamila? Yet it's true he has kept her out of his mind! If he hadn't, wouldn't he have known it's been a long time since she was here—in the month of Aghran, for just two days! Wouldn't he have tried to bring her back once or twice in these eight months? How could this have come about? Why doesn't he pine for his beloved Jamila? Is it because of this appropriator of his love for her? If she hadn't come to this home and occupied Jamila's place in his heart, could old Kadir go on living after giving away his daughter?

Romu's mother Khushi is still fuming. "No wonder they call it living in another's home! Of course, it is another's home. The home where one is called poison-mouthed and one's father a thief, that's not one's own home! Isn't it another's home?"

"Oh, sure it's another's home!" says Kadir. "How can the muhuri's daughter say that? When she gets up before dawn, cleans the twenty-cow shed, feeds the cattle their bran, sweeps the entire house and the yard, fetches pot after pot of water, cooks, feeds the family, dries the paddy, keeps the crows off it, goes over the yardful of drying paddy, turning it by foot several times in the hot sun, then dries the straw, dries the jute stalks, keeps rats away from the stored jute, husks so much paddy in basketfuls, then cooks again, and does a thousand other things every day! Does anyone ever do so much work for another's home? The home you ruin your health working all day for is another's home indeed! As if calling it so makes it so. There's no fee for using words—say anything."

Now tears come to Khushi's eyes twice as hard, and she bursts into sobbing. After a long, hard cry, it occurs to her that there is relief, even happiness, in this kind of crying.

In the end Kadir says to his son, "Go ahead, send your son to the maqtab, but let me tell you this right now. If he learns to lie, if he learns to fake and swindle, if he learns to cheat others, then I won't scold him. I'll only crack your skull open, Chhadir Mian."

Next day Romu goes to the maqtab, wearing a new sarong, a new shirt, and a new cap on his head. After coming home and taking some food from his mother, he remembers he hasn't shown his new outfit to the carpenters. The boys at the maqtab looked at it with appreciation; those four must also take a look.

Seeing Romu, dressed in new clothes, get to work preparing the hookah for them, one of them is moved to say, "No need, munshi's son, no need for you to mess with the soot of coal to light the tobacco."

The day is waning, and not far from the work shed, along the path down to the ghat walk wives and daughters, some in red-and-black-bordered saris and some in striped ones, some carrying a rice basket, some with a water pitcher perched on the waist, some wearing silver anklets.

Watching them, one of the carpenters is inspired to sing his plebeian song:

> Mornings and afternoons the poor folks eat,
> the higher-ups' dining is late in the night,
> cries Dewan Katu Mian's poor Ma, alas, in her plight.

The head carpenter interrupts him. "Look here, you son of a smarty, aim your singing at them and you won't be able to return home with your head on."

"Then I'll leave my head behind."

Romu can't understand how a man can leave his head behind, but he likes the song.

"Don't stop. Please sing your song."

The head carpenter looks at him, pleased. "If you come at noontime, then I can sing for you, but not in the morning or the afternoon."

"Noontime I go to school to learn to read."

"Then you can't listen to songs."

"Why can't I?"

"When matters are such that either you study and not listen to singing or listen to singing and not study, then it's better you study and forget about listening to songs."

On Friday, when the maqtab is closed, around noontime Romu puts on his new sarong and cap, though he forgets the shirt, and comes expectantly to the workmen. The head carpenter turns him away saying they're extremely busy now. He also asks Romu to go home and tell his mother they don't have the time now to boil milk anymore and would like to have boiled milk sent to them with the parched rice and molasses.

Using a scrubbing stone Romu's mother thoroughly cleans the pot in which she boils milk for her family. Then she boils the milk, pours it into a large metal pitcher, ties a string around its narrow neck, making a loop with the string to carry it, and sends Romu back with the food. The carpenters can't help laughing at the sight of Romu in his new garb, balancing a bundle of parched rice on his head and the milk pitcher by its loop in his hand.

In a few more days the construction of the entire boat is done, and the work still remaining is to lay the boat on its side and polish and varnish the bottom. Leaving that work to the three juniors, the head carpenter sits down one day with the hookah in his hand and starts to sing softly, solemnly:

> Staff in his hand and umbrella on his shoulder, Buruj goes
> on a journey that is very long.

Then Buruj grows tired from the strain of walking and . . .

> In Chaitra or Baisakh month, in the parching heat of sun,
> his thirst grows very strong.

Then he looks this way and that for water, but he sees no river, no pond anywhere. But suddenly he notices . . .

> A clean wiped hut, marks of sandalwood paste at the door.
> Is it a Brahman home, he pauses to ponder.

Being a Brahman himself, Buruj doesn't take long to recognize a Brahman home. So clean and tidy, it can't be anything other than a Brahman home. Buruj approaches it and calls . . .

Householder friend, do you have water? I want to drink,
am dying of thirst—I'm a traveler here.

His call does not go unanswered . . .

Water jug in right hand, plate of betel in her left,
out comes a maiden to quench his thirst.

Thirsty Buruj takes the drink of water, and . . .

Refreshed, he asks the maiden her caste; she says:
we're of the peasant-gardener caste.

That, alas, means the Brahman Buruj has now lost his caste. The hands he drank water from, without asking beforehand, belong to a maiden who's not a Brahman's daughter . . .

Buruj cries, he flings himself on the ground and he cries,
for he's lost his caste in a gardener's home.

Now that Buruj has lost his high caste, what will he do? He does not go on to the destination of his journey; he does not go back home; he returns to live in the home where he lost his caste. He stays there and says to his travel companions . . .

My friends, companions, take this word to my parents back home,
that I've lost my caste in a gardener's home.

Hearing how a man lost his high-caste status so helplessly, Romu feels really sorry for him. He has never seen a Brahman, but from what he has heard, he concludes they must be well above ordinary people. He has heard they chant mantras and have finished reading many thick books. And gardeners! All they're asked to do is plant banana trees in a Hindu home for a wedding, not really a prestigious job. In such a gardener's home, so learned a man loses his caste. Losing his Brahmanhood, he now lives in the gardener's home as a gardener. Will he ever chant mantras at weddings or memorize thick books? From now on, he'll only plant some banana trees in people's homes at weddings. Doing such an insignificant task, he won't get any attention anymore. But he had this high caste, why did he lose it? That is terrible.

"He was thirsty, he drank a glass of water, and he lost his caste?"
"Yes, he did!"

"Why did he lose it?"

"I don't know why, but he lost it."

"How did he know he lost it?"

The head carpenter does not answer, but one of his juniors gets angry. "Tending cattle is all he'll ever do, but look at the peasant's son's way with words!"

Ignoring his detractor, Romu asks the head carpenter, "Will you lose your caste if you drink water from my hand?"

Difficult question. After a moment's deliberation, the head carpenter resolves it and says, "No."

"And from my mother's hand?"

"No."

"And from my father's hand? And my grandfather's?"

"No, no, no. We know you. You're not strangers."

"Drinking from the hand of someone you know doesn't make you lose your caste?"

"No."

"If Buruj-thakur knew the gardener's girl beforehand, then he wouldn't have lost his caste by drinking water from her hand?"

The head carpenter says nothing, yes or no, in answer.

Seeing him without an answer, Romu suddenly claps his hands and laughs happily.

"Why're you laughing?" The head carpenter is irritated.

"Because I just thought of something. It's this: it would be very nice if you could lose your caste after drinking from my hand."

"What do you mean?" the head carpenter asks with big, shocked eyes.

"Then you'd have to stay with us, just like Buruj-thakur."

Having lost the argument, the head carpenter gravely turns his attention to work.

The carpenters are overjoyed the day they complete the boat. Many days of work and effort reached fruition today. They finished making something that will be on water for a long, long time—so many people will ride it, sit on its platform to cross the river; so many times it will race and win prizes, proudly bearing the name of its owner, someone other than its makers. No one will know who made it, whose diligent labor and store of skills bit by bit brought this boat slowly into existence. But the boat? Will it forget these four carpenters? Certainly not!

That day the carpenters are so happy—they have the villagers come and watch the four of them dance together in step, clapping and singing. "Listen to us you town folk, oh the pleasure we get from making a boat."

The boatmaking over, the carpenters settle their accounts and one day pick up their toolboxes on their heads and actually leave. They cross the canal, gathering their clothes above its water, and then slowly walk away along the cow path, farther and farther away until they look little, like four crows, and then disappear.

On another day three craftsmen come from somewhere. Working all day and evening with brushes and color, they paint the boat all over, and on each side of the stern draw designs consisting of vines, leaves, snakes, peacocks, and a pair of wrestlers.

Finally the day comes to launch the boat. Chhadir brings a group of men from the neighborhood and a pot of raw sugar drops. The men position themselves on both sides of the boat, grasping the oars points. One shouts, "You have strength?" All answer, "We have." Then all shout at once, "Put all your strength in here, or dead wood will eat what you spa-a-a-re . . .," and give one mighty pull that takes the boat into the water, but before it comes to a stop they give a strong push that sends it to the middle of Titash, where it dances and sways on the little waves. Romu's eyes shine with joy at the sight. Such a marvelous thing has never been seen before! Such beauty, such lovely colors! Floating there, the boat looks as if the rainbow of the sky has dropped on its back into the river.

On the first day of Bhadra, Kadir's house bustles with people and excitement. From early morning all the strong young sons of farmers gather in scores in their house. Then, each holding one of the colorful oars, they go and take their seats at the oars points of the boat.

Romu has been hanging around them the whole time. At this point, finally catching his father alone, he asks, "Ba-jan, you're going to race the boat, aren't you going to take me along?"

"The boat race is not now. We're going only to practice. The race is in the afternoon."

"Will you take me then?"

With a brief "Yes yes," Chhadir storms out to join the rest.

The young men are very happy with the practice trip through the river and the wetlands, past many villages. They all agree the boat is well made and races well too. When they pull the oars at exactly the same time, it moves on hissing like a snake, whizzing like a hunter's arrow, lapping like a river's current.

After the midday meal when they get back in the boat with their oars, Romu also gets ready like them, putting on his colorful sarong, vest, and bright cap, and comes to the side of the river amid the bustle of all the people. The young men sit with their oars in two rows along the two sides of the boat. In the middle, several older men stand on a few boards around a low mast-like post. They are going to sing the shari songs. A drum and several cymbals are also taken aboard. And some fighting poles are stacked in!

After arranging everything else, when Chhadir is about to get in, Romu grabs him with arms like the pincers of a crab. "Ba-jan, take me along, Ba-jan, take me along."

"Don't bother me when I'm busy. Can't stop now." Impatiently, Chhadir jerks himself free of Romu's arms, pushes him away from the water, climbs in, and takes the pole of the steering oar.

Chanting "Ali Ali," they untie the boat; scores of oars rise and fall in the water together, causing a mist over the water, and then it shoots onto the river like a hunter's arrow. When Chhadir holds the pole of the steering oar and dances, stamping his feet on the boards with the rhythm of shari singing and the rising and falling of oars, Romu sobs by the empty bank of the river. His grandfather tries to console him, his mother tries, but he doesn't listen. He still says, "Ba-jan, take me along."

On that day many sailboats glide on Titash, all going in the same direction, toward the place where the boat race is to take place that afternoon. In most of these sailboats, of different sizes and shapes, there are more women than men. It is so in Banamali's boat too. There are two other men besides him, both from the "big house," and there is Ananta, and among the female passengers are the women of the same big house and their daughter Anantabala, and there is Banamali's sister Udaitara.

When they reach the place of the boat race, they see a grand spectacle. For the length of about a mile the river is very wide here. Hugging the two banks of that wide stretch, thousands of boats with sheds have struck their posts. In places, large boats left partly submerged in water offer shelter to ten or twenty small boats that huddle on each side and in front of them. As far as the eye can see, the edges of the water teem with covered boats, each packed with people. In the middle is the stretch for the race boats to compete.

The afternoon has just begun; the race will start in late afternoon. The race boats now roam all over the wide open stretch of the river, their oars swinging unhurriedly with the many different melodies of shari songs. Spectators from the thousands of boats along the two banks admire the decorations on the race boats and the way they move, making puffs of misty spray.

Ananta's heart jumps with joy at the sight of so many race boats together. Suddenly one flies past very close, and a bit of brisk singing leaps at him.

Made of worthless wood, the jingling boat's no good.
Oh I did win that race, but the stern left no trace.

The singing that goes on in another boat is truly marvelous in melody
and rhythm. The boat glides slowly: the oarsmen lower their oars and
barely touch the water before turning them up again as all lean forward
to tap the handles on the platform at exactly the same time. The boat
moves like a thousand-blade knife, blades rhythmically slicing the air, up
and down. In the center platform a group of men are singing and the
oarsmen repeat after each stanza in a chorus:

Call him, sisters, go out and call my sweetheart.
For my friend to eat his rice, a catfish I got,
With a rupee some milk too I bought.
Call him, sisters, go out and call my sweetheart.
To Dhaka he goes, he cooks his food on the shore,
The tide comes and his pots and bowls are no more.
Call him, sisters, go out and call my sweetheart.
A perch in the lake my frolicsome friend made;
Udaitara, the morning star, he has it named.
Call him, sisters, go out and call my sweetheart.
When the door for my friend I kept open,
My youth, not money, is what was stolen.
Call him, sisters, go out and call my sweetheart.

Udaitara laughs, "What a song! Put my name in it, too."
Everyone now breaks into a laugh. But not all the boats have such
beautiful singing. From one comes the sound of an utterly prosaic song:
"Who cut the head off Chand Mian, the inspector asks, I say who cut off
the head of Chand Mian." Someone from one of the watching boats remarks, "Oh, I know, the boat's from Bijeswar village. They're the ones
who fought and killed when they went to occupy a siltbed. Made a song
out of that incident."
Two more boats pass by them one after the other, singing shari. From
one they hear:

In Jaishtha and Asarh, when it flows over,
do not ever go near the Jamuna river.
Clouds darken the path to the bank of Jamuna,
having lost our way we cry and call out to Krishna.
Going to Jamuna means trouble at home and outside,
the black boy of Nanda's house pulls you aside.

The next boat has people who sing of Radha's disappointment as she
waits at the tryst and Krishna doesn't turn up:

Why pelt the mango tree before it's time,
when you never come to me why wink and sign!
Away under the kadam tree you and I become lovers,
the hostile neighbors here go and tell on us.

From one of the covered boats alongside theirs, they all hear a comment: "There are two villages near Gosainpur called Radhanagar and Kishtonagar—these two boats are from those two villages."

At this, Banamali remarks, "Then why didn't one sing Radha's words and the other Krishna's?"

"Radha's everywhere, brother, everywhere is Radha," comes the reply from the same boat.

The quick reply draws laughter from the spectators' boats nearby. At this point one of the women from the big house calls Udaitara's attention to another song. "Listen—this one's so amusing."

O, the whole of last night where were you gone!
The watchmen were out on their neighborhood round.
Some woman had luck when mine burned down.
O, my luck burned, where were you all night gone!
On the Habiganj-Nabiganj path I came in,
The fish-design nose ring my darling gave me fell in.
O, my nose ring fell, all night where were you gone!

Udaitara smiles a little and, listening keenly for some time, remarks, "So many others sing that sort of song . . . there, listen to the singing in that fat-middle platform boat . . .

Banana grove in front, a hut with east-facing door:
Come in the night, dear lover, these signs you must look for."

Another song makes everybody look at Anantabala. It's coming from a long, arrow-thin boat that moves at a leisurely pace, just gliding with the singing.

The daughter has long hair, done in buns with such care,
that the bees hover as if on a flower.
By the river to wash and groom, back home to oil and comb,
the girl is lost in love—for whom?

Udaitara smiles and gives a gentle twist to Anantabala's hair bun, so large for her age. But the eyes of Ananta and Anantabala are elsewhere. Out on the water are two men rowing two large, gaudily painted clay vats. Their lips have no song, their rowing has no rhythm. With hair and beards cut in a fancy style and their hair well oiled, they wear clean dhotis and white tops. Smiling self-consciously, they paddle haphazardly. The

vats soon catch up with their own boat and come so close that they could
hit the boat's platform and break. Anantabala extends her hand to touch
the vats, and the men lift their paddles to her. Banamali remarks, drawing
the attention of the womenfolk, "Others race boats; those two race clay
vats." Ananta says to them, "Why don't you race with each other and
show us who can go faster?" But the two men pay no attention to these
words. They are happy just to draw the attention of all the women come
from so many different villages.

"Wish I'd brought a vat along. Then I could race paddling it," Ananta
says.

"Do you think you could do it alone? Are you clever and alert like that
man? With the paddle in your hand suppose you're looking at some racing boat, and a passenger boat hits you? What happens if the fragile vat
breaks? If you and I are together, then there's no danger. When you're
looking elsewhere, I can watch the vat. And if the vat breaks, you can
save me. Right?"

"Right."

While the two children are busy talking together, Udaitara laughs
abruptly. She's like that. Her train of thought just races on until it hits
something, and then she suddenly breaks into a giggle, unmindful of those
around her.

Anantabala's aunt turns to her and asks, "What made you laugh?"

"Something just came to me."

"What thing, toad's brain, why don't you tell me?"

Udaitara says to herself, How can I tell you what I haven't told anyone
else yet, what makes me smile every time I think of it!

Anantabala's aunt is young, her eyes sparkle with curiosity, and she
doesn't let go. "Tell me, sister, please?"

"What do you want to know?"

"What just made you giggle to yourself."

"I giggled because a giggle came over me."

"Why mislead someone who's won over? All right. Don't tell."

"Listen then. The thought that made me smile is this . . . so many
boats ply the river; people go singing so many kinds of songs, good songs,
bad songs—nice songs, filthy songs. Don't they?"

"Yes, they do."

"A little while ago you heard some go by singing a weird song. And
then you heard another go by singing a beautiful song."

"Yes. So I did."

"Well, the bad songs and the nice songs, neither leave any mark on
the bosom of the river. Do they?"

"No."

"That's the thought I smiled at."

"I also see what you mean."

"If you see what I mean, then I'll tell you the truth. Ananta and Anantabala, their names match and their minds too. Just that."

Just then comes the voice of a woman from another boat tied near theirs. Her words offer another woman consolation: "Don't ruin your health worrying, sister. So many people go about on the river singing so many different songs. Do they leave any mark on the water?"

Ananta, with a start, whispers in Anantabala's ear, "Aunt!"

Her eyes big with curiosity, Anantabala follows his eyes and sees his legendary aunt. A widow, she is still in her youth, but the grace has washed away from her body. Her face is beautiful, but melancholy, and touching.

"This is the aunt who threw you out!"

"Yes, she did."

Hearing the word aunt, Subla's wife at once turns her head and sees Ananta. Instantly, involuntarily, she cries out, "Ananta, my Ananta!"

The two boats' hulls partly touch. She quickly steps into their boat and eagerly holds out her arms to him. Ananta, too, holds out his arms, calling out, "Aunt!" Seeing the tears stream down her face, his eyes too fill with tears.

Udaitara steps forward, unmoved, unstirred, like a stone figure.

Paying no attention to her, Ananta's aunt hugs him tighter, eagerly strokes his back. She clears her choked voice with difficulty and says, "Where were you all this time?"

With her eyes closed, she keeps saying, "Where were you all this time, who with, where did you sleep, who fed you, who told you stories before sleep, who put you to sleep?"

In a ruthlessly cruel, high-pitched voice, Udaitara breaks in. "Of course! The one she threw away like chaff off the winnowing fan, she now asks who put him to sleep!"

Reminded of the past events, Ananta feels the muscles of his face and his two wrists harden. He takes his arms away from her and, eyes downcast, says, "Leave me alone, Aunt."

"You too become a stranger to me, Ananta!"

"I was never yours, Aunt! You were my mother's friend. As long as my mother lived, you had love for me. After mother died, your love left me just like people at the end of market day."

"My love left you! How do you know my love left you?"

"Don't think I don't know. From the day my mother died, everything left me. From that day I became a stranger to all, a forest dweller. My home is the home of anybody who calls me in, and I keep away from the home of anybody who hates me and throws me out."

"Oh, you ungrateful crow, who taught you this kind of talk—what slave woman?"

Udaitara now explodes. "You, the moonlight of slave women's delight! Be careful what you say, if you want to go home with your chest covered today. Better keep those words in, don't untie that sack's string."

Subla's wife can't take it anymore. At the edge of something terrible—what it is she has no idea—she leans forward and grasps Ananta's hand. Ananta jerks his hand free and moves to the safety of Udaitara's shelter, saying, "No, Aunt, don't show me your love anymore."

His aunt's patience snaps. Her head reels in humiliation. Udaitara's abuse goes on, unrelenting. All this for Ananta. Set ablaze head to foot with anger, she says, "I certainly will show you my love—not with words, but with hands." She grasps Ananta by the hair and pounds his back with the fist of her other hand. Ananta fearfully looks up at her eyes. Overwhelmed by the burning anger he sees there, he lowers his eyes and resigns himself completely to its raging flames. Under her furious pounding, he collapses to the boat's platform. Everyone watches, stunned. Udaitara suddenly wakes up and, with something like a roar, lunges in and frees Ananta from his aunt, like freeing a fawn from a lioness. Ananta trembles like a captured pigeon about to be slaughtered.

What follows is almost beyond recounting. Udaitara and the other women in their boat join forces, pull Subla's wife down on the platform, and beat her mercilessly. At length, when she is completely overpowered, they finally stop and let her go. Dragging her body up with great effort, Subla's wife covers chest and thighs, stands up disheveled, and staggers back to her boat. From the surrounding boats thousands of people look at her. In her shame and humiliation she can no longer hold her head up. When her companions help her sit down in their boat, she slumps lower and sobs uncontrollably.

Udaitara's group of women puff with righteous victory. But Ananta still trembles all over. Seeing the men in his aunt's boat try to move it away from theirs, and knowing he may never see her again, he turns back fearfully to look and sees her lying with her face buried on the platform, her body shaking with sobs. The men of that boat are still at their wits' end. Now they exchange a few words and decide to go back instead of staying on to watch the race.

They turn away and move off. They have a long way to go back but
no need to rush, as the afternoon has several hours left. After leaving the
crowded area of the boat race, they sigh with relief. And they notice a
lone race boat going toward the racing area—so late. The oarsmen do not
seem hurried; they row and sing in a chorus their shari song . . .

> They all have their own ones, but I have none,
> thundering inside me are the waves of the ocean.
> I came to the river's edge hoping to go across:
> an empty boat with no boatman helplessly bobs.

IV

Double-Hued Butterfly

A terrible storm has left the world of Subla's wife in ruins. When she was little her parents loved her dearly and never raised a hand against her. Women in Malo neighborhoods sometimes quarreled and hurled angry abusive words at each other. But no one in the neighborhood ever had a harsh word for her. She always enjoyed a certain prestige. She had pride. Today it has been leveled.

Today she is devastated in body and mind. All over her body is pain, and in several places swelling. Climbing out of the boat, she somehow manages to go home and without a word to anyone spreads out the mat and lies down. From the other women who were in the boat, all the neighbors presently come to know what happened. Her mother hears everything, prepares a bowl of warm turmeric paste, and comes to her. "Turn back the cover, show me where it hurts. Let me see. Oh, your body's burning hot!"

The loving touch brings tears back to her eyes. Her mother wipes her eyes and says, "You—you, with not a single enemy in the world, you're reduced to this condition! He's not of your womb, not of your back, why do you suffer on his account?"

Subla's wife says nothing.

"What made you show love to that heart-chewer? You got disgraced before so many!"

Subla's wife still does not answer.

Her mother says nothing more and lies down beside her. The old man has gone out to cast the night net. The old woman keeps lying next to her daughter, even as she smokes for a while.* Then she puts out the lamp

---

*She smokes a hookah, as elderly women in lower castes would sometimes do.

and cradles her daughter through the whole night. Her dried old breasts are like two knots of rope, yet the daughter finds deep comfort in nestling her full breasts against them. When the mother presses her dented and hollowed cheek to the daughter's smooth cheek, soothing sleep comes over the daughter's eyes. The pain in her body wakes Subla's wife from time to time, but she falls asleep again. In the gaps between waking and sleeping that night one thought returns again and again: in this world only a mother remains true to the end, nobody else.

The next day the swelling subsides, the pain grows less. Her mind too starts to feel a bit lighter. To ease what remains of its burning she sets herself to the task of reeling thread and weaving net. But she does not get back her lost prestige in the neighborhood.

From their neighborhood the account of the incident spreads to the neighborhoods of other caste communities. After this incident Subla's wife feels embarrassed to appear before the young men of even her own neighborhood. On top of that, now even Brahman and Kayastha young men glance at her hut with curiosity when they pass by. She takes to staying inside and keeping the door closed all day. Still she does not escape harassment. One day as she goes to the ghat to wash plates, Mangala's wife sees her on the way and remarks, "Well, sister, our homes are next to each other, our rooms are next to each other, still I don't see you at all. What's the reason?"

"I don't feel too well, sister. I feel feverish on and off. And father's net is old—it can't stand the thrashing of the fish. He needs a new net. Do I have five brothers in my home and five sisters-in-law? I've got to do everything by myself, as you know."

"So why does the door have to stay closed?"

Subla's wife does not answer this.

"Whether or not you keep the door closed, sister, the word's all over town and market."

Subla's wife ignites at once. "What word, Mohan's mother, what word do you mean?"

"It's not my doing, sister. People near the market, those who play tabla at Tamasi's father's place, they've been talking about it. They're Brahmans and Kayasthas, they're educated, they know better than Malos. Malos buy things on credit from their shops, hand them a deed of mortgage for a loan of cash when they go on jiyal fishing. They lend money for their weddings too. Most Malos of the village are in their control. How can Malos ignore what they say—their words seem to Malos like Brahma's script. Those folks are saying, 'Don't we know why a widow stays in behind a closed door all the time and doesn't show her face to anyone?' ''

Subla's wife is stunned. The ground seems suddenly to fall away from under her feet. But she does not lose control, somehow she makes her way back home.

After this, she takes to glaring with such red-eyed ferocity at anyone who glances in her direction that she forces the person to flee. One day she directs an hour-long volley of abusive shouts at the tabla-playing men near Tamasi's father's place by the market. The other women in the Malo neighborhood remark to each other, ''Mother, oh mother, looks like the widow's declared all-out war.''

She keeps trying to rid the Malo neighborhood of intruders. But she finds no way to achieve that. The leaders of the old days can't do much now; if they could, a solution would be easy. Ramprasad of Jatrabari is subdued after his attempt to make widows' remarriage acceptable in the Malo community. The Chakravarty priest of the village persuaded Malos, by quoting from his priests' handbook, that getting a widow remarried was bound to take a person to hell. They listened to the Brahman pandit and ignored Ramprasad. Now he does not have as much influence in the Malo community. Dayalchand used to speak up with courage. He plays the role of a sage in those others' jatra performances, and by taking their jatra show to the town, they gave him the chance to get gold and silver medals from the rich. Now he too shifts in their favor. He will not speak up for the right thing as he used to.

But inside Subla's wife lives a rebel woman. She does not know how to give up.

''Listen, Mohan's mother, I'm a daughter of this village, I was married in this village. I'm not one to be afraid of marketplace men.''

''But you're a woman.'' Mangala's wife tries to reason with her. ''What can you do, sister?''

''I can do anything. If nothing else, I can set fire to the village and burn it down.''

''When one home in a village catches fire, a thousand homes burn. If the neighborhood near the market burns, the Malo neighborhood will burn too. Your home will burn, and mine too. We'll die just as they will, sister.''

''It's better to die with honor, sister, than to live in humiliation.''

The statement strikes a chord in the minds of Malo youths. Catching hold of three men on their way home from tabla playing late one night, they give them a good beating with their bare hands. Those who were beaten up then mobilize the people of the jatra group and get together to decide what to do. After much debate, they decide against direct revenge. As the lives and possessions of the Malos are practically in their hands, they'll destroy the Malos by means other than a mere beating with their hands.

From that day a black cloud hovers in the sky over the Malo neighborhood. Its inhabitants remain unaware of the terrible things its shadow will bring them.

The new race boat Kadir's son took out that day to the racing stretch of the river never comes back. Every year some such incident invariably occurs: a boat from some village attacks one from another village. If there is a quarrel from an earlier year, then of course one of the boats takes advantage of any opportunity that comes its way to drive its bow into the belly of the other. Once the boat breaks, clubs and poles that are kept on board with this kind of situation in mind come out. Legs and arms and hips are broken, heads are broken. Every year at the race some boat rides over another. This year Chhadir's boat is done in.

Chhadir's party does not even know who the others were, whose boat broke theirs. Everything happened in an instant. A moment before, his boat looked like a peacock with unfurled plumes of oars, moving at the speed of a snake. In the blink of an eye they found themselves thrown into the water.

The people in their home are silent. They all hold their breath listening. No one has words to say. A storm has blown over the fate of everyone in this household, leaving total stillness in its wake. Though the kerosene lamp dimly lights the inside of the room, everything seems motionless. Romu is in front of them all and devours his father's every word. His father seems to him to be of enormous stature tonight: the man who has come home after surviving such an unimaginable danger seems far beyond his reach.

Kadir Mian finally gives a deep sigh and says, "Merciful Khuda saved you. Who knows what happened to all the others."

"I don't know, Father. I wouldn't have lived either. Thrown into the water, I found so many boats speeding around me, one going left, one right, one over my head. Spray from one, a blow from the oars of another, in the end I saw darkness in front of my eyes! And then I noticed him. I recognized him and held out my hand. He jumped into the water, caught hold of me, and finally pulled me into his boat. That same fisherman brother who saved us when the potato boat was sinking."

With grateful eyes they all look once again at Banamali. Romu feels infinite reverence for him.

Cries of anguish and loss are ready to break out in the neighborhood. Almost all their young men were in Chhadir's boat. The news of what happened overwhelms all the families. Seeing some of those young men return one or two at a time, Kadir asks them to be patient a little longer. "If Khuda saves them, they'll all come home unharmed, you'll see."

His hope is borne out. In almost every boat passing this way they come back in twos and fours. Romu keeps thinking, if only the boat too would come back like those lost in the water! Suddenly regret overcomes Chhadir. "Ba-jan, I've dropped your five hundred rupees to the bottom of Titash." After Kadir lightens the weight of loss in his son's mind with earnest words of consolation, Chhadir takes Banamali's hand in his and says, "Brother or friend, you're really my own. I can't let you leave until you have some fresh soaked parched rice here." Kadir too grows aware how much he wants to offer his hospitality to Banamali's group. Its members are unable to turn down the combined entreaty of father and son.

The home of Romu's mother's father is near a Hindu neighborhood. She immediately sets about wiping clean the floor of their large cow shed. Then she takes out a winnowing basketful of parched rice, which she quickly sorts and cleans. Chhadir milks the cows. And Kadir Mian runs to the potters' neighborhood and brings a new clay pot.

On the cleaned floor of the cow shed Udaitara sets the clay pot on three lumps of earth to bring the milk to a boil on a wood fire. The fire dims from time to time and starts up again. When it burns well, the glow lights Udaitara's face, and when it dims she lowers her head and blows until it flares up again, throwing its red glow on her face. Watching her from a distance is Jamila, Kadir's only daughter. She watches for a while until she is absolutely certain. Pulling Romu's mother aside, she says, "Oh sister-in-law, this is the one I talked about so many times, the one I saw on the way as I first went away from here with my husband. The one who was dipping and dipping her water pot to fill it."

Tired from the whole day's travel, the quarrel, and hunger on top of all that, they sit down in the cow shed and eat off banana leaves a satisfying meal of parched rice soaked in hot milk and sweetened with raw sugar drops. After they finish eating, Jamila holds Udaitara's hand and takes her to the inner room of their home. She seats Udaitara and explains. "I was on my way to live with my husband for the first time after marriage, sitting inside the dome, the opening in front of me covered with a sari. The wind blew a bit of the sari that was tucked in. You were at the ghat then, making waves with your water pot before filling it. I saw you and it felt as if I'd known you for ages. I don't know why the sight of someone, a total stranger, felt so pleasant. I kept my eyes on you as long as I could, but you didn't spot me. Next time I came back here, I told father I wanted you as my friend. But he said, 'Don't know the name, the place she lives, how can I find her?' Since then, every time I went past your ghat on the way to my husband's—not a new bride any more—I removed the sari cover with my own hand and looked. I searched thoroughly, but I never saw you again. And today, how amazing it is: you've come on your own to me! Now that you've come, stay on here for a few days, then take me to your place for a few days."

Udaitara says nothing; she only lets out a sigh. She likes the name Jamila but feels sad, finding her so inexperienced in matters of social life.

When happiness comes once again after a major danger, like the moon from behind dissipating black clouds, its sweetness is hard to describe to anyone not present in Kadir Mian's home this evening. The grace of hospitality wipes out all residue of the unpleasantness and unease from the quarrel and violence earlier that day in their boat. Carrying a peerless imprint of affection and friendship in their minds, they return to the boat.

The moon has risen in the sky, and the rippled surface of Titash sparkles in its light as the boat moves on through those small moonlit waves. Only Banamali and Ananta are not with them. At the earnest request of their host, they stayed on for the night.

Next morning Ananta goes outside as soon as he wakes up. He hears the cows calling in the cow shed and sees the calves, released after the night, leaping around for no reason. A short way from the yard is low land flooded with water from the rainy season, with trees and shrubs of all sorts stranded in waist-deep water and a dinghy tied to one of them. In an open stretch a long bamboo pole is suspended horizontally, with lengths of jute hung from it to dry that make it look like a great wall of jute. A strong smell of wet jute fills the air there and has attracted swarms of dragonflies flying about and landing on the jute. Ananta walks on attentively watching these and, as he takes a turn, finds Romu standing and watching too, his eyes also filled with wonder. Romu was all excitement about the two visitors here overnight and was dying to talk to Ananta. Searching for an excuse to start conversation, Romu finally asks, "You don't catch dragonflies?" When Ananta says no, Romu says, "In that house over there on the other side of the bamboo bridge lives my cousin Gafur. He catches dragonflies, pierces them with a shuttle stick, and leaves them to thrash and die. It makes me sad. You don't catch dragonflies, you're so good."

Romu's mother, going with a basket of dung from the cow shed to dump on the compost heap, is so happy to see the two boys talk to each other like close friends that she stops, picks a cucumber from a vine, and gives it to Ananta. "Here, take this, Ba-ji." Ananta takes the cucumber and looks at her in surprise. When Romu says she's his mother, Ananta promptly bends down and touches his head to her feet.

After returning to the village Ananta puts his mind to studying. The day Gosain-babaji first teaches him the "black letters," his mind overflows with joy. A new world swings its door open and calls him in. Soon he learns how to put two and three letters together to form words, such as those he knew how to speak and now, to his utter amazement, learns how to express in writing. Practicing those letters in various shapes, round and square and triangular, on a length of banana leaf gives him enormous enjoyment. Even at night, when he is about to fall asleep, the shapes of the letters appear shining before his mind's eye.

Very soon he finishes the first-level primer, *Shishu-shiksha*. Banamali, proud of his achievement, places his finger at random spots in the book and asks Ananta to read. Ananta reads without halting or stumbling. Listening to him read, Banamali sometimes sighs and says, "Now I see the value of the black letters I didn't learn when I still had the time."

Ananta then moves on to the second primer, *Balya-shiksha*, and the counting manual with it. "Man rides and again he falls"—the letters are all familiar to him from the earlier primer, but the words that put them together are new as well as the conjugated sentences made by using those words. With the sentence is a picture of a man riding a horse. No picture of his falling though; maybe he climbed back too quickly to be seen well enough for drawing a picture. After this he comes to the conjunct letters. These are complex and difficult. But the fascination inherent in their complexity and difficulty grips Ananta. They playfully return to his imagination in all sorts of novel forms.

Anantabala too is sent to learn to read and write with him. But the girl's mind is not quite on the book; she doesn't make much progress, because she doesn't study and her attention is elsewhere. Most of the time her eyes are either on Ananta or outside in the distance where paddy fields merge with the sky or where she notices another village. And whenever she gets a chance she talks—about things that seem to Ananta meaningless or unimportant—and her talking once it starts is hard to stop.

One day she says, "Today in our home there was a lot of talk about you and me. Our names are nicely similar, but they think too similar. If they change your name, I'll ask them to change mine too. You want to know what your name's going to be? Mother suggested Haranath, but Little Aunt didn't like it and suggested Pitambar. Big Aunt didn't like that one, and so after a lot of arguing they agreed on the name Big Aunt suggested. Your name's going to be Gadadhar."

"My aunt won't like that name."

"But as they've already named you this, it can't be changed again."

"What need is there to change my name?"

"Seems you don't know. My mother knows, my father knows, I know, and you don't. But they asked me not to tell you, and so I won't. They talk about you a lot in our home. You'll have to stay in our house for good. They won't let you leave and go away elsewhere. They say you will look good only with me and with no one else."

"And if I don't want to stay?"

"They'll make you stay. They'll tie you up."

"Huh, tie me up! They won't even know when I'm suddenly gone or where."

Indeed Ananta is getting ready to leave. One day as he returned from lessons, past a barber's house with a guava tree, the barber's wife gave him some guavas to eat and asked him to come back on his day off to read the *Ramayana* to her. A remark the barber's wife made, as she listened to his *Ramayana* reading, lighted an inextinguishable fire in his mind.

"Ananta, your reading of the *Ramayana* is really wonderful. Let me give you some good advice. Go away. Here they'll let you study maybe up to the second grade and after that just put you to work in a fisherman's boat. There's no way to study much further here. But you've got to learn a lot more, to gain knowledge and earn college degrees like the sons of Brahmans and Kayasthas. This three-cornered human world, the sun and the moon, the round earth and the universe—you must learn about all that, you must learn about the seven seas and the thirteen rivers, about the mountains and the great bodies of water and grasslands of the world. There are thousands of books, and each one is about something different. You need to read all those books and you need to gather all the knowledge they contain."

"There are so many books in the world?"

"Yes. How can you know about those when you sit here? How many books will you be able to read if you stay here? Go to the city—not the little town near here, but away. Go all the way to Comilla."

"How am I going to live there, what'll I eat, where'll I get the money to study?"

"You must address someone else's mother as yours, someone else's sister as yours. God will not leave you without food. Once they see you've got a talent for learning, they won't charge you any fee, and they'll even spend their own money to buy you the books you need."

Ananta would come back from listening to those words and turn them in his mind day and night. An unknown world of great mystery beckoned him endlessly. In his eagerness for the joys his mind had yet to taste and know, from time to time he felt a tremendous restlessness.

Soon he would take the path toward the object of his desire.

Bad times for the Malo community of Gokanghat start from the day cracks appear in its unity. Until now that unity has been tight like thunder. In their neighborhood Malos have had a cohesive social life constructed like strong brickwork. No one has dared to bother them openly. When the jatra drama group enters their neighborhood, so does dissension.

The patrons and impresarios of the jatra group have far more money and cunning than Malos do. They hold a lot more power. Instead of using the full force of that power all at once, they apply it in small doses. The day after the beating incident that opens their hostile designs, the jatra group's presence in the home of Tamasi's father grows more energetic. Before there was only tabla playing. Now come a harmonium, a flute and a fiddle, followed by three different song books for staging a jatra. Rehearsals for an opera no one has ever even heard of begin. Tamasi's father used to play mostly the commander-in-chief; now he receives the role of the king. They send out word that young boys from the Malo neighborhood will be given the female roles of heroine's confidantes. The boys' fathers forbid them to take part in jatra and fraternize with those men: they smoke *bidi* and crop their hair at the back of the neck, they use indecent language in the presence of elders. Instead of songs about the gods, they launch into tunes from those cheap and immodest confidante songs anywhere on village paths. All this corrupts their character.

At this point the confidantes are recruited from other caste groups. But the rehearsal takes place in the Malo neighborhood. Many Malos become even angrier with Tamasi's father. But many others, especially Malo women, are won over after they watch the first rehearsal. They shed tears and vow they'll have their young sons and brothers play the roles of confidantes at the next rehearsal of the new jatra.

In the next rehearsal a few young Malo boys join young boys from other neighborhoods to practice the transvestite dance of confidantes, one hand coyly placed on the hip and the index finger of the other on the chin. They sing:

> Hush hush, tiptoe, girls, or our friend will shy away.
> She throws dust in our eyes and hides her love away.
> But now the bee'll fly to her, before the night's over,
> Hush hush . . .

And so on. Their mothers and sisters are enchanted. They tell each other how charming the dance is and how novel the song. The sentiment, the words, and the style of singing are so very different from the kind of songs Malos sing, and the tunes are so different too. The women are fascinated and from the next day become ardent fans of the jatra group.

Other Malos oppose and argue with those families, they threaten to ostracize them, they try to persuade them how worthless those songs are: with such indecent suggestions and bad meanings, those will only turn the heads of Malo youths and harm the minds of Malo women. But the fans are not perturbed. Instead they say: "Oh, keep quiet. Malos' songs are awful, can't even be called songs compared to theirs. We sing: 'In my dreams tonight Shyam's black beauty came to my eyes as light. Crumpled are Radha's clothes and the flower bed of her tryst.' Such boring songs! The jatra songs have such pretty tunes and novel words, so charming to listen to. We'll send our boys to play the roles of confidantes, we don't care if you ostracize us for that."

As a result, the Malo neighborhood splits into two bitterly opposed camps.

One day, finding her alone at the slope, Mangala's wife informs Subla's wife, "There's danger waiting for you, sister. Be careful when you step out. Someone'll accost you. My Mohan heard about it."

Asked if she heard who her would-be assailant is, Mangala's wife says it's Aswini of the ferrymen's neighborhood. A squat young man with bushy hair, he used to row a passenger boat and now plays the part of the king's younger brother in the jatra troupe.

The proof turns up shortly. As Subla's wife walks to the ghat with water pot and change of clothes for a bath, she notices him watching her from a little distance. As soon as she sees him, he starts to sing:

> When my friend on a white horse is riding, I come out then for
>   bathing.
> An ill-timed wind comes, my bosom it uncovers, my friend
>   sees everything.

The aim of the song is transparent to her. And at noontime she is cooking inside when another couplet of the same song comes from someone who passes the yard:

> When my friend goes to royal court, I sit here cooking food.
> And I weep behind the smoke from clay stove and wet wood.

It has been possible to tolerate it so far. But another day still another couplet of that song is heard while she is eating.

> When the friend goes flute playing, this woman sits here eating.
> Afraid of the in-laws I say to him nothing, tears soak my clothing.

Then Subla's wife cannot take it anymore. Leaving her food, without even stopping to wash her hands, she rushes outside and shouts. "I don't live with any in-laws, and I'm not afraid of any fellow. I'm telling you without fear to come, if you're a father's son you come right now. I can take you inside in front of all the neighbors in broad daylight. Come at once if you dare."

Hearing her voice, the female neighbors—among them Mangala's wife, Kalo's Ma, Dayalchand's widowed sister—all come out. Hearing the cause of it, Mangala's son Mohan and the two brothers Ramdayal and Gurudayal come out with their poles. By then Aswini has cleared the neighborhood and taken the path to the market.

"Am I right or am I not right, Mohan, and you Sadhu's and Madhu's father! This is the place of my father and my brothers. Here I speak in fear of no one. The person who can accost me here is still in his mother's womb. Forget about me, I'm talking about the Malo neighborhood. What is it becoming, you tell me!"

Ramdayal, Gurudayal, and such others are indignant. They also manage to rouse the others in the neighborhood and resolve to punish the transgressor appropriately. But in the next jatra rehearsal, when that same man applies his full-throated voice to a long note and chastely sings, "No more tears, sing Hari's name, O daughter of mi-i-i-ne," then the Malos' outrage evaporates. In the mind of Mohan alone, the anguished words of Subla's wife still smolder like live coals.

Malos have a cultural life of their own. In songs and stories, in sayings and folklore, that culture has a distinctive and vital beauty—woven into their festivities and religious celebrations, into their jokes and riddles, and into the language of self-expression in their everyday life. The songs that pass from generation to generation express feelings that are as sweet as their melodies are moving. People other than Malos themselves have no easy access to the heart of that culture to partake of its nectar, because the

Malos' way of lyrical appreciation is unlike that of all the other communities. What the Malos have woven into their hearts, others treat with ridicule. But now this feeling of cultural identity begins to erode. The songs, the tunes, sung in their soaring soulful notes, somehow no longer activate and crystallize the moods within the solitary recesses of their minds. What was tightly knit somehow feels slack somewhere and keeps slipping. Perhaps the vicious axe of the jatra group severed the tree's life-giving root underground.

Many lose hope and let themselves drift with the current of time. Only one young man does not lose hope: Mohan. He has a good voice and dedication to singing. From singers of his father's and grandfather's generations he learned many songs in the tradition of bhatiyali, Haribangsha, and *naamgan*. Young Malos in recent years are forgetting those songs. Taking the place of those songs—serious, soulful, and rich in deeper feelings—are new songs in lighthearted moods and written by shallow composers. Many times Mohan felt this sense of loss deep inside his mind. But who can fight the tide of the times? The times are just like that. Good, durable things are treated as old and outmoded and thrown away, and light things take pride of place in people's gatherings. Mohan refuses to give in. He calls a few singers together and, with tambourine and stringed instruments, starts a singing session right away in the early afternoon.

But just as they begin, "The peerless grace of Gaur is unforgettable once seen, I went to the heavenly river's bank for my eyes to sink in," from the next yard come the shrill voices of two Malo youths joining in with two youths of the basket-weaver caste, who sing, "Get ready soldiers, onward to the battle, Prepare an attack, soldiers, on to the great battle." The loudness of that song, drowning the mellow beauty of theirs, pains Mohan. His accompanists and fellow singers, too, seem distracted, almost as if in their minds they appreciate that song. They leave the session, with an excuse: these days daytime singing doesn't take hold anymore.

The dreaded news spreads one afternoon: the evening's rehearsal of the new jatra opera will be held in Kalobaran's house. Those among the Malos who are still eager to save their cultural identity feel desperate and go to Kalobaran to dissuade him.

They argue: "Listen, merchant, some of our Malo leaders—Dayalchand and Krishnachandra and Harimohan—they've all been leaning toward the jatra. Where we were one, now we're two, constantly bickering and vying with each other. We fear some day we'll start to fight and use our oars and poles against each other. You too, you're following in the footsteps of those who brought ruin to the Malo neighborhood. Don't do it, merchant, stay with us. Come with us, let's persuade the leaders, and reclaim the unity we had before. Why should we sing jatra songs? Don't we have songs of our own? Are the songs our ancestors left for us too few? Compared to those songs, jatra songs are like slave girls. We see dark days ahead. We're worried about what a terrible end this jatra thing in our neighborhood's going to bring us. We need you. Letting jatra rehearsal be held in your home tonight means letting it be held at the heart of the Malo neighborhood. You know that!"

Kalobaran says nothing and looks as if he doesn't even hear what they just said.

They come back depressed. "Mohan, O Manmohan, there's no hope. The deadly snake claimed this one too."

In a defeated voice, Mohan says, "They're all deserting us and crossing the sea. Dayalchand's gone, Krishnachandra's gone. Gaurkishore, and now Kalobaran, too. They'll all leave."

"Not all, Mohan, not all will leave." The strength in Subla's wife's voice startles everyone. "Dayalchand left, Krishnachandra left. But don't you see, Mohan, you haven't left? You're here, Sadhu's and Madhu's father is here. Of the six times twenty families, three times twenty may have left. But we still have three times twenty families, and we'll survive. We won't let ourselves drift helplessly into wrong channels. With the help of those who stay with us, we'll fight to the end. We're not going to accept defeat from those who brought harm to the Malo neighborhood, those who split this betel nut in two. If there's going to be a jatra rehearsal in Kalobaran merchant's house tonight, then you too hold a singing session in your home. Let it be a test today."

Subla's wife sits down with Mohan. The two of them open up the doors of their memory stores and call into their minds all those good songs at the edge of oblivion. Then they carefully go over them, pick out the ones they know are most moving, and talk over the list of their final selection.

"These are the songs of separation. Sing them after those on the theme of body-spirit. Late in the night start bhatiyal songs. And Haribangsha songs shortly before dawn. Then have the coming-of-dawn songs, and in the morning have pasture-play songs, and end the session with a song of eternal union."

In the evening when the jatra-wallahs come to Kalobaran's yard with their harmoniums and tablas and start to slap the tom-tom, Mohan's group also sits down with their tambour and stringed instruments. The distance between the two homes is the length of just a couple of huts; even the talking in one is audible in the other.

When in that yard some heroic lecture is being delivered with gusto, in this yard Mohan's group finishes the body-spirit songs and moves on to the mood of separation:

> Tell him, bumblebee, that away from her black one,
> heart's pain makes Radha's golden body burn.
> She takes no food, no water, nor will she do her hair.
> Without you, Shyam, Radha's like a madwoman.

The entire Malo neighborhood divides into two groups and collects in those two yards. Larger numbers go to Kalobaran's yard, the expressions on their faces showing the excitement of greeting the new. The expressions of those who join the gathering in Mohan's yard reflect devotion to their own culture and the resolve to save it.

Radha's pain of separation wells up in the melodies, flows in waves and radiates in layers of the lyrics. The pain of separation from the beloved touches and stirs the deepest recesses of the hearts of all in the audience.

The participants bring forward their favorite songs. Udaichand, one of the main singers, retunes his strings and suggests, "This song might work here—'Who else can soothe this life and heart? Kind Krishna is the only friend in this world.' " Sensing hesitation, he mentions another. "How about this:

> Why, black moon, why with your flute name Radha, not Krishna?
> With whom, Hari, do you now leave your poor Radha?
> In no home in Braja today can she find comfort or shelter."

Mohan remembers well an even better song in this mood and says, "Let's sing this first—'In Brindaban today, the eyes of the Braja women are raining, The birds and the beasts all in silence for Krishna are crying.' "

Today Krishna leaves for Mathura. Everyone in Brindaban cries from emptiness and loss. Birds and animals, cows and calves, the twelve groves, the lovely bank of the Jamuna river, and the seventy miles lined with the yards of all the Braja homes he passes by shed tears. The tears of the milkmaid make the path wet and slippery and cause the wheels of his chariot to sink again and again, as she sings, "Take me along, heart's dearest, Stop your chariot on Jamuna bank for a moment." But the entreaties do not stop him. His chariot goes away, trampling the milkmaid's brimming desire and love; it crushes her heart to the dust. The milkmaid has lost everything today but hope lingers on and still she sings: "Maybe I'll have you after I die, To soothe this heart's painful cry."

When the song ends the air is heavy with sadness. From the other yard then comes a pompous heroic verse about battle between gods and demons.

Stopping for a moment, Udaichand remarks, "Since the battle has started, let it be in earnest. Think of a bhatiyal song now, Mohan."

The night advances. A roll of laughter comes from Kalobaran's yard, perhaps to punctuate a humorous role. Malo children, young wives and daughters, even some middle-aged women crowd there. The assembly in Mohan's yard has thinned out. But the singers are so absorbed that they do not notice whether the audience diminishes or increases. It is now quite late in the night—the hour to sing the soaring bhatiyals, the unique hour when consciousness can perceive the rare moments of the transcendent within ordinary life. Listening quietly to the heartbeat of the night, we almost feel the mysterious brushing of wings of thought in the innermost chamber of our minds. Unrevealed mysteries, in their cosmic essence, murmur in the quietude of human minds at this hour of night. The hint of that murmur which exists at this moment in a bhatiyal song can be felt at no other time.

Now Mohan's group opens a melody that resounds in hearts even on the other side of the Titash river.

> O Kanai dear, it's growing late in the afternoon,
> Radha's heart trembles: the selling in Mathura will end soon.
> O Kanai, lovely ferryman, taking her across the Kangsa river,
> Radha's pot of curd is spoiled by your touch, Kanai dear.

This Radha is not the Radha of Brindaban, who ventures in love. She is the human soul crossing between this world and the other. This river Kangsa or Jamuna flows between life and death. The soul has left the temporary home and is on its journey upstream. The two banks of the river lie in blank, infinite darkness. In the familiar form of Kanai, the Omnipresent leads the soul across. The soul is unblemished but still holds on to the material pot of curd. To free the soul from all polluting attachment to material possessions before taking it back in, God spoils her pot of curd through the low-caste ferryman's touch. Perhaps some Malos may not understand the composer's meanings and associations, but in the soaring melody they all sense the transcendent voice that comes as if from beyond this life. They lose themselves in the song's passion.

> Black is the blackbird, black like Braja's beloved Hari,
> the black of the wagtail's chest brings back his memory.
> Lying down brings no sleep, sitting makes my tears flow.
> Sleeplessly I hold to my bosom my head pillow, side pillow.

The climactic moment of union with the supremely desired approaches, signaled by the growing depth of the night that covers everything with the deep black that is also the color of the beloved Krishna. The deepest desire in the waiting soul is for the disembodied beauty of the infinite. The thirst grows stronger by the minute and causes such restlessness that lying down brings no sleep and sitting up makes the tears flow.

Not much is left of the night. This is the hour to sing a Haribangsha song. Malos do not know the reason for the name, which they picked up from their fathers and grandfathers as they learned the songs. The lyrics are solemn yearnings of the human spirit for reunion with the Sublime. The singing has to be open-voiced for the soaring melodies. The right voice carries the high notes and makes the air resonate far and wide. Not many these days can sing these vocally demanding melodies. In this village only Udaichand has a voice that can carry the notes.

> Trees inhabit the top of the ground,
> branches inhabit the top of the tree,
> birds' nests inhabit the top of branches,
> how long I'll be apart from the life that is thee.
> Her Kanaiya is on the other side of the river,
> Radhika knows this in her longing to be free.

If not by the sophistication of the words, then by the power of the open-throated melody, life-Radha finds deliverer-Krishna in order to transcend death-river. With this song the night approaches its end. From Kalobaran's yard still comes the sound of singing: "Garlands I string all night and kiss the face, O, that sugar-sweet face." But finding the bhatiyal singing more attractive, people move away in droves from Kalobaran's to Mohan's yard. Encouraged by the influx, Udaichand begins his favorite song. They all know that every time he sings this song, he gets up and dances along. And a few from his audience also get up and dance with him.

In the other yard they just listened as the singers sang other peoples' songs. But the songs going on here they know by heart. Wherever Malos are, the sound of these songs never fails to resonate inside their minds. If they are nearby, they join their voices to the song. If they are away, they hum to themselves. Once again they sing with spontaneous joy along with Udaichand's vigorous singing.

> Listen friend, friend, friend, O dear friend—
>> You Shyam, you brought stigma to the pure Radha,
>> All buying-selling ends in the market of Mathura.
> Listen, O friend—
>> With no oil or wick, how's the lamp alight?
>> Who made this house, whoever has its right?
> Listen, O friend—

The yard is dry and hard, the porch drifts in flooding.
Ganga is dying of thirst, and of cold Brahma's dying.

At this moment they hear the first cawing of crows waking up as the darkness outside begins to clear, and someone puts out the lamp inside. Kalobaran's big yard is totally empty and quiet now. Mohan's small yard overflows with people. Flushed with the happiness and pride of victory, Mohan asks the audience: "Respected ones, before you leave let's sing a little naamgan together.* I'll bring the cymbals and the khol."

This is an even harder kind of singing and for that reason is rarely attempted. Equally rare is the gathering of so many Malos in one yard to sing and to listen. It may not happen again soon; perhaps it never will. That's why Mohan is so eager to have some naamgan in his yard today. The scale for this singing is high and the volume has to be high too. The singers divide in four groups and take turns to sing a stanza apiece, using the full range and combined power of their voices. It takes almost an hour to complete one song in this manner.

Mohan asks the participants to choose between two episodes—"Krishna's stealing of the bathing maidens' clothes" or "the constant companions of Radha." Then he proceeds with their choice. It is an elaborate song of Radha's laments to her female companions: Had she known he'd go away, she would not have fallen in love and sacrificed all she had, her home and her place in society; still, with much effort she kept herself distracted from the pain of his absence; but now what have they done, they've reminded her of him by showing her his image in a portrait they've drawn; now she won't be able to live anymore and they should support her body as she is about to depart from it.

When the collective rendering of this song is over, sunlight is everywhere. The minds of everyone gathered there have grown clear as this morning's sunshine. At long last they've been able to rejoice to their hearts' content and sing to cleanse their minds.

But two days later, when boxes of costumes arrive at Kalobaran's house, and in the evening when the performers actually put them on to perform the jatra opera, then all the Malos flock there, forgetting everything else. The only two people who do not go are Subla's wife and Mohan. Subla's wife stays in bed with a feeling of utter humiliation, and Mohan sits alone in his yard with the tears of bitter pain in his eyes.

*Also known as *palagan*, this passionate, eloquent form of narrative singing revolves around particular incidents from Krishna's earthly play or from Radha's passion in love and in separation.

Floaters

After this defeat the Malos lose their self-identity. Their sense of personal integrity, distinction, and culture fades. The social ties of morality that had bound their community slacken and begin to fall apart. Rather than do things together, they come to blows over them. Even tying their boats by the ghat produces quarrels, and sometimes fights, about who is to tie his ahead of whose. When laying their nets in the river, they vie meanly among themselves and often end up in factions, fighting and hitting one another's heads. None of this happened before.

Their young men quit the hookah and take up cigarettes. They stop respecting their elders as they did before. And their sympathy for their fathers and uncles diminishes. They begin to dislike the work of their traditional livelihood. In earlier years during the slack season in Titash, young fishermen went enthusiastically on distant fishing trips. They do not anymore.

In their neighborhood now the jatra-wallahs rule, fops who take to visiting Malo homes at will and hang around chatting. Even women start to join those chats. The Malos sometimes feel uncomfortable about it but do not find the courage to object in strong enough terms. To Malo women, these players of the roles of king, prince, commander-in-chief, and "conscience" character appear to be amazing men with adorable ways. Young married women are even more pleased to be addressed by them as "Boudi" instead of the Malos' "Bou" for elder brother's wife. The jatra players then go back and tell juicy stories about young Malo women to the other young men of their own communities. Out of curiosity these other men accompany them to Malo homes, sit down, and talk. The talk seems innocent. But when young women are on their way to the ghat, the men watch and at suitable moments whistle or suddenly belt out a tune of separation. Thus the Malos start to lose even the sanctity of their inner home life.

The Malos see all this and are aware of the effects, but they do not find the strength to protest. They take it silently and sometimes let themselves move with the flock. At times they get into fights over it. A member of one family might make snide remarks about the goings-on in the family of another, who then snaps back, "Stop buzzing here. Put your own home right, then come to salt others' cooking." That, of course, is right. But when you try to straighten out your own home, that brings tension and loss of temper there too.

Eventually, the women also indulge in expensive luxuries. Seizing this opportunity, jewelers frequent the homes with samples of fancy designs and cosmetics sellers come with their wares of soap, oil, and towels. Whatever little money Malos make during the good months thus gets misspent, and nothing is saved for the hard times. They must then starve for days; small children cry from hunger; women threaten husbands with their ideas of doing this and that. The men keep silent, ashamed of their inability to feed the family and, helplessly looking in only one direction at nothing in particular, puff hard at the hookah.

Gradually they slide below the standards of ordinary human dignity, so much so that when an enemy perpetrates atrocious acts—sitting right there on the tip of the nose!—they are unable to face up and fight back. Fixing angry red eyes on the ground and spitting, they only say, "Go away, dog! Go away, crow!" Day by day they slide further down. It comes to such a pass that when loan-company babus come with a gun-carrying attendant and tyrannize them unspeakably on the pretext of re-covering loans and take away all their possessions, they do not even object. Years ago some enthusiastic rich people of the village brought in from town a branch of a loan company for Malos here. Attracted by the low interest, all the Malos borrowed on impulse. Every year they pay through the nose and just cover the interest that grows at a compound rate. Now to collect the principal a tough babu comes, along with his underlings. His name is Bidhubhusan Pal, related to the Pal family of this village. With briefings from that source about the Malos' real condition, he comes to the neighborhood and assumes a destroyer-god stance. The older fishermen are dragged by their beards into the water of Titash and asked with much eye rolling to confess how much money they have. Even shivering wet in wintertime, standing in the water of Titash, these men cannot utter lies; it is impossible for them to lie in Titash's water even if they can lie everywhere else. Some confess they have two rupees, some say one and three-quarters, some confess they have none at all. After collecting every bit of their cash with this fine sieve, and still finding it too little, they take away even the metal plates and pots, bundles of nets and spools of thread from their homes, loaded into a horse-drawn carriage. After the raids there is much crying in the Malo homes. Even Ramkeshab, the oldest fisherman in the village, whose only son became insane and died, and who drags his worn body every day to catch fish in the river—even he is not spared. His long beard is easy for Bidhu Pal's man to grasp, so he is pulled and twisted in the water more viciously than the others. But he does not cry. When the others wipe their tears and come to comfort him, he says, "What good is crying when the Almighty has put me under a stack of fourteen clay plates!"

The Pals are shopkeepers in the marketplace. As Malos buy things from the store on credit, the Pals are careful to stop short of making the fishermen completely destitute. They come and console the weeping Malos, saying, "Bidhu Pal may have a tough temper, but he's a kind man. Maybe he took your other things, but after all, he didn't touch your boats."

Such terrible times have an end. The time of year comes when there are fish in the river. The Malos again see a little money, with which they buy new pots and plates to replace what they lost. The reeling of thread goes busily on in the homes, and the weaving of new nets. With those nets Malos catch many kinds of fish. Their faces have smiles again.

But one day before the year ends, even those smiles disappear. Radhacharan Malo of this neighborhood had a bad dream. Some Malo men listen intently to his account of it. After listening, a few say, "Don't be silly, it can't be true." Others' faces dim and they repeat, doubtfully, "It can't be true. But suppose it turns out that way!"

"Dreams come at night and leave at night. How can dreams ever come true?"

"Well of course they can. Jashoda Rani dreamed Gopal would one day go away to Mathura. Didn't he? Subla's mother-in-law dreamed Subla would die crushed under a boat on the jiyal-fishing trip. Didn't he?"

"Yes, but she talked about the dream only after Subla's death. She couldn't tell beforehand. So you see. You too should talk about your dream—but not now, only after it comes true. Keep quiet now, don't get so worked up."

But the one who had the bad dream does not keep quiet. That it did not belong just to the night's sleep, that in broad daylight with open eyes he noticed plenty of evidence to go with it, all this he now proceeds to relate.

"I didn't mention anything for so long because I thought, they won't believe me. Beyond the jutting bend of Jatrabari, near the mouth of Ku-rulia canal, a little farther upstream where that whirlpool is, you know. From the days of our fathers and grandfathers, we all know by heart the direction of the current there. Don't we? The other day I lowered the net there, and it turned the opposite way. The current there was turned around. What a strange thing to happen! Not many of you go night fishing any-more, so you don't keep track of changes in the river. I roam the river through the night, laying the net upstream and downstream. I know every twist and turn of the river. For several days since, I've been noticing something amiss, something different in the river's flow pattern—famil-iar calculations just don't seem to hold. The current where we've known it to be slanted is now straight, where we've known it to be straight it's now slanted. From that day I had this terrible thought—something's going to happen. No more peace in my mind, only a strange anxiety. Last night I lowered the net near the bend of the cremation ground: no fish there. Went to the bend of the five homes: no fish there. Went near Garibullah's tree and still couldn't get fish and net together. Wherever I went, the current was slack as never before. The fish leaped a little away but not where I laid the net, where I expected the flow. Finally I went near the mouth of Kurulia canal. Found the current there turning round like a top. Lowered the net and lay down on the deck. Couldn't sleep, with the same thought turning, something strange is going on in Titash. I don't know when my eyelids closed. All of a sudden I had this dream, Titash has gone dry. How can this dream be untrue? I saw, in the middle of the river where you can't touch the bottom with a twenty-cubit bamboo pole, a tiny fellow walking across, and then I saw the places he walked over, all those were without water, dry, hard dry. My heart leaped up to my mouth, my hands and feet were trembling. Alone in the boat, I was so terrified I let out a scream. Then after uttering *Rama-naam* three times my fear calmed. But does sleep return after a dream like this? I stayed up."

His listeners express sympathy. "Poor Radhacharan had a terrible dream last night. Go massage the top of your head with oil and take some dips."

They dismiss his bad dream as just a dream; nobody really believes it. But a certain curiosity mixed with apprehension comes over them like a dark shadow and takes hold of them. Whenever one of them goes to lay his net upstream from the mouth of Kurulia canal, he holds the two poles of the net upright and lowers them deeper than he needs to and counts with trembling heart the moments that pass without the poles touching ground. And carefully searches for any change in the pattern of the currents. After days of searching, the fishermen do find strange discrepancies from what they've always known. Malos have known this river over generations. It is their constant companion day and night. To the lanes and passageways of its mind they have unrestricted access. Its ins and outs they know as if they could see them on the mirror of their thumbnail. Hence from even a slight feel of the pulse of its currents they know if disease enters its body somewhere. They sense that somewhere nearby, a very large siltbed is growing, moving closer.

They are not mistaken. One day, the pole of Mohan's net catches the floating siltbed. It is the last day of an ebb tide: the big river has drawn down Titash's water level, as it always does before the tide turns and reverses the flow. During the ebb, even after giving away much water, Titash still has a deep, solemn body of water. The abundance of its midstream never diminishes.

Mohan's heart pounds like a hammer. In childhood he heard the story of a sage who walked across this Titash on his wooden clogs. That was possible with the power of his mantra. From the script reciter he heard about how on a night of rain and storm Basudeb, with infant Krishna in his arms, stepped into the vast river Jamuna and waded across, splashing as if through a puddle. That was possible only because they were gods.

And this—this is in broad daylight, right before his human eyes. As soon as he lowers the net, even in midstream its bamboo pole hits ground at the bottom. The boat shudders, and so does Mohan.

After coming home, he remains in stunned silence. When the neighborhood folk call him for something, he explodes. "Let Malos do jatra, watch the versifiers' duels, dance, fight and squabble, let them do whatever they want. No need to worry about the future anymore. The river's dried up."

"What are you saying, Mohan? What did you just say? Oh Manmohan!"

"You heard what I said. Go out on the river and check for yourself."

Half a mile from their village is the jutting bend of Jatrabari village. The men take their boats near there and lower bamboo poles. Starting from that bend a vast underwater siltbed has formed, stretching far upstream, how far they cannot figure out. They notice that a bather, prompted by the desire for a deep dip, has slowly waded almost to midstream and still stands in water only neck-high. For the first time in their lives they see this amazing sight.

Large rivers wash away from one bank and form siltbeds along the other. That is their nature. But the river Titash does not act that way. It does not erode either bank. Therefore when the siltbed started to form, it started inside, at the center of the riverbed, expanding outward and rising upward.

During the rainy season Titash is again full to the brim. At the end of it the water level goes down and the siltbed reappears above water like a chest that rises after a deep breath. Where has so much water gone? Where have so many fish gone? Only two narrow channels remain near the two sides of Titash, the only evidence that a brimming river once flowed here.

Farmers from distant areas appear on both banks one day and, armed with bamboo poles and clubs, descend upon the siltbed. They fight over portions of the siltbed and stake their claims. The fishermen simply look on from the banks as if at a show. As long as this land was under water, Malos moved on it, it was theirs. The moment it floats above water, it becomes the farmers'. Those farmers will plant seeds here, they will harvest and take home the crop. This right will always be theirs, no one can steal it. This right is staked in solid reality, rooted in soil. And the Malos' right was in the flowing water, in its formless, groundless, ever-moving fluidity. That right never had the solid touch of real ground, it never had a stable support, a firm foothold. Hence they are floaters. No matter how much they, the fishermen, love the trees they tend and the homes they raise on the ground, they remain floating there like vapor. No matter how hard they cling to the bosom of the earth, the soil forever pushes them away: "No space for you, no place for you!" As long as there is water in the river, only that long do they float on the water. When the water dries, they too evaporate and disappear.

Even now the high tide comes; the siltbed then submerges. Looking out at the water-filled bosom of Titash, the Malos try to think: here is the brimming river—this is the truth—what they saw a short while ago was only a bad dream. But when the ebb follows, bad dream becomes naked truth. From each Malo's heart rises a deep sigh. Titash seems like an enemy; turned hostile and merciless. It has become a total stranger today. After holding them to its bosom with such affection all this time, it suddenly pushes them away into some abyss of swirling black waters. Ending its close relationship with the Malos, it seems to say in a merciless voice: "Don't come near me. I'm not yours anymore." Then in the rainy season it brims again. From far away comes new water, surging in waves. The current flows and laps pleasantly. Once again lively fish ride the current and move upstream with exuberance. In the new water, Malos splash and dip to their hearts' content. Giving themselves to the cool embrace of the river, they say, "How could you dry up and push us away when you love us so much!'' Tears come to their eyes as they say, "So distant you seemed then! You don't now. If you have so much love and affection for us, why did you then appear so cruel? What game is this of yours? This game, play it with anyone else you wish, not with these fisherfolk. They're so easily overwhelmed. Taking your momentary whim as the truth, they suffer self-torment. They are humble people. Kind as you are, don't play that game with them, don't turn that fearsome look on them. They are used to seeing only your kind face.''

The law of nature fixes the duration of the rainy season. When that time is over, Titash again recedes, turns distant, exposes the siltbed at its heart. This time the bed has grown even larger, extending from far upstream down to the ghat of this Malo neighborhood.

Soon bands of farmers will come armed with clubs and occupy it again. Ramprasad goes around among the Malo fishermen and tries to work them up. "They are farmers, they've got land of their own, they're going to take more land. As long as there was water here, it was ours. The water is gone, but the land under the water is ours too. They come from far away and take it all—and we fishermen, so close to it, are we going to just stand by and make no effort to fight?''

As a result of the long disunity and factional fighting, the Malos have completely lost their ability to work together. So they are terror-stricken at the mention of fighting, even for their rights. They say: "When the river dried, we died. We're not going to fight and bite over land. You go alone if you feel so strongly about it.''

Ramprasad does go alone. To occupy a piece of the siltbed that directly faces his family hut he comes out to fight, fairly certain of losing his life. With his young brothers at his side, the old man fights hard. And he dies the death he expected. Landless peasants like Karam Ali and Bande Ali also come, but they are beaten back. None get a handful of that siltbed. Who are the ones who get it then? Those who already have lots of land, those who are mightier, they also become the owners of the new land in the middle of Titash.

The fishermen don't feel too worked up about that, because they feel they're finished anyway, from the day the river's yearlong water left.

Several years pass one after another. At the end of the wet season this year the fishermen of Nabinagar upstream find the floating siltbed now extends even beyond their village.

Anantabala's father is worried also about something else. One day he talks to Banamali about it. "Can you try and find him?''

Anantabala is grown. Most other Malo girls of her age have gone to live with their husbands. She still observes every year the unmarried girls' Maghmandal rite. Ananta told her that when he returned after finishing his studies he'd do what she said. "What will I say to you other than what my mother and aunts say already day and night?" Anantabala answered. That was the childishness of an innocent age. Now as she grows up, her anxiety intensifies. Watching all the other girls her age with the grooms who have come for them, she thinks every time of her groom who will come to her too, and he will be none other than Ananta himself.

Every day she looks a little more grown up, and now even her mother and aunts begin to find her unmarried appearance somewhat improper. Younger girls now make a different kind of rhyme about her: "A fixture in her father's home, What a problem Anantabala's become." Her mother reproaches her father one day. "Why don't you get your daughter married? Is she a wooden door that you keep her attached to your home?"

"Banamali, listen. I'll give you the train fare. You go to Comilla city. See if you can find him."

Banamali does go as her father asked. Two nights he stays in a hotel and two days he looks through the streets for Ananta but can find no trace of him.

Not until seven years after he had left. Anantabala has turned seventeen. As no Malo home has ever had a girl of this age still unmarried, they speak ill of her father and her uncles. When she was younger, they hoped for Ananta and turned away good matches. Now that hope is lost, and the proposals they get are from widowers, even third-time or fourth-time widowers, illiterate and ugly on top of that. One day when her desperate father cruelly tells her he has no choice but to give her to one of those, she wants to die in sorrow and humiliation. After much crying she resigns herself, under the scolding and entreaty of her mother and aunts, to the prospect of being married to someone else. At this point Banamali brings the news.

"When the train pulled in to Comilla station, it was late in the afternoon. Seeing the checker get in at the station, I got off at the other end. With weights slung from the shoulder pole, I couldn't run. I'd be ruined if I broke those two clay containers with young fish in water. To the west of the station is this open field where the sun was setting. I went there to get away from the checker. Trying to hide, I saw Ananta—sitting on the grass with three other young men, arguing. His clothes were clean, even the shoes on his feet were polished. I was so ashamed to appear before him wearing only this. Still I went and stood near him. He didn't recognize me. Then, with my face turned to the pots of fish, I said as if to myself, 'Don't know where our Ananta is now. Doesn't he know Titash is dry and Malos are like fish out of water! They've got nothing to eat; they're going out of their minds too. Ananta's become educated; why doesn't he come to the Malos and help them by writing a letter to the government! Oh Ananta, if only you'd come once and see the condition of the Malos on the banks of Titash!' The medicine worked. He came up and looked at my face for a long time. Then recognizing me, he put his arms around me and said, 'Banamali-dada, what've you become!' 'Not just me, little brother, all the Malos have become like this. At least I'm still alive, can still carry pots of water-and-fry and walk; so many Malos have died; so many have lost all their strength and faculties and can't move.' He said nothing for a long time, lost in meditation. When he came out of it he asked, 'How do you make a living these days, Banamali-dada?' I said, 'The Malos' life of fishing died the day the river dried. They left their own work and took up work for wages. I did too. One day a big-city moneylender from Chattagaon visited the Malo neighborhoods, a man by the name of Kamal Sarkar. He said, "I'll supply fry to this area. My agent will stay here, he'll put them in the ponds and tanks here. Since you people can't live by fishing anymore, work for me." We carry their big clay pots filled with young fish and water, slung on shoulder poles. They get us a train ticket and some parched rice to tie in our towel for the day's meal. When we go back and give the account to the agent, we get one rupee per delivery. I still have the strength to do this work; most other Malos can't. This time he didn't buy me a ticket, he said: "You look like a beggar in your worn cloth and towel, with your beard and hair. The checker won't stop you. Go without a ticket, you'll get a rupee and a quarter in wages." I came almost to the station that way but felt so afraid I got off just before.'

"Ananta gazed at my body, my cloth, my hair and beard. Then he said, 'You don't have even a good towel, Banamali-dada!' I said, 'Yes, I've got a good towel and a good dhoti too, but I saved them. For traveling away from home, this worn cloth and towel are all right.' He took me to an eatery and fed me. From a shop he bought me a dhoti, a sari for his aunt in Gokanghat and one for Udaitara. He made me sleep in his bed beside him. Next morning he bought me a ticket, put me in the train, and before leaving said that after six months, as soon as the final examination for his B.A. was over, he'd come and see us."

Anantabala later sees him alone and asks, "Banamali-dada, he gave new cloth for you, for his aunt, and for Udi-didi. He didn't give any for me?"

"I'm sure he would have, but I didn't tell him about you."

"You didn't tell him about me? Why didn't you?"

"He wouldn't remember you. He had trouble remembering me."

"Why not? Have I grown a beard or become old like you?"

Banamali's sister Udaitara too seems old. The youthful beauty of her body is gone, but nothing has erased the color of her mind. The rainy season now brings new water in Titash, water that is beyond all imagination as in a dream. The water is so transparent that when you stand in it up to your chest and look down, you can see the ground underneath, the ground that is the reality. At first, when this ground emerged and stayed up, it seemed like the stuff of a nightmare. Now it seems normal. And the water that now flows over it seems like a dream, an enchanting dream. But when the flooding goes, it will leave behind a harsher desert. Searching that desert even grain by grain will not yield a single fish. Still, Udaitara feels overjoyed as she immerses her body in this water. Anantabala too bathes in the water and lingers. Watching the ripples play with the girl's tresses, Udaitara speaks in rhyme. "Luscious in coils all syrupy, without water who wants even the sweet Jilapi? Whatever you find in cream and sugar, nothing cools as well as water. Ananta is forever, but not this water!—now let's dip, sister, let's go under."

"Why, sister, are we towels or bars of soap from the market to end ourselves under the water? If you're burning and want to cool off, why don't you go under?"

"For me, sister, 'the teeth loosen, the hair's gone, youth's flow is ebbing down.' Nothing can burn me anymore."

Fearing the talk will now turn to her age, Anantabala gets out of the water and, putting the dry sari in folds over her wet sari, proceeds to go home.

"Look at her, as if I hit her or scolded her." Udaitara gets out too.

As she steps out in wet clothes and loose hair and proceeds homeward, she hears two people talking near the boat landing. One person has just arrived in his boat and drives in the tying post. The other man standing by the ghat asks, "Come to take her back?" "Yes." "You've been missing her, haven't you?" "Yes." "Well, that's the wise thing, to come now. Better take her back while there's still water in the river. You didn't come in the good season. Like the river, your love too dried up, didn't it?" "That's one way of putting it." "But how could you come when the river went dry? You couldn't carry the boat on your back." "No." "Whatever you may say, let me tell you the truth, 'If the friend'll only remember, the river can be no barrier.' If you don't remember, even a deep river doesn't help. If you remember, even a dried river is no barrier. Think of that song, 'This much Radharaman knows, The boat of love even on dry land goes.' Am I wrong about that?" "No, you're not wrong about that."

Udaitara's husband has come to take her back.

Today she looks at Banamali in a new light. And what she sees breaks her heart. Every time she looks at her elder brother, she longs to hold him, cry and cry. Banamali's getting so thin and withered. Not that old in years. But he already looks so old, and on top of that, a headful of hair and a faceful of beard, a worn towel around his waist and another on his shoulder. The river dried not just for him; it dried for all the fishermen. Aren't they worried too? Or does he take on himself all their worries and stoop under the weight? A few rupees still come in, and some food still goes in the stomach. Later on, when there's even less, is he going to die before all the others? Behind the affection and compassion for her brother that well up within her runs a muffled howl of despair.

"Dada, say the name of a flower!"

A wan smile comes to Banamali's worn face. "So now you can read my future? You used to be the groom-teaser. Now you're the astrologer-madam."

"Stop joking. Why are you getting so thin? There's still water in the river."

"Yes, like sparrow's piss. We used to cast five different kinds of net in five seasons of fishing in a year. Caught fish with the ease of kings. That time's gone. Even in a dream it seems incredible. I worked on my own, lowering and lifting nets. Now I slave for others. Carrying the weight of the pots of fry, the shoulder is all calloused, the back bent. Still that's not what I worry about. I worry about what's going to happen to the Malo community in the coming dry season."

Distressed by the pressure of an impatient husband's prodding, Udaitara puts her arms around Banamali's neck and breaks down. Banamali, as he takes her arms off his neck, says, "Don't act crazy. Listen to me. Are you a little girl that you're crying so?"

Sobbing hard, Udaitara says, "Dada, will you never wear the sola cap on your head?"

"Yes, I will. When I'm finally at the cremation-ground bend, I will. Don't cry."

This is the last time Udaitara sees Banamali.

When the boat starts back, Udaitara silently sits inside the cover. She does not say a single word. Her husband, tired and impatient with working continuously at the scull, finally speaks himself. "Nitya's aunt, oh Nitya's aunt, can you prepare the hookah for me?"

After many years they are alone with each other on the river today. But Udaitara feels no enthusiasm at all. Indifferently she puts tobacco in the top, lights the pieces of pressed coal in the bowl of ember, and holds the lighted hookah out from inside the cover, saying in a detached voice, "The hookah is ready."

An unexpressed pain for Banamali tosses and rolls within her, uncontrollable. Her husband pulls the scull and watches the villages they pass. The villages of peasants on both sides are green as always. But whenever a Malo neighborhood comes in view, the sight of its loss and ruin wrings the heart. Trees and plants are there, but where huts used to be are mostly empty hut bases. By the ghat where rows of fishing boats used to be, now there are but one or two. Where the nets used to dry, cows graze. The huts are gone and on the empty hut bases can be seen the holes for bamboo posts, the broken hearth, the crumbled steps where the water pot and the spice grinding stone were kept. The yards are littered with fallen leaves, their altars of sacred basil broken into pieces, with no one to bring the evening lamp there anymore. The few homes left have small huts in place of larger huts as hut parts were sold.

"Everywhere the same pathetic condition. Radhanagar, Kishtonagar, Manatala, Gosainpur—everywhere," he remarks, picking up the hookah.

When the boat comes to the ghat of their village, Udaitara steps out and looks around. "I see your village too is in the same condition."

She's back to live with her husband—it has been a long time. Near the ghat she sees Subla's wife bathing, her body immersed up to her neck, and showing no eagerness to leave soon.

"So Basanti—the water's got you under its spell! Aren't you going to come out? There's something I wanted to tell you."

Staying in the neck-high water, Subla's wife turns her head and says, "There was a time when I was little and they called me Basanti—that was when I used to set a float on the water in the month of Magh. Then I became someone's wife, then I became a widow. For a while I became Ananta's aunt. Now I've become Basanti again."

"I too was married when I was a child. I came to this village and found you. Our homes next to each other, we lived back to back. You're Basanti to me now just as you were then. Now, will you come out of the water? I want to talk to you."

"Didn't we have a quarrel eons ago? Try to remember. I can't talk with you ever."

Pain wrenches Udaitara's mind. The person nobody had ever hit even with a bouquet of flowers, how mercilessly they beat her that day. Today she looks so dimmed and helpless. Her neck grown so thin, her cheeks sunken, not even half the long hair she used to have. Like Banamali, she too is old when still young. Today even to look at her stirs Udaitara with pity and compassion. If that quarrel came today, Udaitara wouldn't be able to raise her hand against her even if it meant her own ruin.

So Udaitara herself gets into the water, letting it rise slowly up to her neck. She says, "I'd feel better, sister, if one day I got a good beating from your hands. It would cool the burning in my chest. The fire that started after hitting you never went out. That's the truth, Basanti. Will you hit me?"

"I'll hit your enemies, you enemyless woman. May you die pierced by the thorn of a gourd, may you drown on dry land."

The weight of pain in both their minds grows light.

"Don't you want to know anything about Ananta?"

"Ananta? Oh, Ananta. Who takes care of him now?"

"Ananta isn't a little boy anymore that he has to be with someone to take care of him. He's grown up now. Lives in the city, has passed examinations. My brother saw him when he went there carrying loads of small fish, heard him talk about so many things. He lives with gentlefolk. He looks like a gentleman himself."

Subla's wife says in a detached voice, "Mixes with gentlefolk. Won't they make him bad by teaching him the manners of jatra?"

"Oh, no no. They're not marketplace gentlefolk, they're learned gentlefolk. He bought a sari for you and one for me. I'm wearing mine. Yours is there on the dry ground. Wrap it around yourself after the bath before going home."

Subla's wife suddenly looks distracted, thinking of something.

"Well, Basanti, the thought of him hurts, doesn't it? Hurts me too. Our condition, sister, is like that of the Braja women without Krishna. But he's someone else's son, not of your womb, nor of mine."

"Silly enemyless woman! I'm not thinking of him. I'm thinking of something else. Before the last rainy season the siltbed was over there. Now it's come all the way here, right up to where I am in the water. Next year you'll see even this'll rise up as dry ground, and there won't be enough water to cover our bodies. I want to soak as long as I can this time, for the last time."

By the end of that year, in summer, the Malos are paralyzed. The siltbed rises closer to the banks. Only a thin stream of water is left along the edges, too thin for a fishing boat to move through. The women go to bathe there, but the water no longer covers their bodies. By squatting and digging for hours, they've made something like a hole where they lean forward and backward, turn this way and that to wet their bodies and fill their pots. Stuck out on dry ground under the sun, the fishing boats crack; too little water in the river to keep them afloat. The Malos still do not give up fishing. With the triangular pushnet on one shoulder and a narrow-neck fish basket on the other, they desperately roam all day from one village to another looking for a pond or a tank. When they spot a clogged pond in some village, they scan it with hawk eyes. Their bodies are skin and bones, their eyes sunken in their sockets. Those eyes have a crazed glint, a murderous rage. Dipping the tip of the net into the murky water, they push it and wade in those clogged ponds. A few tiny fish get caught and a bunch of frogs. The frogs leap out, and the few small fish stay in—these they collect to sell in the market for a few coins. Only if they manage to do so can they bring home a little rice for the day's meal.

Throughout the day Mohan pushed his dipnet into one clogged pond after another but found no fish, only frogs. He is back home without rice. Throwing the basket in a corner, he props the net against a fence. His old mother has become thin like rope. He married only a few years ago. Without food, his wife also grows emaciated. He cannot bear to look at her anymore. His father silently sits on the porch smoking. His mother and his wife both come out of the hut when they hear him come; silently they go back in when they see no bundle of rice in his hand. They must all pass the day without food; no way to know if there'll be anything to eat tomorrow either. Yet his father smokes tobacco, unworried. Mohan takes the hookah from his father's hand, takes a few deep puffs, and finds that he feels better.

Many of the Malo families left the village. Those who left early on, when there was still water in the river, took their belongings and hut parts piled into their boats. Those who went later left behind their huts and belongings. Those who are still here have little idea where the others went. Some left to harvest paddy for farmers. Others went to the side of the big river. There the moneyed folk have arrangements to catch fish on a large scale for their business. The Malos gone there will catch fish in the river on their behalf in exchange for subsistence.

Those in the Malo community who had sided with the upper castes in factional fighting now, with fishing in the river disrupted, take jobs offered by the shopkeeper Pals, the jobs of bringing sacks of goods on their backs from the town to the village shop in exchange for a few nickels per trip. Carrying those sacks so bows their spines that many grow unable to do even that. They now stay home waiting for death.

Udaitara's husband is in this state. He can no longer walk even one step without leaning on a stick. With his tired sunken eyes he only looks silently at Udaitara.

Subla's wife has so far provided some food for her feeble parents and herself by reeling thread. No one comes anymore to buy thread. Now taking Udaitara along, she goes to sell betel leaves, betel nuts, and baked clay in village homes.* All day they go from house to house in village after village and walk back home through the fields in the evening with a little bundle of paddy each.

But even such petty selling requires a few annas in capital. Those who have none grit their teeth and go away to beg. Jaichandra's young wife is one of them. After Jaichandra's death a few days ago, her last few coins used for his cremation, with one baby at her breast and the other constantly crying from hunger, she takes to begging in distant villages and comes back after nightfall to avoid notice. But the day she's found out, she is treated as if she has shown a new way. Many other young women follow her example and start begging.

But that way is very slippery! Some stumble and fall there and can never get up to show their faces back home. They disappear without a trace from the Malo neighborhood.

Those who died are in a way saved. Those who are alive only wonder, how much longer! From the side of Titash, the answer seems to drift in, not much longer!

The rainy season is indeed not very far away now. The coming of the new water in Titash would soothe a little their long-suffering bones. But separated from water, Malos gasp like fish. Will they be able to wait any longer? The ebb tide that reduces their life-river is now in its all-draining last draft. The life wasting away bit by bit now runs out.

Inside the huts they take to their beds and lie down restlessly. Knees sinking, eyes receding far into their sockets, jawbones sticking out, chests reduced to rib cages, they still drag themselves to the ghat at the river in a procession of skeletons. They go there hoping to see the current from the south come and the fish swim upstream. But what even if the current brings high water again? They can't float the boats and cast the nets with these hands, shaking and wasted as they are.

Becoming more and more gaunt, Udaitara's husband says one day, "I can't stand on my feet anymore," and takes to his deathbed. Basanti's parents follow. By dying they release Basanti. And his father's death releases Mohan. But quite a fuss his father made before dying.

---

*Pregnant women sometimes crave baked clay and thus might buy it to eat.

"So many times I begged, let's leave the village, but nobody paid attention to what I said. When I still had the strength, I didn't leave myself. Now I'm under a stack of fourteen clay plates." As he shouted these words at Mohan, he staggered and fell off the porch into the yard. Falling, he held out a hand to Mohan, but Mohan did not take it. At the time of death he had a terrible grimace on his face. His eyes stayed open and made him look as if he was ridiculing Mohan, not dying.

Subla's wife herself hardly gets up anymore. Her feet falter, her head swims, the color of the world shifts before her eyes. But she has thought it over, what happened to all the others will happen to her, no use worrying about it. But she must have some water stored in the hut. The moment before death, they say, is horribly painful without water. When everyone is dying, who will bring water from whose home to put in her mouth? Unable to carry the water pot, she takes a couple of ewers to the slope. New water has come to the river. The siltbed is covered with a dense growth of paddy plants. Alongside that, the new water flows in a current. Sheaves of paddy ripen where the deep water used to be for them to catch fish. A boat slowly comes to the slope and docks. Anantabala, her father and uncles, her mother and aunts have come in that boat. Recognizing Subla's wife, Anantabala comes to her. She says they're leaving the native place. From here they will walk to the town and take the train. They will go away to Assam.

Even at a time as painful as this, Subla's wife cannot help asking about Ananta. She heard those two were very fond of each other when they were children, and later on—like Uma's penance to gain Shiva—Anantabala too lived in penance for him, looking at the path and waiting for him, bearing so much censure for remaining unmarried up to an age so late for a Malo home.

"Has there been no news of Ananta?"

"Lots of news," she says and gives an account. He is going around with educated gentlemen, trying to help the people. "When he first came on this work, no one recognized him. He stopped his boat in Birampur and asked the villagers there about their troubles. Kadir Mian said to him, 'We're mostly peasants here. We've brought home paddy from the field; we're not in trouble. The Malo community is in trouble with the river dried up.' No one recognized him there except Romu's mother. She came up to him and said, 'Ba-ji, I know you. Your name's Ananta. When you were little you came here in Banamali's boat. You played with my Romu. Come to our home.' She took him home and fed him with care.

"That very day Banamali-dada died. After settling the fish delivery account with the owner, he was walking back home along the side of the river with the empty pots, and he just collapsed on the ground and died—

very near Kadir Mian's house, in fact. Many gathered around him when he died. Kadir Mian saw him, Ananta also went and saw him. Kadir Mian could not hold himself back. Saying, 'This man helped me so much,' he opened his store of paddy and asked the babus to take his paddy and distribute it to the Malos. Taking that paddy and rice in his boat, Ananta came to our village. He stayed at our home for one night and he talked about so many things to my uncle."

"He talked about everything, and didn't he talk about that one thing?"

"No. He didn't have the time to talk about that thing. Next day he left for another village. He may come to your village, too."

To Subla's wife, all this seems as unreal as a dream recalled. Even Anantabala's standing before her eyes seems just like a dream. The only reality is these paddy plants on the siltbed, so plentifully are they loaded with paddy. Earlier the new water came in waves from far south, from the direction of Shibnagar village, and ended up here by this Malo neighborhood. Now the very same waves from far south seem to come transformed as the windswept tops of the paddy plants. Looking out in that direction, Subla's wife slowly closes her eyes.

It was the month of Magh then . . . The drum plays, and the brass plate; and the women are singing. Titash brims with water. In that water she sets her beautiful float, and at once the two of them tackle each other and snatch it up. Subal and Kishore. Then comes one spring. An unknown beautiful maiden, as if from a story, comes to dance in the Dol festival in a fish-drying stretch in the north and loses her heart to an unknown young man. From that was born Ananta. And today, a girl named Anantabala spends her youth, grows thin, waiting for him. Will he not come! He comes. When he was studying for his B.A., a Kayastha girl enchanted him. Later her mother found out about him and said, "Ananta is a good-looking young man, and he's good in studies. But he's a fisherman's son, how can you have anything to do with him?" That girl was persuaded and told herself, I can't have anything to do with him. Hurt by this, Ananta became a renouncer. In the end, he remembers he is not worthless. "My Anantabala is waiting only for me." Then one day Dukhai the drummer plays his drum again and his son the brass, in the same rhythm of celebration as always. Only the drum is a lot more worn out, and Dukhai's son is now a grown-up man. But who is to be the groom's mother? Death saved the unfortunate woman back then. Had she lived then, she'd have died of starvation by now. Come to think of it, I have the prior claim now. I'll be his mother and sit under the eaves in front of the hut, and he'll sit in my lap. The women, singing, will put sugar in his mouth, he will take it in his mouth and spit it out. Then from my lap he will get into the palanquin. But Udaitara may also want to be his mother. And Romu's mother is over there. She may come and say, "I love him the same way I love Romu. If I'm Romu's mother, I can be his mother too." Then even if Subla's wife concedes, Udaitara will not. She'll create a scene on the eve of the groom's departure. No! What kind of dream is this! Udaitara is dying, Mohan is dying. She has to put water in their mouths. Are they to die thirsty while she is still alive?

Waving the surface of the water, she fills the ewers. The paddy field is right in front of her. Their stalks now halfway in water, the plants wave their tops. So close! Do the waves made by her ewers reach out to push at them? They are the enemies. They're the killers of all the Malos of the village. Her eyes start to close again.

In the whole of the Malo neighborhood only two persons still live—all the others are dead. The huts have disappeared. On an empty hut base, rice is being cooked. A very large pot full of freshly cooked rice. The gentlemen from the city will distribute it. Old Ramkeshab staggers to them with a clay bowl in his hands; they put rice into his bowl. When Subla's wife comes with a bowl in her hand, one of the gentlemen comes to put rice into her bowl. It's Ananta! Afraid he might recognize her, she averts her face and comes away without a word. What a dream! At the sound of a splash, Subla's wife looks with a start and sees that the filled pitcher has slipped from her slack grip.

The paddy has been harvested and taken away. Not one paddy plant is on the siltbed anymore. The swimming-depth water of the rainy season covers it. Looking at the river now, no one will believe there's a huge siltbed underneath. As far as the eye can see, it's filled with water. From far south the current pushes upstream in small waves and ends here in the ground of the Malo neighborhood, as always. But now the ground is all that is left of it. That Malo neighborhood is no more. The empty hut bases are all covered with wild growth. The wind blows through them and makes a rustling sound. Or it may be the sighing of those who fell and died here.

Afterword:
An Appreciation
of the Novel

In my reading of *Titash*, repeated countless times through the years, I find myself absolutely fascinated by its use of images to form patterns of parallels and variations. The recurring images give meaning and emotional density to various situations. Let me briefly note some of them.

A late-night kitchen scene occurs twice; in each, three women talk as they make sweet cakes, treats for the next day. In the scene in chapter three, the women are friends, though they address each other as sisters. Two of them are linked in a tragic misfortune, a link they grow aware of but know is perilous to reveal openly, as they tell each other veiled stories about their own lives; though each pieces together the tragic events, neither wants to speak. The three women in chapter five are sisters who constantly played together as children but spend their married lives in different villages and rarely meet. They keep sleep at bay by telling and solving riddles, playfully. Each kitchen scene is brought about by a lonely man's longing for grace: old Ramkeshab seeks to transcend the bleakness of his sad home; young bachelor Banamali wants to evoke fond filial memories. At the end of the sweet-making night in Ramkeshab's kitchen, one woman offers food to the lunatic in the yard whose wife she is, in the manner of invoking a sleeping god, the man's lost sanity. In the second scene at dawn, a minstrel walks by outside singing his invocation, which awakens Ananta. He comes out and follows the singer, who sees him as his dead son reincarnated and who later helps Ananta go to school to awaken his mind and go on to develop his creative gifts.

There are two scenes of Holi festivities with more or less intoxicated revelers singing. Each forms the background for the blooming of passion between unfortunate lovers, unseen by almost all the others. In chapter two, almost as soon as the couple fall in love they are overwhelmed by the impersonal stampede of a riot. In chapter four, almost as soon as their love rekindles, the lunatic stumbles on the threshold of remembrance, and the volatile frenzy of a mob ends his life. The parallel ends here, as one scene brings the young love to bloom, the other to its destruction in death.

The shattering of a joyous moment occurs also at the boat race, in two parallel yet different incidents. The emotional impact of the explosion of a personal fight humiliates Basanti and tears her link with Ananta, both to the breaking point. The relief of surviving the random violence to a race boat and its crew leaves in its wake a sense of grace and renewal, of friendship gained in a crucible of danger; a hope dashed (to win the race) is offset by a wish unexpectedly fulfilled (to meet a person once seen).

The river trips that take place are highly significant. Two involve the first adventure for the person through whose eyes and mind we experience the trip: Kishore's upstream Meghna trip to Shukdebpur and back, and Ananta's to Gokanghat (and the longer, later one to Sadakpur). Each offers a metaphor for the traveler's mental transition. We follow Kishore's journey through his sensitive eyes and note the stirrings of his heart—the river's awesome destructiveness or tranquility in the soft light of dawn, the various encounters along the way that include a boatmen's night camp filled with singing and reciting but end with the horror of the pirate raid and Kishore's descent into madness before he is back home.

On the creek-and-river trip of little Ananta with his mother from Bhabanipur to Gokanghat, we glimpse homes, farmers and yoked bullocks along the creek side, and then at the mouth of the river, in the clear shallow underwater bed, the little fish and snail tracks that lead toward greater, darker depths; the visible merges into the mysterious as the boat moves into midstream. "All his sensations are absorbed in the river that flows around him. Ceaselessly and as lightly as gossamer, the river draws out all his feelings, all that is the essence of his existence . . . he floats in the continuous flow of this freshly awakened, eloquent present." A trip that contains similarly evocative and magical moments is Ananta's to Sadakpur; the boy of seven, given to wonder, not disbelief, eagerly reaches out for the mysteries of both the celestial universe and the one within the river. We see through his eyes the starry sky, freshly emerged from gray clouds, and its reflection on the river's expanded mirror. He thinks of walking the starry paths of heaven reflected on the calm water; his companion tells him the story of a mythical journey to heaven through the interconnecting rivers. Another trip takes place during a downpour on Titash, which brings together a Muslim peasant and a Hindu fisherman, strangers until then; their souls embrace as they silently huddle to wait out the rain in one of the most heartwarming scenes in the novel.

The image of the rainbow joins an orphan boy with an older brother figure, who eventually helps him on his journey of self-discovery, and forms the bridge in chapter five between Ananta's present and the alternative future that opens out before him. The rainbow leads to a series of repositionings that take Ananta from Gokanghat to Sadakpur. The rainbow later on leads to the image of the colorful race boat, like the rainbow descended on its back into the river. The race boat becomes the vehicle to move the narrative from Sadakpur to Birampur, links the two boys' separate worlds, and develops the friendship that first stirred in a downpour on the river.

The riverside ghat scenes, punctuating the entire length of the novel, wonderfully serve to express moods, frame events, link the cycle of seasons with that of human life, stage transitions and junctures in the characters' lives. Among the most significant are the arrival of Ananta and his mother at the same time that the lunatic, unknowing father and husband, is dragged out to the ghat by his parents for a bath; the departure of Ananta with Udaitara, which foreshadows the violent rivalry between the two women; the return of a sadder Udaitara after many years to the ghat where she and Basanti reconcile; and the dying Basanti who comes to the ghat to fetch water and lingers with the sweet memory of festivity when Titash was always brimful and their life so vibrant. It seems inevitable and right that the novel ends at the side of the river, now empty of humans: "The empty hut bases are all covered with wild growth. The wind blows through them and makes a rustling sound. Or it may be the sighing of those who fell and died here."

None of the novel's many incidents of violence (individual fights, unpredictable mobs, water pirates, oppression by the mighty, tricks by both Hindu and Muslim moneylenders to make poor people destitute) arise from religious intolerance. Significantly, the author ends the account before the shadow of the 1947 partition falls on the community. He was writing it during the preceding decade of rising religious communal tension in the region's politics and finished it during one of this century's most devastating religious riots and massacres. Some of his Malo kin became refugees along with hundreds of thousands of others. But he was writing about a people in a place and a time when they were still innocent of communal violence. In *Titash*, the scenes between old Kadir Mian and young Banamali, between Baharullah and Ramprasad, between Romu and Ananta, between Jamila and Udaitara are some of the most moving and humane portrayals of affection that transcends religious barriers.

Kadir's son reflects: "Peasants and fishermen have a link nobody can cut even by hacking or erase even by scrubbing." *Titash* details with care the portraits of cross-religious affinity, the barriers transcended, the sentiments shared.

Aside from these scenes and portraits, the novel is filled with rituals and gestures reflecting the cross-religious culture of Bengal. The Malos push their boats off chanting the names of Pir Badars, patron saints of Muslim boatmen; they are invited to the jari singing of Muslim peasants; both participate in and watch with shared excitement the annual boat race, during which violent incidents happen, but not because of religious differences. Many of the songs are permeated with the panreligious harmony of the mystic philosophies of Sufism and of *dehatatva* (see the appendix); both see emancipation in the fusion of body, soul, and god. Wandering singers circulate songs from the intermingled traditions by composers of both religions, their names inserted in the songs like signatures. The poor in this novel—singers and listeners alike—regularly place humanity above religious differences. Theirs are not simply the liberated notions of a high-minded elite, as one might think; they live these ideas. The portraits of transreligious friendships in ordinary lives and of transreligious cultural fusion constitute an element of abiding significance in Bengali culture, even aside from the novel's immense literary and ethnographic value.

Appendix:
Background Notes

Adwaita Mallabarman (1914–1951) was born in a Malo family in Go-kanghat village beside the river Titash, near Brahmanbaria town in Co-milla district of Bangladesh (known as East Bengal until 1947, then as East Pakistan until 1970). The second of four children, he lost his parents when he was a small child. His two brothers died shortly after, and his sister (widowed soon after marriage) died before he went to Calcutta at twenty. As a boy and a teenager, until he left for college, he lived in the village with his uncle.

He was the first child from the Malo community of the village and nearby area to finish school. Members of the Malo community collected subscriptions to support his school expenses (mainly books, since his school fees were either waived or covered by scholarships he received). He at-tended the town's elementary school and Annada High School, from which he matriculated in 1933, and went on to Comilla Victoria College. In part because of financial difficulty, he left college in 1934 and went to Calcutta to work as a literary editor. Throughout his teen years he wrote prodi-giously, mostly poetry, and published in student magazines. Those early writings were highly acclaimed, so much so that peers who aspired to be writers sought his opinion on their work before sending it to a publisher.[1]

Mallabarman's first job in Calcutta was as assistant editor of a literary and news magazine, *Navashakti*.[2] After three years with the magazine,

1. Motiul Islam, a well known Bangladeshi poet, sent his first collection of poems to Mallabarman, then in Comilla College and only twenty; he received comments and advice from Mallabarman in a letter addressing him as brother (Shantanu Qaisar, *Adwaita Mallabarman* [Dhaka: Bangla Academy, 1987], 12, 72).
2. Narendra Datta, a Comilla-based educator, founded *Navashakti* in Calcutta under the editorship of a young avant garde writer named Premendra Mitra. Mal-

he worked as an editorial assistant for a literary monthly, *Mohammadi*, in which he also published a number of his poems and parts of what was evidently the first draft of *Titash*; he continued to work for *Mohammadi* until its Muslim publisher closed the monthly and migrated. During this period he also worked for the newspaper *Azad*. In 1945 he joined the literary weekly *Desh* and the daily *Ananda Bazar Patrika*. From 1945 through 1950 a number of his poems, stories, essays, and translations were published in *Desh* and other magazines.[3]

His growing career as a literary editor and a writer ended abruptly with his death at age thirty-seven. He was diagnosed in 1950 as suffering from tuberculosis; he had felt increasingly unwell for two years. Entrusting the just-finalized manuscript of *Titash* to friends, he went for hospital treatment. Soon after his release he suffered a relapse and was readmitted. Before the second phase of his treatment was over, however, he walked out of the hospital. Two months later, on 16 April 1951, he died.

Descriptions of Mallabarman all mention his mild manners, polite reserve, reticence, and reluctance to accept material help from affluent acquaintances; they also comment on his collection of books, which constituted his single largest personal expenditure, and his generosity toward Malo relatives and acquaintances who moved to West Bengal after the country's partition. As a child he was known to turn down offers of food from his upper-class schoolmates and teachers, even when he was starving. If pressed, he took as little as possible. Evidently, he never lost an acute sensitivity to the condescension with which affluent upper-caste villagers and educated townfolk regarded the fisherfolk. To this day they refer to the Malo neighborhood of Gokanghat as the *gabor* (stupid laborer) neighborhood.[4] Although Mallabarman became an educated intel-

---

labarman was with *Navashakti* throughout its brilliant three-year life. In Calcutta he formed an abiding friendship with another young writer-editor, Sagarmoy Ghosh, who later urged and helped Mallabarman to join him at the weekly magazine *Desh*.
3. His published writings in Calcutta include *Ranga Mati*, a novel serialized in *Chatuskon* magazine; another one, *Sada Hawa*, in a special issue of *Sonar Tari* magazine; his translation of Irving Stone's *Lust for Life* under the title *Jiban Trisha*, serialized in *Desh*; his translation of Karel Capek's essays published also in *Desh*, along with two travelogues, several short stories, essays that included one on T.S. Eliot's poetry, and a partly serialized collection of folk songs.
4. Qaisar (*Mallabarman*, 9, 75) reports from his own experience on a 1981 visit to the Malo neighborhood in which Mallabarman lived, as well as the visit in 1980 of a professor and a photographer from Brahmanbaria town; they were faced with local people's perplexed embarrassment about what on earth gentlemen like them might want to do with illiterate fishermen. We can imagine what life must have been like fifty to sixty years earlier for a Malo boy who went to school, the domain

lectual and worked in a more cosmopolitan environment at a time when progressive secular movements were on the rise (inspired by Marx, by Gandhi, or both), the Malo within him was never quite at ease with the urbane Calcutta intellectual and literary community, whose members (mostly sons of Brahmans and Kayasthas) came from families with generations of higher education. In Calcutta elites, accent and verbal style have always—next to a family's professional and literary prominence—had more importance than caste or religion.

Bimal Mitra, a rising young editor-writer at the time Mallabarman came to the magazine *Desh,* wrote this impression. "A diminutive man, he could be seen sitting at a very small desk, giving meticulous attention to his daily editorial work for *Desh.* Most days he could not be seen, though, because those of us writers outside the magazine came to its office in the afternoon, when he had finished his work and left. Some people are always trying to hide themselves. Adwaita Mallabarman was one of them. Hence in the writers' afternoon get-togethers, he was quite regularly absent. We heard that in his rented small room in a large building in north Calcutta, he hid himself in a mountain of old books and spent his spare time studying antiquities. But we did not know that behind it all he was writing a novel."[5]

Although during his sixteen years in Calcutta Mallabarman shied away from the literati's favorite pastime of talking and talking in informal group meetings at familiar haunts, he had a small number of very close friends, particularly those few who were natives of the Comilla region, alumni of Annada High School and Comilla Victoria College. One of them, Subodh Chaudhuri, was closely involved in the production of the book from the manuscript and has been an invaluable resource for my understanding of Mallabarman as a person, as well as of the local terms and usages in the novel. With him and a small number of other friends from his Comilla days, the author often talked in his native dialect, discussed the material of his novel, and sang the region's village songs.[6]

---

of educated gentlemen's sons; he felt constrained to protect his self-respect with a boundary of unyielding reserve, which to his classmates from the upper strata might have come across as abnormal shyness. From interviews with Mallabarman's school and college friends, Qaisar notes their impression of Adwaita: he seemed to feel awkward in their company.

5. *Desh,* Sahitya Sankhya (literary issue), 1978; reprinted in *Desh,* golden anniversary issue, 1983; my translation.

6. Subodh Chaudhuri, also a native of the Brahmanbaria area, talked with me at length in Calcutta between 1989 and 1991. He said Mallabarman's close friends were aware of how real the novel was; how deeply rooted his artistry was in intimate knowledge and love of his native way of living and being—its details of location, weather, customs, and speech. Old fishermen of Gokanghat who remember

THE WRITING OF THE NOVEL

Mallabarman worked on *Titash* over at least six years, from 1944 through 1949, finishing it in 1950. He may have worked on it much longer, for seven to eight years, in time spared from his jobs. Some songs used in the novel, most notably the Buruj song, are from a collection of village folk songs that he compiled; parts were published in *Mohammadi* in 1944. In August through October 1945, three chapters of an earlier version of the novel were published in *Mohammadi* before the magazine closed. Shortly afterward he lost the only handwritten copy of the manuscript and, by all accounts, was broken-hearted. His friends and readers kept pressing him to rewrite what was lost. A year later he started again, in the process apparently reworking the novel entirely. In the final 1950 version that he left with his close friends, the serialized parts were re-arranged, developed, and redone along with the portions lost earlier.

His friend Chaudhuri, closely involved with the book's production, told me about certain passages the author had crossed out by hand in the final manuscript. Most notable of those was a detailed description of the profit-sharing arrangement of visiting Malo fishermen who worked collectively in the fish-drying stretch of Ujaninagar, processing the fish hauled from fish ponds leased by the village chief. Although Mallabarman felt strongly about the ethnographic-institutional accounts in the novel, in the end he decided to leave some of them out—perhaps because he saw them as impeding the dramatic flow.

THE TIME SPAN OF THE NOVEL

When the novel begins, Basanti is seven; when Ananta comes to the village at age three, she is perhaps seventeen. At the end of the novel, Ananta

---

Mallabarman as a boy and youth said they saw him spend much time singing and making songs, little time fishing. At times we seem to catch glimpses of this young man who became a writer in Calcutta: behind Basanti's assertive pride in Malo culture, Mohan's musical talent and aesthetics, Kishore's and Ananta's rapt absorption in people and places. The circumstances of Ananta's and the author's lives have many similarities.

Mallabarman wrote his novel for an educated urban Bengali audience with little knowledge of the Malo community and culture, but he wrote from within that community. Asked by some close friends his opinion of an already famous novel written in 1934 about a fishing community facing extinction, *Padma Nadir Majhi*, by Manik Bandyopadhyay, he said he greatly admired its artistry, but since its author came from an educated Brahman family he knew about fisherfolk's lives only from the outside; it reflected (Mallabarman remarked to Chaudhuri) "a Brahman's son's romantic view."

is probably almost twenty, so Basanti would then be in her mid thirties. I calculate that this span of approximately a quarter century ends with the 1930s. I base my supposition on four things: the autobiographical parallels between the author and the boy Ananta in the novel; the approximate time of the first appearance of siltbed in the lower of the two double-S bends of the Titash river, near Gokanghat village (the late 1930s); the author's absence from the area between 1934, when he left for Calcutta, and 1951, when he died there (except for a brief visit in 1948, when the writing of the novel was largely finished); and the approximate times that he started writing the novel in Calcutta, that the earlier version was partially serialized, and that the final version was completed.

TITASH IN FILM AND DRAMATIZATION

Ritwik Ghatak, a preeminent film director of Bengal and a native of Comilla, made a movie in 1973 from his own screenplay based on the novel. The movie was shot in Bangladesh with the help of Bangla Academy but was not commercially released because Ghatak became ill and could not go back to Dhaka to finish editing it; it was shown in his movie retrospectives. Ghatak was also involved in the earlier dramatization by Bijan Bhattachayya (of Bharatiya Gananatya Sangha). Utpal Dutta (of Little Theatre), himself a native of Brahmanbaria and one of the foremost playwright-directors of West Bengal, staged another version at the Minerva Theatre in Calcutta, and most recently Manzural Alam (of Brahmanbaria Natyasangstha) staged it in Bangladesh.

THE CALENDAR

The Bengali calendar starts with Baisakh (mid-April) and ends with Chaitra. The traditional division of the year is into six seasons, two months each, starting with summer (*grishma*—the months of Baisakh and Jaishtha), followed by the rainy season (*barsha*—Asarh and Sravan), early autumn (*sharat*—Bhadra and Ashwin), late autumn (*hemanta*—Kartik and Aghran), winter (*seet*—Paush and Magh), and spring (*basanta*—Falgun and Chaitra).

The blooming of flowers occurs mostly in the mild winter through spring; the relatively mild summer heat brings the ripening of fruits, not flowering. Local inhabitants most often distinguish the seven months of (more or less dry but navigable) "good season" from the wet season, midsummer through early autumn. By this time the rains cease, but the Meghna floodplain, particularly the lowland of the Titash basin, does not dry out until midautumn.

THE SONGS

The region's village folk songs have a distinctive philosophy of life's paradoxes and contradictions that several songs in the novel illustrate. They come from a genre known as *dehatatva* songs, of which *baul* songs constitute one stream.

Dehatatva songs include a wide range of rural folk songs, with philosophical messages that evolved through a blending of elements from Buddhism, Sufism, other related non-orthodox Islamic sects, and the devotionalism of Vaishnava sects, whose followers in Bengal rejected the rigidity and ritualism of orthodox Brahmanic Hinduism. The composers are often folk-religious figures, both Hindu and Muslim, from peasant communities; their names are included in their songs like signatures. The name of the genre (*dehatatva* means the truth of the body, or body-spirit) comes from the lyrics' use of philosophies about the human body and soul. The metaphors, in the oral tradition, have seeped from the songs into speech: for example, the metaphor of bird in cage for soul in body, of bird freed from cage as death; human body as hut or boat; and God as maker and owner of hut or boat, as householder or oarsman. Dehatatva songs in the novel include the verse quoted by the Meghna village sadhu whom Kishore and his companions meet, the Murshida baul song in the boatmen's night camp in the inlet, the song of Udaitara's brother-in-law, and some of the songs from the session in Mohan's yard, at least the two sung by Udaichand.

In the songs, riddles, and verses sung or recited by the novel's characters and by the common folk in the region, end rhyme is considered highly important. The rhyme is simple and pleasant, the rhythm even and smooth. In translating the rhymed songs, I try to keep a sense of the rhyme as well as fidelity to the literal meaning and the rhythm of the original.

Jari songs, commemorating the siege of Karbala, are sung on the occasion of Muharrem. Although lines from a couple of jari songs are quoted in dialogue (in chapter 3), none is actually sung in the novel.

Shari songs, which often accompany the harvesting of paddy and the rowing of boats, are sung in groups (as at the boat race scene on Titash in chapter 6).

Jatra songs that accompany this melodramatic form of opera—with its profusion of histrionics and its chorus made up of the heroine's confidantes (traditionally played by young men in female costume)—were often composed by urban or pseudo-urban songwriters, rather than by traditional singers, be they wandering singers or those living within the community. The fact that jatra operas and songs became available in book form shows their origin among and dissemination through literate impresarios; the use of harmonium, tabla, and violin for accompaniment instead of folk-style string instruments and khol reflects rural elite tastes.

Jatra performance and singing achieved professional excellence and earned respectability during the 1920s and 1930s in Calcutta under the direction of highly talented manager-director-actors and later on gained widespread popularity in both urban and rural Bengal. But initially village communities that had their own distinct singing traditions naturally regarded jatra as an insidious urban or bohemian influence that undercut traditional values, codes of behavior, and singing styles (as it turned out, their fears were not unfounded). The Malo community in the novel also found it a threat to their own singing tradition and culture (as in chapter 7).

Kabigaan (the singing poets' duel or versifiers' tournament) was a popular literary entertainment that proliferated in Bengal during the late eighteenth through mid-nineteenth century. Rival performers (*kabi-wallahs*) would sing improvised verses before patrons or a general audience. In Bengal's long tradition of song literature (*mangalkavya* and *Vaishnava padavali*), kabigaan is a relatively recent form.

THE PRINCIPAL SCENES AND PLACES

The Malo neighborhoods of villages Gokanghat and Sadakpur, the peasant neighborhood of Birampur, the marketplace of Gokanghat, the old canal near that marketplace, the boat-racing stretch of the river, parts of Titash and the Meghna—these are the locations in which the novel's principal scenes and events take place, all in Comilla district, near Brahmanbaria town beside the river Titash. Only Shukdebpur village is more distant; it is upstream on the Meghna, bordering Mymensingh and Sylhet districts.

In March 1990 I went to Brahmanbaria and the village of Gokanghat and talked with people from different social strata, including many members of the Malo community that remains. One of the things that absolutely fascinated me was the authenticity of the novel's description of places, time, speech, customs, folk music, and climate. The locations referred to and their descriptions felt eerily true to life: the named villages, the Bijoy river (now silted up and under farming), the market of Anandababu, the canal near the market, the location of the Malo neighborhood in the village, the field of Kalisima, the area for boat races. The songs, the riddles, the proverbs, the rituals and customs are minutely authentic. So are the dialect, the terms, and the speech modes. Dozens of terms and idioms in the novel are local usage, not even alluded to in most dictionaries; my visit to Brahmanbaria and Gokanghat helped me greatly with these and also gave me a truly wonderful sense of the lilt and rhythm of the speech, of the pleasantly dignified bearing of the people there—Malos and others—and of the novel's visual images that met my eyes.

GOKANGHAT VILLAGE: THEN AND NOW

When Mallabarman was a child, a hundred and twenty of the total of about two hundred households in the village were Malo households. The novel, too, mentions one hundred and twenty Malo homes in Gokanghat (in chapter 7). The Malo neighborhood of the village now has about fifty Malo households, as a result of the migration to West Bengal. The upper-caste groups, and the Kaibarta and the Namashudra fishing-caste communities, have all left, except one Brahman family that shifted its home to the Malo neighborhood. Of the homesteads that the Malos left, only a few were bought by the remaining Malo families, some of whom also acquired farmland, although they lease it to Muslim farmers for a crop-share rent.

Not many of the Malos now make a living solely as self-employed fishermen, and their young men are rapidly moving away. Of the fifty Malo families in March 1990, only a quarter owned a fishing boat. Some had had their boats stolen, others had lost them to moneylenders. Six of the fifty families owned some farmland, in the lowland and in the siltbed, which they rented to Muslim farmers. Fourteen Malo young men had shifted from fishing to other work. In all, ten worked as carpenters in the woodworking factories nearby, six were self-employed carpenters who made small items of furniture to sell at the weekly market, two were tailors. Several others in their early twenties were in vocational training, intending to work in the small industries that have come up in the Titash area (now the preferred career goal for Malo young men in Gokanghat, if their families can afford the training cost and the indirect cost of their earnings being postponed by a few years). Women no longer spun thread and wove net, as wives in the novel did. They bought nets from shops; I saw only some older men repairing nets.

The dry-fish business has expanded with the growth of export to India. Much of the dry fish comes from damming the waterways through which flood water goes down in late autumn, trapping the fish; this kind of fishing is done mostly by other communities. Nearly 60 percent of the fishermen living in the village in 1990 were Muslims. Only three or four Malo men would take the trips to a fish-drying stretch in spring, usually up north. The fish drying work in Ujaninagar (in chapter 2) was a large-scale commercial operation involving the collective leasing of ponds with grown fish from powerful, affluent Malos (like Banshiram Modal), and the sale of dried fish to wholesale buyers; some visiting fishermen caught fish on their own (as Kishore did) in the open river and used the drying stretch. The few who still go upstream on trips to the khalas combine both these methods.

Since 1929 a motorized long-distance ferryboat service has made regular stops in Gokanghat; it has largely supplanted the use of individual ferrymen and Malo fishing boats for family travel (and thus the mode of travel between native and marital villages for young wives like Jamila and Udaitara). Gokanghat also has a cycle-rickshaw service from Brahmanbaria. Eight years ago electricity came to the village from a thermal electricity plant fueled by gas extraction, and now all the homes in the village have electricity; four of the fifty or so Malo homes have television. The town has grown a lot and the village is now part of the municipality. The villagers no longer drink river water, which is far more polluted today than it was seventy years ago. There is a common tube well in the Malo neighborhood, and one Malo home has its own tube well.

Although unmarried Malo girls still perform the Maghmandal rite, their usual marriage age is now between seventeen and nineteen, no longer at puberty. In 1990 about a third of the Malo girls (also a third of the boys) attended primary school, and one girl was in the sixth grade; three boys attended high school beyond the middle level, but no girl in 1990 was in high school. Only one young man from the neighborhood was in college, although several others were in vocational training.

The temple of Radha-Madhab mentioned in the novel has been shifted to the now smaller Malo neighborhood. Holi singing on the full moon of Dol still occurs there every year, as does the annual Kali puja, with subscriptions collected from the Malos.

Only a quarter of the hundred or so Malo men in the village smoke a hookah these days, most of them older men. Once in a while a father and a grown son can be seen sharing a hookah.

The Malos of Gokanghat formed a fishermen's cooperative society in 1970. The society has few resources to undertake anything beyond repairs to fish stalls in the marketplace. For some years until 1987, however, the society could lease bodies of water from the government. Now the leases are auctioned to individuals.

In times of need Malos still borrow from moneylenders; many of these are fish traders, who give a three-month credit against the future sale of dry fish. Now some of the large Muslim farmers in the village also lend money to the Malos.

GLIMPSES OF WOMEN'S LIVES

The novel gives us vivid pictures of women's lives—from various angles, at various emotional planes—in a situation where marriage for them is universal, usually exogamous, and occurs at a very early age, arranged by parents or brothers.

Village exogamy with patrilocal residence is a common custom all over South Asia. It perhaps derives—aside from the consolidation of patriarchal control—from the need to preserve a community's cultural identity and homogeneity of life-style. It may also ease the transplantation of women to their marital homes as adolescents and prepare them for infrequent visits back home—in a context of primitive transportation where a fifty-mile trip is very long, and hazardous if it involves pirate-infested stretches of rivers. In more recent times, as bridges and speedier ferry services become available and as more village girls attend school (still fewer than boys from the same socioeconomic stratum and girls from upper strata), Malo girls in the same community are now married years after puberty, although patrilocal exogamy persists.

In the novel's Malo community the norms of female seclusion are less constraining than among the upper castes and Muslim farmers. Brideprice, not dowry, is the practice in this community, paid by the groom to the bride's father to feast his neighbors. (Kishore was expected to marry after returning from his trip with the needed money; Banamali, without money, might perhaps marry without a bride-price if someone within his extended kinship group would give a daughter or sister to him.) A Malo woman does more of the work of spinning thread and weaving nets than do women in other communities. In her neighborhood or when she travels a Malo woman is less likely to cover her head and part of her face, and she need not cover her head in her home or yard. She is more likely to walk alone at night or with a small child. A Malo woman who comes into a new village where she has no marital or kinship relations may receive welcome and consideration, and she might even receive support if as a widow she wishes to remarry (at least one Malo elder in the novel advocates widow remarriage, and one woman counts on some support for remarrying).

If a name is part of a person's identity, a young woman lives a dual existence: in her native village she is referred to by her own name or as her father's daughter, her brother's sister; in her marital village she is referred to as someone's wife or mother. Even a man is often addressed as someone's father or son. In neither case is harm or insult intended or perceived; in both the custom is considered proper and shows honor and respect. A woman married in her own village within her own community is still referred to and addressed as someone's wife; this custom obtains even for a childless young widow—but perhaps causes her less sadness than being referred to as her husband's widow. Women seem accustomed to having two identities (in Gokanghat childless Udaitara is Labachandra's wife, in Sadakpur she is Banamali's sister, to her peers and juniors she is Udi or Udi-didi). For men, the title Malo's son or sheikh's son conveys respect or formality; in informal usage a man with a child is sometimes called his son's or daughter's father.

Women live and juggle their dual existence of names and appropriate behavior, seemingly at ease and with some enjoyment. A newly married young woman, for example, comes to her native village to visit—brought by her brother, father, or other close kin—with head uncovered; she may run from the ghat all the way home to hug her little brothers and sisters. If she travels with her husband to her marital village, she arrives with head covered and face partly covered; she walks at a modestly slow pace (and a Muslim bride like Jamila is chaperoned by several females). The arrival of a husband to take his wife or of a brother to take a married girl home is more than protocol; it is a measure of and an occasion for joy and pride (Udaitara remains at her brother's place not entirely by her choice but because her husband does not come to take her back).

Although Malo girls are socially conditioned for early marriage, it is not always a strictly arranged one. Malo boys and girls play together much longer than those in upper-caste and Muslim communities. A seemingly arranged or approved marriage may follow a girl's affection. A girl may dream of love in her preteen years and her parents, out of sympathy, might defer her marriage to wait for the loved one's return. Occasionally, a Malo girl may fall in love with a Malo stranger and marry him with the help of a sympathetic parent; such a marriage, though unusual, is treated with kindness.

The novel depicts the wrenching pain of young girls separated from filial relations and familiar environment, and the sense of dichotomy between a nurturant parental home and a duty-bound marital home.[7] *Titash* also shows the sisterly camaraderie between unrelated women in their marital village that lightens the pain of filial separation. When a young wife leaves with her brother for a visit, all the young women in the neigh-

7. The filial relations that "celebrate the values of affection . . . as opposed to the patrifocal values of duty and obedience" may constitute the humanizing subculture within patriarchy, as Lynn Bennett noted in a different South Asian context (*Dangerous Wives and Sacred Sisters: Social and Symbolic Roles of High-caste Women in Nepal* [New York: Columbia University Press, 1983], 314).

borhood gather to watch her happiness, and another young wife who has
not been back home for a while may grow sad-eyed.

Beyond the personal level, countless songs (mostly composed and sung
by men), proverbs, and metaphors in the folk culture commiserate with
and dwell on a young woman's separation from her natal home and filial
relations; they unfailingly strike a sympathetic chord in men and women
alike. The heartache of a lonely woman married away from her natal
home is an abiding theme of moving songs everywhere in riverine rural
Bengal. A daughter-in-law's pain may strike a patriarch and make him
see her in the place of his own daughter similarly married away from
home.

The novel's most intensely portrayed character is Basanti, who does
not know how to back off or bow down, who would rather set fire to the
whole village than accept humiliation for herself and her community.
Articulate, headstrong, and rebellious, she is an unusual woman who lives
all her life in the same village, the same community, as daughter, wife,
and widow, without fear of in-laws or of the constraints of the usual
norms of propriety. In the end she rises from the ruins of personal life to
mobilize the disheartened Malo male singers in a quixotic campaign to
celebrate their traditional songs, to resist the intrusion of jatra.

Being a daughter, a wife, and a widow of the same community, Basanti
is an exception to the pattern of exogamous patrilocal marriage that produces docility. Any culture of subordination has its exceptions, one might
argue. But local or neolocal marriage is not a great exception within the
laboring classes in Bengal (or all over the subcontinent). And among the
novel's vivid female characters we must include two other young women
who also show strength and ingenuity in the face of constraints and adversities: Ananta's mother and Udaitara. The first hides her identity and
ventures out in widow's garb to live on her own, with her child, in a new
village where she has no relatives and where her kinship and husband's
identity remain unknown. The second, married at ten and stuck in an
unhappy childless marriage, away from her dear sisters married off in
other villages, nonetheless uses her talent for lively speech, rhymes, and
proverbs to enliven any gathering of neighborhood women.

In general, in their relations with one another and with the men in
their lives, these young women reflect the author's keen sensitivity to the
complexities of the human condition. A true artist's mind has an incan-
descent quality, a harmony of male and female powers within the soul or
brain, unimpeded in the ability to perceive and create (Virginia Woolf, *A
Room of One's Own*). This quality of deep empathy, neither judgmental
nor detached, comes to us through the novel's female and male charac-

ters; we see it in their response to all that constrains and uplifts them, the painful and the joyous in their culture, and the conditions of their time and place that allow them to seek autonomy through sources that lie within.

The harmonious relations depicted in the novel between Malo (low-caste Hindu) fisherfolk and Muslim peasants in the Comilla area persisted to a remarkable extent even through the period (from the 1910s through the 1940s) of accelerating rifts and devastating riots elsewhere in East and West Bengal. Although a great many Malos migrated after the country's partition, many stayed on in Gokanghat village, in the Titash area, and in Comilla generally. There have been few riots and little religious communal hatred among the poor in the area, compared to other places in Bengal and other parts of the subcontinent. After one major riot, in 1950, more Malo families left the village, but not all. What I observed and heard during my visit in March 1990 corroborated the novel's description of Hindu-Muslim amity in the area. Intellectuals, artists, field workers of various development agencies, and ordinary people, including some of the Malos of Gokanghat, all expressed bitterness about the corruption and tyranny of officialdom and about the increasing incidence of crime—but never about religious hostility.

The relative absence of religion-based conflicts in the Comilla region may derive from the patina of a thousand years of cultural influences of Buddhism, Hinduism, and Islam over the indigenous peoples of Bengal. In the northeastern part of Bengal especially, the Buddhist influence was once important. The Buddhist towns of Mainamati and Debagram, founded a thousand years ago (their ruins were discovered in the 1940s), are relics of the local Chandra dynasty that ruled the east of Bengal in the ninth and tenth centuries, midway through the long rule of the Pal dynasty in Bengal (from mid-eighth to mid-twelfth centuries). The Pals, the subcontinent's last Buddhist monarchs, sheltered the remnants of Buddhism before it went to Tibet and Southeast Asia. During the twelfth and thirteenth centuries the Sen dynasty squeezed out Buddhism and with patronage and protection fostered Brahmanical Hinduism with its emphasis on the caste system of social stratification.

Islamic influence first came to Bengal through Arab traders and proselytizers along the coast of Noakhali and Chittagong in the eighth century, then through the military-political control of the pre-Mughal Muslim dynasties centered in northern India during the fourteenth through mid-sixteenth centuries, and finally from the Mughal dynasties, from then until the British came. During the reigns of the Delhi sultans and emperors, Bengal was ruled by regional governors, mostly Muslim but sometimes Hindu. Throughout that period, close interaction and mingling of Hindu and Muslim cultures took place in important and very striking ways.[8]

Over the centuries Bengal has fostered powerful streams of rebel religious cults within both Hinduism and Islam. The political atmosphere created by the independent nawabs and sultans of Bengal during the fifteenth through the seventeenth centuries in particular allowed Sufis to settle in various areas and come in contact with the common people.[9] Disciples of Kabir and Chaitanya contributed to the Hindu and Islamic cultural fusion in philosophy, literature, and music. The sects of Baul, Kartabhaja, fakir, and others with a strong musical component drew both Hindu and Muslim followers and contributed to an increasingly transreligious folk culture. At the popular level, the greatest and the most abiding form that this Hindu-Muslim cultural intermixture took was folk music.

Aside from this long-term historical layering and intermixture of the cultures of the three religions in eastern Bengal, two locally important developments in recent history explain the greater degree of religious tolerance and cultural fusion in the Comilla region.

One factor is the relatively recent origin of the Meghna floodplain, which may explain its settlement by migrants, both Hindu and Muslim, who lived by manual labor. They saw the moneylenders, traders, and educated gentry who later came to the region—mostly Hindu but Muslim also—as tricky exploiters. Shades of that past find an echo in the antipathy toward traders in the conversation of Banamali and Kadir Mian (in chapter 5). Thus the groups that Malos as well as peasants most distrusted and avoided were shopkeepers, moneylenders, and educated upper castes, skilled at cheating illiterate common folk and contemptuous of their life of manual labor, their tradition of oral culture and songs.

Another important factor is the politicization of the poor in Comilla. During the 1930s in particular, a peasant movement spread in large areas

8. In the first half of the fifteenth century Bengal was ruled by Jalaluddin Shah, who, though the son of a Hindu prince, converted to Islam and yet was the patron of Krittibas, the composer of the Bengali *Ramayana*. His son and successor, Shamsuddin Ahmad, was the patron of the Hindu poet Chandidas. Nawab Murshid Quli Khan (1714–1727) was a Brahman's son brought up as a Muslim. More generally, since many Muslim nawabs had Hindu wives, cultural intermixture historically enjoyed much royal support and patronage.
9. See Muhammad Enamul Haq, *A History of Sufi-ism in Bengal* (Dhaka: Asiatic Society of Bangladesh, 1975), 156.

of Comilla district under the leadership of a number of noted grass-roots leaders. Eventually the (peasants') Krishak Party formed in 1936 under Fazlul Huq, who as chief minister legislated peasant debt relief and arbitration procedures. It was not until 1938, after Muhammad Ali Jinnah's visit and Fazlul Huq's change of affiliation, that the Muslim League and its communal appeal gained the upper hand in Comilla, supplanting the call for class struggle among peasants.[10]

The secular, class-focused movements were not, however, totally extinguished in the area, even during the communal riots that preceded and followed the 1947 partition. In the aftermath of the 1946 carnage in Noakhali, at the call of the socialist Kisan Sabha Party, close to ten thousand peasants of Comilla, armed with bamboo poles, marched in a procession to the border between the two districts to stop the entry of rioters.[11] Estimates of the relative strengths of the peasant movement and the religious communal movement in Comilla diverge, but no one disputes the fact that concern for the plight of the have-nots, irrespective of religion, took pride of place in the mass politics of Comilla during the 1920s and 1930s. An indirect gain of the region's peasant movement was to moderate the communal hatred that pitted sections of the laboring class against one another during the second half of the 1940s.

THE MALOS' OPEN-RIVER FISHING

The novel refers to different kinds of fresh-water fishing livelihoods; they involve cultural differences as well. There are the closed-water Namashudra fishermen and the open-water Malo fishermen. Among its characters the novel includes a few affluent Malos (such as Kalobaran of Gokanghat) with large boats and money to hire boatless Malos (like young Subal) to go out on the big rivers to catch the large kinds of fish; there are a few (for example, Bodhai of Nayanpur) who lease ponds and other closed bodies of water, then stock and harvest them using hired Malos (such as those who live near a river like Bijoy that dries in the summer); a few others (like the chief of Shukdebpur village) operate a large drying stretch and rent its use to groups of Malos visiting from distant villages, who come to catch and process fish from the river and the stocked ponds and then return home with money from selling the dry fish to merchants.

But the majority of the Titash Malos described in the novel, with their typical lifestyle of close family relations and a rich abundance of com-

10. *Comilla Zelar Itihas* (History of Comilla district), ed. Mobesher Ali (Comilla Zela Parishad, 1984).
11. *India's Struggle for Freedom* (Calcutta: Government of West Bengal, 1987), 208–9.

munity culture, are independent full-time river fishermen who do not
have to move constantly or stay away from home on a regular basis.[12]
Although young Titash Malos (like Kishore) take trips to an upstream
fish-drying stretch, it is an occasional event rather than a regular activity.
Nor do the majority of the Titash Malos farm part-time, own farmland,
or engage in other supplementary occupations.

The Titash Malos' somewhat unusual combination of small-scale non-
migratory fishing as a regular livelihood[13] and a rich family-and-com-
munity life is—or rather, was—possible only because of the perennial
fullness of the river. So, when the siltbeds finally formed and spread, the
result was devastating for their established ways of living. The difficulty
the Malos have encountered in getting reestablished as fishermen derives,
however, from two other factors. One is the country's partition. The other
is the recent institutional changes regarding fishing rights in bodies of
open water.

The traditional ways of fisherfolk who cast nets in open water, using
their skills and generations-old close knowledge of patterns of waves and
currents, have been disappearing. All fishing in ponds, rivers, and marshes
is now regulated by leases granted or auctioned through the district-level
committees of the fisheries administration. The lessees are often influen-
tial moneyed people, many of whom sublease, not necessarily to those
who have been fishermen for generations. The land reform slogan *Hal Jar*

---

12. The relation between nature and human labor holds a key place in the novel;
it affects the quality of life and the living culture of a laboring community. As a
yearlong source of subsistence, the river affords the Malos free time for community life and culture. Later it becomes a source of despondency and harshness in
their lives, and the Malos lose the spirit of their culture. They must struggle,
leave, or move to menial wage labor. The Malos' oral culture that thrives on a
stable and secure subsistence environment perhaps impedes their adaptation in the
face of drastic natural change; fishing communities that live along the changeable,
violent Meghna or Padma learn to survive under harsher conditions, but their life
of constant stress and vigilance exacts a cultural price.

The novel does not, however, take a natural deterministic view of the Malos'
end. Kishore sees a prosperous Malo village on the Meghna that does not depend
on passive river fishing alone; Ramprasad tries to persuade the Malos to protect
their livelihood when the siltbed forms, to fight for social justice. Ultimately it is
their disunity—not just natural adversity—that makes them vulnerable to pred-
ators and unable to act collectively for the survival of their community.

13. Part-time fishing combined with farming is more common in the larger flood-
plains of the tropics, including parts of the Meghna floodplain. Except for the
occasional upstream trips in spring for dry-fish business, most Titash Malos did
not migrate, unlike communities of full-time fishermen in river basins in most
parts of the world, who constantly move up and down a river, from the river to
the margin of the floodplain (R. L. Welcomme, *River Basins*, FAO Fisheries Tech-
nical Paper 202 [Rome: Food and Agriculture Organization, 1983], 11).

Jomi Tar (land belongs to the tiller) has found an echo in the slogan of *Jaal Jar Jol Tar* (water belongs to those who cast the nets) in Bangladesh, but in fact those who have cast nets for ages have been pushed out by affluent lessees of the open water, some even in the name of the fishermen's associations that qualify for leases.[14]

Ownership of the new land from siltbeds (*chars*) has been determined entirely by might, the ability to hire or keep a retinue of *lathiyals* or stick wielders (effectively securing *Jore Jar Jomi Tar*—the mighty get the land).[15] Neither small fishermen nor small farmers and landless laborers have managed to be ng the major beneficiaries. At the end of the novel, y the new siltbeds that dislodged the fishermen, those lot of land acquire them. Landless peasants and fishy are intimidated, beaten back, or die fighting.

long channel (in places, a set of channels) that sepana and meanders in two long S-bends through the lowlands to the east of the Meghna. Hill streams feed it from the east, and it casts off canals for irrigation and navigation before it rejoins the Meghna downstream (see maps that follow). The long course of the river, which has modified over the past two hundred years, meandering farther east and silting up in parts, is part of the Meghna floodplain that gets inundated during the rainy season. The silt carried by the Meghna,[16] and by the hill streams that join Titash from the northeast, is the main factor in the flow reduction and siltbed formation in the meandering river Titash.

The characteristic of the middle-Meghna floodplain is that silt obstructs the main stream and overflows to form new branches, which over time silt up and divert the water farther. The slope of the floodplain of Titash is slight. The contour difference between the Meghna and the easternmost reaches of the river Titash is less than ten feet. The resulting slow flow also promotes the deposit of silt.

14. This information was corroborated by fieldworkers of non-governmental agencies like Proshika.
15. "Riverbank Erosion Impact Study: Symposium on the Impact of Riverbank Erosion, Flood Hazard and the Problem of Population Displacement" (Jahangirnagar University, Dhaka, 1987).
16. Near Ashuganj, the siltbed of the Meghna has expanded rapidly in the last forty years—since the time of the novel—substantially cutting down the flow coming into Titash from the north.

The regular ebb and tide of Titash come from the Meghna in the south. During the monsoon, the swollen waters of the Meghna as well as hill streams in the high-rainfall northeastern region contribute to the inundation of the Haor Basin (consisting of the many lowland *haors* or lakes to the northeast of the Meghna).

When the swelling of the Meghna from upstream sources coincides with local rains, almost the whole low-lying plain is subject to sheet flooding. This inundation is actually beneficent: it does not come in sudden destructive surges as in the estuary close to the Bay of Bengal; the floods renew the croplands with fertile silt; and the deposits of silt are not so extreme. Because of the relatively small silt content of the flow of Meghna, silt deposits take longer to raise the lowlands through which it flows. A meandering river like Titash, one hundred fifty miles long, could therefore keep flowing for over two hundred years, in spite of the mere seven to ten feet of elevation difference and the annual sheet flooding. Had the silting occurred faster and the siltbeds in Titash formed earlier, then the Malo lifestyle, intensive in community interaction and recreation, based as it was on local yearlong fishing, would not have developed; more fishermen would have had to go away for longer periods, fishing or working as wage laborers in town or on bigger rivers.

The water of the Meghna is relatively clean and drinkable, because the hill rivers that feed it originate in an area with abundant crystal rocks and silica. They carry relatively little silt, or at least they had little before the recently accelerated deforestation in the eastern wing of the lower Himalayas. After coming down from the hills, those rivers flow extremely slowly through the immense lowland haors. Some of the silt in the water settles there and the clear water becomes the flow of the Meghna. However, the intensive use of chemical fertilizers in the last decade has polluted the water, and tube wells are now the chief source for drinking water.

Maps

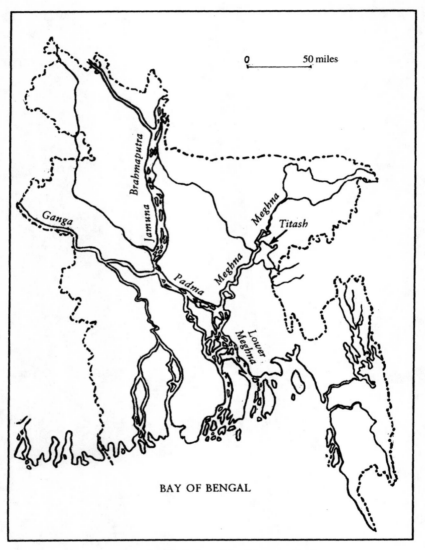

BAY OF BENGAL

Bangladesh and Its Rivers

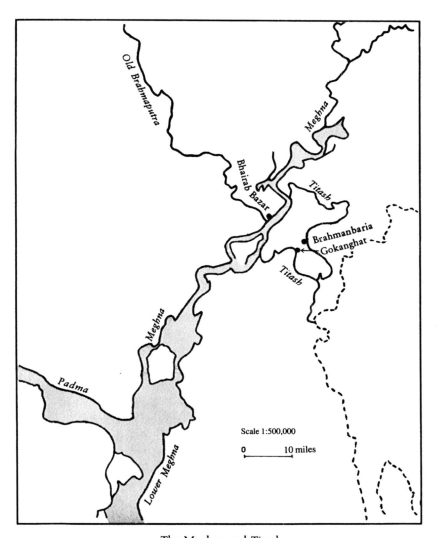

The Meghna and Titash

CPSIA information can be obtained at www.ICGtesting.com
Printed in the USA

237637LV00002B/28/A